ONE RED
SHOE

ONE RED SHOE

The Story of Corporate America's First Woman

PEG WYANT

gatekeeper press™
Columbus, Ohio

One Red Shoe:
The Story of Corporate America's First Woman

Published by Gatekeeper Press
2167 Stringtown Rd, Suite 109
Columbus, OH 43123-2989
www.GatekeeperPress.com

Library of Congress Control Number: 2020947383

ISBN (hardcover): 9781642375138
ISBN (paperback): 9781642375145
eISBN: 9781642375152

To Jack, our Secretary of State, Captain of Fun and Cheerleader.

CONTENTS

ABOUT THE AUTHOR

A native of Cincinnati, Ohio, Peg is Founder and CEO of Grandin Properties, a real estate development firm and an alum of The Procter & Gamble Company. She graduated Phi Beta Kappa and Magna Cum Laude from Smith College. Peg and her husband Jack live in Cincinnati and Sea Island, Georgia. They have four grown children and nine grandchildren who live in Wilmington, Delaware; San Francisco; Brooklyn and Chicago.

FOREWORD

YOU ARE ABOUT to embark on a bracing journey spanning over five decades with a remarkable woman, Peg Wyant. You will meet a woman who from her earliest years followed the precept that, "When you are truly comfortable in your own skin, not everyone will like you, but you won't care about it one bit." A woman who followed the precept, "The secret to winning is start before you're ready and then persist."

You will read about a woman who was ahead of her time, not always to her advantage but rarely with regret and ultimately achieving a life of success and fulfillment.

I came to know Peg Wyant over 50 years ago. After already launching a travel business as a young 22-year-old, she was applying for a job in marketing at Procter & Gamble. I was a brand manager. No woman had ever been hired directly into marketing before Peg. She went to take her entry test. She was asked to start with a "typing test." Her response was, *"I don't type. All I can do is think. Don't you have a test for that?"*

I met Peg later that week. I hadn't met anyone in recruiting at P&G who was smarter and no one with more energy. So she went on to a day of interviews. She was hired.

At The Procter & Gamble Company, Peg would achieve a series of *firsts*. She was the first woman to go into the field on sales training. She was the first female brand manager and the first female promotion and marketing services manager. She was the first woman to work all the way through pregnancy. In fact, she addressed P&G's annual year-end meeting only a few days before giving birth to her first child.

And she was the first woman manager to report directly to the CEO, then John Smale, researching and recommending areas of strategic focus for the coming decade.

Wyant tells her story frankly. She pulls no punches. She spares no words in describing the challenges she faced as a woman, navigating one role after another in a corporate world where female managers were rare to non-existent. You will see the skepticism and no small amount of harassment she faced, but also the empowering support she received from many other executives.

While I was no regular fan of the television show *Mad Men*, Peg's story strikes me as *Mad Men* brought alive through a young woman's eyes.

Along the way, Peg had encountered a bigger challenge than anything at work – an unsuccessful first marriage. She is unsparing in describing what led to her divorce. Fortunately, a few years later, Peg met Jack Wyant, a charismatic young man also working at P&G. He became the love of her life. They remain together 47 years later.

By the time Peg concluded her work with CEO John Smale, she and Jack had four children, all under the age of 10. Jack had entrepreneurial instincts like Peg's and was working hard, forming one new business after another. Peg concluded she could no longer balance doing the right thing for her family and for P&G. She became a fulltime mom. I don't think you'll ever read a more honest portrayal of the challenges of managing the responsibilities of work and family than what you will read here.

The journey continued. Financial challenges for the family emerged. Peg concluded she needed to go back to work. She also missed the challenges of working. She was about to break more barriers. She became a consultant for several Fortune 500 companies. Seeing that venture capital firms weren't focused on investing in women's businesses, she formed a venture capital firm to find she was ahead of her time. So, she started a real estate business. First, flipping homes then acquiring, renovating and managing apartment and commercial properties. It has proved very successful.

Later, Peg and Jack invested in a squash academy to help disadvantaged children on their trajectory of learning. Through the brilliant success of their four children they had discovered that squash can inspire young people to pursue their overall educational success.

You will read about how, having been barred from entering several all-male social clubs because she was a woman, Peg brought together a group of women leaders to form their own social club which did investing over good meals and conversation. That was 26 years ago. It lives on today.

You will learn about how she and Jack raised their four children. It was not a simple or easy path but one marked by one of Peg's core values: "Never have a bad day, even though you know you will."

Toward the end of her book, Peg concludes with a list of *lessons learned* compiled by her administrative assistant, Betty Douglas, with whom she worked for 13 years. These are lessons which Peg lived. "You are the maker of your own destiny. Don't let anyone hold you back."

As you accompany Peg on her journey, you'll find these lessons embedded in chapter after chapter of her life, through challenges, sometimes setbacks and, in the end, fulfillment and success. Peg's and her family's stories are unique, as all lives and families' are. I believe you will find Peg's story has much to teach us as we pursue our own lives.

– John E. Pepper, Jr.
Former CEO, The Procter & Gamble Company
Former Chairman, The Walt Disney Company

PREFACE

O N THE MORNING of December 12, 1973, I walked nervously across the stage of The Procter & Gamble Company's year-end meeting and began speaking to an audience of several hundred men, from all over the world. Preceding me was the company lawyer who had just told these men about their obligation to comply with a new federally legislated program called "Affirmative Action." They were going to have to start hiring women. That was the stick. The intent of putting me, Procter's highest-ranking woman but lower ranking and younger at 29 than everyone else in the room, on the dais was to sell the idea, to be the carrot.

I was nine months pregnant, something no one at P&G knew when the company invited me to speak.

For years, I had worked for an opportunity like this. In Cincinnati's Hillsdale and Smith College, both all women's schools, students were treated equally. After graduation, when there didn't seem to be any good jobs for a woman with a liberal arts degree, I started a company, which helped open the doors of Procter & Gamble. When I learned P&G had never sent a woman on sales training, I worked hard enough to be the first. At the initial sales district annual meeting, I dressed in a bright red suit with matching pumps and strode with all the confidence I could generate into the room where it happens.

Now those experiences faded into silence. As the applause softened, I tried to steel myself with flashbacks of recent events. In May of 1973, Ruth Bader Ginsburg won her first case as a litigant in the Supreme Court. Frontiero vs. Richardson decided on the basis of sex that a military law limiting dependent benefits to wives discriminated against men. It was a landmark gender case although the decision generated few headlines. I only knew about it because of my constitutional law courses in college and the fact that my Dad was a federal judge.

Just three months ago, in September, Billie Jean King won the highly publicized Battle of the Sexes in Houston's Astrodome against Bobby Riggs, an outrageously boastful and chauvinistic tennis professional. The event attracted 90 million television viewers. I was among them.

Now, I was more than nervous. I was petrified as I gazed upon their serious faces, crisp white shirts and dark wingtips resting on the floor. I took a deep breath and started slowly to speak.

"Good morning, gentlemen. The whole idea of bringing females into the professional ranks is new. People are understandably skeptical. Many think the movement is a fad popularized by female extremists. Most view it as a governmental thorn that will be costly and time consuming to execute. It will take time and money."

"But, today, I hope to share some information and experiences that begin to suggest females might represent a valuable human resource."

The talk included a number of facts from credible sources – the University of Michigan Institute for Social Research, a Wharton professor's speech, the U.S. Census Bureau and the Harvard Business Review. Facts explained the social, economic, scientific and industrial changes, advances companies like P&G made, that created *"far better educated women with fewer children, fewer household responsibilities and a longer life . . . who were interested in applying their talents to the most challenging jobs."*

Everyone in the audience knew the company's competitive edge was its people. What I tried to suggest was that the way to stay ahead was opening our doors to 51% of the population still left out. It was smart business:

"The major thrust of the equal opportunity movement for females will be to strengthen this organization and the individuals within it by broadening the options for both men and women. The environment will be more competitive; the company, more profitable; and the people, better human beings. You are in the unique and enviable position of effecting these changes."

I seriously doubt they felt envied.

The idea for putting this and other stories into a book came a few years ago from a Brooklyn Heights breakfast.

My husband Jack and I met at Procter & Gamble during the seventies when men shied away from strong women. Jack was different. While just hired, he applauded my high-ranking brand manager position and became a vocal cheerleader.

We were in Brooklyn visiting our son Tim. Jack had arranged a breakfast meeting at a swishy Brooklyn Heights restaurant on Montague Street with Emily Del Greco, a 30-something Vice President of Sales for one of his venture backed companies. As was his habit, Jack imposed on Emily excessive praise about my accomplishments. Upon my arrival she suggested: *"You should write a book."*

I responded: *"Thanks, but I have no interest in writing a memoir or history book. You flatter me, Emily, but my journey is from a different era. The challenges I faced are so different from those you face."*

Without hesitation, this bright young woman responded: *"Oh but Peggy, they aren't. We face the same issues."*

Emily was right. Women still face challenges. The 60's and 70's, even the 80's, were a free-for-all. Without laws or company policies protecting women, men did whatever they could get away with. Barriers keeping women in the home were like billboards. When I applied after college for a job in Congress, the answer was "We only hire women as secretaries." P&G's management recruiting brochure wrote about becoming a "Brand Man." Men I worked with conveniently forgot to invite me to work dinners. Women couldn't get credit cards, let alone bank loans, or capital for startup businesses. There were no hair dryers in hotel rooms.

Women have lots to celebrate. We have moved from low single digit percentages of graduate degrees to over half for law and medicine, fewer in business and engineering but still substantial, have landed a significant share of management positions, federal judgeships, board seats and partnerships. Congress and CEO offices are more elusive but at least there is female representation where, only a few decades ago, there was none. And a few impressive women are not only heads of state but also outperforming, on critical world issues, their male counterparts.

Now, the laws as well as company policies and politically correct attitudes guarantee women equal treatment. And yet we are not equal. The obstacles are subtle, even invisible. And like the influenza virus, a microscopic enemy is maddeningly evasive.

In navigating a career for more than a half century – from Mad Men through Me Too and motherhood – I have learned how to accomplish goals and level playing fields. As an entrepreneur, corporate executive, consultant and real estate developer, I faced obstacles which only increased my determination to succeed. Fortunately, life had given me the tools.

I grew up on a 400-acre farm east of Cincinnati in a place called Mulberry. There was neither a stop sign nor traffic light. For the cars, trucks and tractors speeding by, the only markers were Clermont county's sign by the side of the road and a small 19th-century brick homestead of about 1,500 square feet. George and his wife Mary lived upstairs and, on the first floor, the couple ran the neighborhood grocery, drugstore and post office. Outside, there was a single gas pump.

There were horses on the farm. The first time I confronted fear was in the fall of 1951 when the galloping steed under me jumped a gully on one of our unmanicured trails. I was nine. My older sister Nancy was a natural rider who led at a pace that was usually fast. That day we were late for dinner, so she encouraged her horse Pal to let go. My horse followed suit. Deep in the woods, turning back was not an option. I had to muster the confidence to control my fear.

Our Irish Catholic father, Timothy S. Hogan, was a brilliant attorney, later a federal judge, who purchased the farm after World War II as a way to find peace and quiet for his family. He was an unpretentious man who drove only hand-me-down cars, often held together by masking tape and barbed wire. Dad drove the 17 miles to the city each day to practice law for corporate clients while dabbling in livestock in Mulberry.

My Welsh, Protestant mother was Evalon Roberts Hogan, daughter of a postal worker and a woman who ran a boarding house. Independent and ambitious, Mom was as beautiful as Dad was brainy. She became Cincinnati's leading model in her 20s and was the life of the party throughout her life.

Nancy, my brother Tim and I had first-class private school educations, economic security, role models and the stability of growing up in the Midwest with its solid values and polite ways. Cincinnatians even say "please" instead of "excuse me." It's softer. It would be fair to assume that I had everything necessary – including connections – to find success wherever my dreams led.

Ample proof of my privileged upbringing hangs from the 14-carat gold charm bracelet my grandmother started for me in elementary school. There are tennis trophies, a cheerleading megaphone, Cum Laude cross, my contract master point number from the days playing tournament bridge with Mom, an Irish shamrock, Nantucket whale, a wishing well and mouse trap from the farm, the aspirational engagement ring and a fish symbolizing the 300 pound marlin caught one spring in Bimini. It was all the rage in the 1950's to wear your accomplishments and happy memories dangling from your wrist.

But also, in the fifties when I was growing up were the narrow definitions of men and women and their roles. What made a woman valuable was taking care of the home and looking beautiful. Corporate success or even deep thinking were not expected or generally encouraged. I didn't fit into that mold. I was becoming a freethinker with thoughts of being a force and a voice beyond the home, just like my Dad.

While my growing independence rested on family history, the tipping point was coming to adulthood in the 60s, one of the most tumultuous and influential decades of the 20th century. It was also going to Smith College, an all-women's institution in Northampton, Massachusetts. In 1960 Harvard, Yale and most of the Ivy League Schools were only for men. Smith was a "sister" school, there to provide women with an excellent education denied them at so many top schools.

In the 1940s, Smith educated Betty Friedan, whose 1964 book *The Feminine Mystique,* about the unhappiness of suburban housewives, launched the modern feminist wave. It also educated Gloria Steinman in the '50's. It is located in the middle of the state which most influenced John Fitzgerald Kennedy. Especially for young people like me, JFK sparked high hopes in 1960 which would only be dashed by the assassinations, civil rights riots, rampant inflation, the Vietnam War and White House lies.

Men obviously ran the world. Women had only had the right to vote for 40 years. But as Bob Dylan wrote, "The times they are a changing." Suddenly everything was up for grabs including patriotism and politics, war and peace, family and jobs, private and public issues, sex and love.

On June 3, 1964, I graduated from Smith College wearing a green linen Jackie Kennedy sheath. Secretary of State Dean Rusk, who would become a target of anti-war Vietnam protests, gave an uninspired graduation address. President Thomas Mendenhall handed out diplomas. It would take 100 years after Smith College's founding for a woman, Jill Ker Conway in 1975, to become its President. He handed me one with Phi Beta Kappa and Magna Cum Laude honors.

My father was never big on pomp and circumstance. He hung a stuffed fish he caught on his courtroom wall rather than the traditional judge's portrait. He preferred law clerks from universities in West Virginia or Kentucky over Harvard and Yale. His highest compliments went to young people who grew up poor, who made it on their own. This bothered me as I did not come from that needy place. I feared he would never truly value my accomplishments. So, on this particular day, I was thrilled to surprise him with an honors degree. Dad, an emotionally restrained man who frequently said, *"silence is a virtue,"* gave me a warm hug.

Rick Knauft, my boyfriend of two years, attended the ceremonies. He would graduate the following week from Harvard, heading in September to Case Western medical school in Cleveland. Women, who were in love with men starting law or medical school, married, got secretarial jobs and supported the new family unit. For reasons not entirely clear to me at the time, I could not see myself traveling down such a path. With a heavy heart, I had broken up with Rick a couple weeks earlier, sending him off to find a better-suited wife – which he did within the year. But he sweetly still came to my graduation.

Just a month after the Smith ceremony, on July 2, Congress would pass the landmark Civil Rights Act of 1964 which outlaws discrimination based on race, color, religion, sex, or national origin. Sex was added almost as an afterthought. The law was ahead of society.

Having planned since childhood to go to law school after college, I applied and was admitted to Georgetown law school. But at the last minute, I decided to take a break from academic rigors, having worked so hard during college. I first became an entrepreneur, founding a global travel company. Then I applied to Procter & Gamble. P&G would take the chance of hiring a "girl" and three years later make me its first female brand manager in the company's then 134-year history.

My first day, February 6, 1967, I was assigned to Bold, a new brand in the Packaged Soap and Detergent Division. There were four men on the brand, a secretary and me. At noon on day one, the men went off to lunch together in the company cafeteria. With no invitation for me, I invited our secretary. That afternoon the Ivory Snow brand manager from across the room motioned with his index finger for me to come into his office where he extolled without a hint of embarrassment: *"Don't do that again. We don't fraternize with the help."* For the next several months, not wanting to eat alone, I didn't go to lunch, dropping to about 100 pounds. Nobody noticed.

Every day I would listen to my boss Gordon Wade and his friends Jim, Norm and Ron carrying on about Ohio State Football or the newest advertising campaign as they walked by my desk. Until they turned the corner toward the elevator, I would put my head down in order to appear focused on a memo to avoid having to confront the fact that I was invisible to them.

I stayed at P&G for 16 years and worked in the world of what, thanks to the TV series, we now call Mad Men, breaking down, with the help of a few visionary leaders, one barrier after another in the all-white, all male and virtually all-American management monopoly that had evolved over the course of the 20th century. During those years I became the "first woman" to go on sales training, become a Brand Manager, marry another P&G brand person, have a baby and return to work, then babies two, three and four, advocate for maternity leave and childcare, move up the corporate ladder and directly report to the CEO.

John Smale, P&G's legendary CEO, called me to his office in late '78 and said: *"I'm looking for someone to help me figure out what Procter & Gamble should be in the next millennium."* CEOs think in quarters, maybe years, not decades, never millenniums, but that was John.

I took on the responsibility for the next five years of helping this extraordinary CEO lead a multi-billion-dollar acquisition program and a strategic plan which thrust the company into quadrupling its market value before the next millennium dawned. Five years later P&G was a different company, in the grocery store, in the executive offices and on Wall Street. The trajectory was straight up. What an exhilarating ride.

However, the pull of family was strong. I had taken a full 12 months off in 1982 when our youngest son, Chris, was born.

Jackie, Missy and Timmy were 9, 7 and 5, respectively. Jack ran a fast-growing entrepreneurial company and, as was the norm in the '80's, it occupied so much of his time that he was unable to take much responsibility for home and children. They needed me. I needed them.

Making the decision to resign was difficult. Everybody knows the power of red shoes. We also know "there's no place like home."

I would go on to work in a variety of fields including venture capital and real estate, serving on boards, founding a non-profit, starting clubs of my own and giving speeches on life balance . . . again and again finding myself the only woman at the table, surrounded by folks usually resistant to new ways of thinking.

Throughout the journey, there were bumps in the road – women need not apply signs, marches and a sit-in, inappropriate advances, a switchblade and gun or two, divorce and a near bankruptcy. But in all those ventures, I found a way (often with the help of men with influence) through hard work, drive and a commitment to excellence – to pioneer. With similar skills, I found ways to avoid ever having to say, *"me too."* I said, *"not me."*

It is said that there are no certainties in life, just stories. I tell my story in hopes that it will advance the idea of equality at work and in the home for men and women. Only then will individuals and resulting society have a shot at reaching its full potential.

John Pepper, who would become CEO of P&G and Board Chair of Disney, asked the head of personnel one question after my interview in 1966: *"Tell me again, why is it that we don't hire women for management positions?"* I'm still grateful to John for asking it.

That was the question that would redefine corporate America's landscape.

PART I

GROWING UP

FAMILY

"Flashback to kindergarten 1947 and in comes some little kid who lived out in the country that was coming to our kindergarten. She was cute, a good athlete, always first pick on our kickball teams and so damn smart that she scared the rest of us."

— *Susan Abernethy Frank, lifelong friend*

MY PARENTS MET on a tennis court when a stunning 17-year-old brunette climbed the fence surrounding Eden Park's Tennis Club and the caretaker and part-time instructor kicked her out. It was 1928 when Eve Roberts and Tim Hogan met. They would be married five years later: a gifted athlete and top model with a fun-loving free spirit, and a responsible law student and future federal judge.

Eve was unique. She knew her own mind and spoke it without filter or reservation. She was independent, especially for that era and ambitious for herself, for sure, but even more for her children.

In the late 60s, race riots swept through many American cities, hitting Cincinnati's urban core near where Mom and Dad had moved. Cincinnati sits on the Mason-Dixon line which divides the North and South. Despite the danger and Dad's pleas, my mother refused to move back to the farm – even temporarily.

We frequently had a drink in their breakfast room under a crystal, aquamarine chandelier. One evening, the phone rang. The angry caller announced that he had just been released from prison and he intended to kill the judge who put him there. Many (I suspect most) judges don't list home phones. My father did. He believed he was first and foremost a "public servant." And the public has a right to access its servants.

In the face of this "clear and present danger" threat, Eve Hogan had several options. She could have called the federal marshal's office as marshals are charged with protecting judges and their families. She could have called the neighborhood police. Instead, she responded: *"Our address is 3810 Eileen Drive. Come on over, I've got my gun out."* Astonished, I asked her why the invite and address? Her response: *"He'll never show up now."*

And she had a commanding, infectious personality. On a trip to Michigan in an upscale boutique hotel where the two of us stayed, we were leaving to find a place for dinner when she spied a wedding reception. To the utter embarrassment of my then 15-year-old self, Mom said, *"Let's go there."*

My reply: *"But we aren't invited."*

Then with flair and bravado, she waltzed into the party announcing, *"That's only because they don't know me yet."*

She would not babysit the grandchildren and didn't want to be called grandma. She was Eve and my father was Judge to all the grandchildren. She frequently invited our family for her gourmet meals, dressed up as the Easter bunny, took the kids to theatrical productions and arranged for Santa Claus to deliver presents in person on Christmas Eve. In many ways, she personified Auntie Mame's slogan: "Life is a banquet and most poor fools are starving to death."

Eve grew up in a large, frame home in Walnut Hills, Cincinnati, located on the streetcar line and a few minutes from downtown. Hers was a Welsh, Presbyterian, Republican family from Oakhill, in the hills of southern Ohio. Eve's grandmother, whom she called "Momgee," spoke Welsh and left their southeastern Ohio farm for Cincinnati when her husband died. A single woman with eight children couldn't thrive on a farm. The city offered opportunity. Mom used to tell us how, as a child, she and Momgee, who was well into her eighties, would scale the fence adjoining their small backyard to avoid paying entrance fees to the swimming pool next door. Breaking into forbidden places apparently characterizes the women in my family.

My grandmother Margaret started her Cincinnati life in her early teens as an upstairs maid in a house on Grandin Road, in the affluent neighborhood of Hyde Park. As fate would have it, in 1982 Jack and I bought the house across the street. My maternal grandparents were devout churchgoers. They had little formal education but succeeded with hard work. Mom went to the Cincinnati public Withrow High School, where she became a self-taught tennis champion. She attended the University of Cincinnati for a semester and found it challenging academically but soon enough was spending full time walking down runways, often modeling as a bride.

Tim Hogan was a child of privilege who, early on, lost the father he worshipped. His grandfather Patrick, a potato famine immigrant from County Kerry, Ireland, arrived in the U.S. in 1852, worked first as a fisherman on Lake Erie and finally settled on farming in Wellston, Ohio. Patrick married Margaret, the only one of her family to survive the Atlantic crossing – she was only 12 – landing in Canada, then New York where a well-to-do British family took her in and taught her to be governess for their children. Somehow, she found her way to Chillicothe, Ohio, met and married Patrick.

My paternal grandfather was born on a Jackson County farm June 11, 1864. As a young man he taught school for a few years while attending university in the summers. At the age of 23, he became superintendent of schools in Wellston. When Hogan introduced Longfellow's Churchyard Scenes into the curriculum, the Board, influenced by the Irish Catholic bigotry which raged in Ohio in the late 1800's, accused him of bringing religion into the classroom. This proud Irish Catholic resigned in a moving speech saying, *"no paltry job is worth it."* He taught himself law "under the old apple tree" and became one of the area's most successful lawyers with clients stretching across Ohio, West Virginia, Pennsylvania and Illinois.

Despite the bigotry rampant in Ohio and evidenced early in the Wellston schools, my grandfather became the first Irish Catholic elected to a statewide office west of New York and became Ohio's "Crusading Attorney General" according to the state's Hall of Fame. He got a favorable outcome in 11 constitutional law cases (out of 13 tried) in the Supreme Court of the United States, including those dealing with progressive labor issues, women's rights and the paramount right of parents to educate their children. He attributed much of his wisdom to what he learned from the children he taught in elementary school. All six of his children became lawyers, including two daughters, who graduated from law school in the 1930's and early 1940's.

After serving two terms as Attorney General, he ran for US Senate. The General, as he was known in the family, lost the race for Senate against Warren Harding – defeated by another wave of anti-Catholic bigotry. Political ads against him showed him digging a tunnel between the Pope in Rome and Ohio.

The General died when my Dad, Timothy S. Hogan II, was

16 and just finishing boarding school at Campion Jesuit School in Wisconsin. With dwindling funds, his mother Mary and two younger siblings moved to Cincinnati where Dad enrolled at Xavier, then simultaneously the University of Cincinnati Law school. He graduated with perfect grades at the top of his class at both universities while holding down jobs as tennis instructor, meter reader and tutor.

When Dad graduated, one of the most prestigious law firms in Cincinnati hired him for the highest salary ever paid in town. He wanted to be a litigator. Two weeks into the job, the senior partner called Tim into his office to announce that he had been assigned to the corporate department.

Tim: *"Do I have anything to say about that?"*
Senior partner: *"No, you work for us."*
Tim: *"Correction. I did."*

Such was his response in the height of the depression with a mother and younger siblings to help support and already knowing the girl he wanted to marry. His confidence and courage proved well-placed.

An independent thinker, he taught by example. Like his father, Dad was described as a common man with an uncommon mind, simple to an amazingly complicated degree. Instinctively he knew how to cut through complicated issues. And he stood for "doing the right thing." Whenever someone came to him for advice, which was often, he would say: *"Why don't we start with the truth?"*

Although I didn't think much about it growing up, perhaps because it was just the way it was, I had admirable role models, including strong and independent women. Beyond Dad's two lawyer sisters, other women in our extended family had jobs. Nana, my grandmother, ran a boarding house from her wheelchair. Aunt Alice, my favorite aunt, who returned to Cincinnati from Kansas City when her husband died, worked at AAA until almost 80. On Saturdays, she would often take me attired in white gloves and a pretty dress downtown for shopping and lunch at the Women's Exchange.

Aunt Helen Nugent (also my Godmother) went to New York in her early twenties and achieved national fame as the first singer CBS Radio Network hired. She sang with George Gershwin, Bing Crosby, Irving Berlin and other New York music greats.

Dad's sister, Aunt Mary, who remained single, practiced law during World War II when the men were at war. The firm let her go as soon as the men came home but she took on service in occupied Japan immediately after the war. When she returned to be with her mother in Cincinnati she taught school in the inner city. Regrettably, I never asked her how she felt being thrown aside. Aunt Mary had a wonderfully interesting life. She taught on a Native American reservation, and at the age of nearly 50 joined the Peace Corps. She met Mother Theresa in India. She traveled the globe and for several years lived with a gay man 30 years her junior.

Mom and Dad married in 1933 during the Depression, soon buying a home on Orchard Lane in Mt. Washington. They married in a small Protestant ceremony. His Catholic mother Mary and her Protestant dad Tom were against the marriage for religious reasons and neither attended nor spoke to the couple for months after the wedding.

Two years later, following a tennis game, Eve surprised Tim by arranging for a Catholic Jesuit priest to marry them at Bellarmine Chapel, Xavier University. The Jesuits are known to be the liberal order of the church. Mom signed the papers promising to raise the children Catholic (a requisite to Dad's being able to take the church's sacraments). Immediately after, she announced that she didn't plan to do that:

> *"My first child shall be raised Catholic; my second, Protestant; my third, Jewish. If there is a God in heaven, he is not as narrow-minded as those of us on earth."*

Mom raised me as a Protestant. We attended the St. Thomas Episcopal Church in Terrace Park. Dinner table conversations were punctuated with lively debates. My siblings argued, relaying what the nuns that taught them, that Mom and I were destined for hell. Dad kidded us about our being "non-union" or "high-society" Catholics. And when the non-union side faltered with Mom oversleeping, Dad always took me to church – sometimes Catholic, sometimes Lutheran, sometimes Presbyterian. Faith and tolerance became part of my DNA.

Before I was born, the Japanese bombed Pearl Harbor. Dad, at 32 years old with a three-year-old child and bad eyesight, was considered too old as well as unqualified to serve. He insisted on enlisting. *"I could never face my children without doing my part."*

The Army Air Force sent Dad to Washington D.C. during the war to help manage procurement in the European theatre. Immediately following the surrender on May 7, 1945, the Army deployed him to Berlin to work for General Lucius Clay, deputy to General Dwight D. Eisenhower, on the division of Germany. At the Potsdam Conference, the Allies divided Germany into four military occupation zones. Dad was part of that process.

During World War II, Mom managed to take me to Florida in the winter. Since only military personnel could get train tickets during the war, she would go to Union Terminal, hand me to a random young soldier, saying: *"I'm your wife and"* – putting me in his arms – *"this is your child."* Upon learning about this story,

I inquired about the wisdom and risks of handing me to a stranger, her answer was that *"No soldier wants a baby."*

World War II ended August 10, 1945. Dad had been in Europe since May. He wrote me a letter from Berlin:

> *"Dearest Peg – Tonight marks 3½ years since Daddy left home and which was even before you were born. It looks like the war of the sword is over. At least it is rumored so strongly over here that all of us (after the usual habit of combining the sublime with the ridiculous or going from one extreme to the other) went first to what was left of a church to say our nickel's worth of thanks to our Supreme Commander, and second to our billet to drink the few ounces of bourbon we had left to join together and celebrate. We hope that what girls like your Mother have gone through as an attendant to war will not be repeated in your lifetime – and perhaps that hope will call for a few more months of sacrifice on the part of us all to that end . . . the job of insuring it will not happen again has just begun. All my love, Dad."*

While in Germany preparing for the Potsdam Conference, Dad saw how the Russians behaved. According to a Cincinnati Post article in 1952, Lieutenant Colonel Hogan warned Clay by writing a speech for him while in Berlin that *"America would be wiser to make friends with the Germans rather than let them be made friends of Russia."* He saw Russia as the real enemy. The Army was tempted to court martial Dad for refusing to re-write the speech. However, as the Lt. Colonel said: *"You control what I do, not what I think."*

Lieutenant Colonel Hogan came home in December, in time for Christmas and my brother Timmy's birth. After the war, the family moved from the suburbs to a farm in the country east of Cincinnati.

The farm was a terrific place to grow up – with acres of fields, rolling hills, virgin forest and icy creeks. We had crazy, wild horses – Pepper, Pal, Goldie and a pony named Bitsy. We rode – often with no supervision – through the woods, swimming the Little Miami River and jumping over gullies and creeks and fences with reckless abandon.

We had chickens until my little brother Timmy lit the chicken coop on fire – not an act of meanness, but rather to see the fire engines come. We had a farmer and, upon those occasions when Mom or Dad mistakenly thought they could manage livestock, there were pigs and cows.

Tim and Nancy have enviable natural gifts. Tim is an outstanding athlete, loquacious and fun – blessed with an engaging sense of humor and commanding personality. Like Mom, everybody wants to be with him. Nancy is the smart one. She has that rare intellectual capacity to understand the globe and all its complexities. However, both rebelled as teenagers. There were car wrecks and wild parties. There were A's and F's on the report cards. There were fights with Mom and Dad, which, hating more than the combatants, strengthened my desire to achieve.

I am a middle child and, like most of those in the middle, I became the peacemaker, the pleaser, the one who, for the most part, lived between the lines and checked boxes. Class president. Cheerleader. Model. Girl Scout. Captain. Honor roll student. Award winner.

Every night we ate dinner precisely at 6:30 pm – with no interruptions. If the telephone rang, we let it ring. Once, I remember my Dad's response to a most persistent caller: *"A retainer guarantees I will never take a case against you. It doesn't mean you have a right to interrupt family dinner."* My usually courteous father once slammed the phone down on one of his most important clients. Family dinner is a tradition Jack and

I worked hard to keep sacred in our family, as do our children today.

There were lively discussions throughout dinner – usually about politics, religion and Dad's cases. The latter would always start with a firm admonition (Dad's early version of *"what happens in Vegas, stays in Vegas"*): *"This stays at the dining room table."* And it did. We learned about secrets and confidentiality early on.

After dinner, we studied. TV entered our lives when I was in fourth grade – long after it became a staple in friends' houses. The parents permitted each of us to choose one 30-minute show per week; I chose *I Love Lucy.*

While my siblings attended Catholic schools, my parents sent me to Terrace Park Elementary, a nearby, small public school in a Norman Rockwell neighborhood. On the surface, it was about as perfect a tree-lined community as one could imagine. Every father had a good job. Every mother stayed at home for the children, a badge of pride in the post-World War II era. Every family went to church, overwhelmingly Protestant. Everyone voted the Republican ticket. Children rode bikes down streets named for colleges like Harvard, Yale and Amherst.

In the 5th grade, I began playing tennis and shortly thereafter was playing with a passion. Dad would drop me off at the Cincinnati Tennis Club in Walnut Hills where I would hit all day long. It led to a lifelong love of racquet sports. Also, it led to developing a desire to play – on a field of endeavor that's level – whether the opponent is male or female, old or young, peer or parent. And eventually, the experience catapulted my desire to level unfair playing fields and win.

Every Thanksgiving and Christmas Eve we drove the 17 miles to Nana and Pop's rambling frame home in Walnut Hills where Aunts Alice and Ruth lived as well. Ruth's boyfriend, Si Bickel, a muscular teamster who drove a truck for Hostess Bakery and

Aunt Mary, the lawyer turned schoolteacher and Aunt Helen joined. Also, Nana always invited a boarder or two who had no other place to go. There was never a meal without a stranger at the table. I remember a police officer and various immigrants.

Given that Nana was wheelchair-bound, we took all the presents to Walnut Hills so she could share the joy. A real Santa would suddenly appear at the door with bells, jollies and a bag full of presents. Aunt Alice and Nana each year gave the girls a single piece of sterling silver flatware which eventually filled an entire set. There was fresh turkey and dressing, mashed potatoes, green beans and homemade pies. "Nothing fancy" as Dad would say. After dinner Aunt Helen would leave for the Catholic Cathedral, where for decades she was the lead soloist at midnight mass.

In 7th grade I had an inspiring homeroom teacher, lots of friends who liked coming to the farm for rides and overnights and finally, a straight A's report card. In 4th grade, I had my first plane ride. We took family trips to Miami Beach in the spring and ventured to a remote lake in Quebec to fish in the summer. Life seemed perfect. Then, my parents "spoiled" everything by making me go to a more challenging private, all-girls school in Cincinnati named Hillsdale (now Seven Hills).

I struggled there. Not only was it much more challenging than Terrace Park, but my sister enrolled me in French II as she didn't want me to be behind the rest of the class. Small detail – I had never studied French and she didn't tell the school.

The girl's school's motto was Qui Vieux Peut which translated ironically to "He who wishes, can." After a couple of years, I became comfortable, dropped French as soon as I could in favor of Latin, became a Cincinnati Country Day cheerleader (a local all-boys school) and began performing better in class. My biggest highs were playing on the city's all-city field hockey team and through the Midwest competing on the Whitman Cup junior tennis circuit.

Dad drove my best friend Leslie Carothers and me to school every morning as she lived near the farm. He drove a white and blue, late forties, Ford convertible. The rearview window was a mass of adhesive tapes, the paint was faded and the floor was so rusty that you could see the road passing underneath. I complained one day. The next day, there was a cookie sheet covering the hole.

On the way to school we would often talk about something relevant to academics. On many occasions, we would ask Dad the meaning of a word which was above our skill level. He always started with the derivatives – Latin first, then Greek. He would go on to give us a synonym, an antonym. He would use it in a sentence, then a sentence in a story. The whole process would often take the entire 25-minute ride. We did not forget any word he defined but sometimes we would think long and hard about asking. No surprise, many of the students to whom he taught the trial practice course at University of Cincinnati Law School on Saturday mornings became able litigators.

On October 4, 1957, the Soviets launched Sputnik 1 – the first artificial satellite to orbit the earth opening up space for peaceful exploration as well as destructive missiles. The announcement came in my sophomore year during English class, intensifying the political and military era known as The Cold War and heightening tensions between the United States and the Soviet Union. As my father had predicted, Russia was proving to be the real enemy. The United States was slow to wake up.

A life changing moment occurred when Hillsdale sent me in junior year as the school representative to an all-city high school conference where the students created and ran a city governance council. Virtually everyone at the event was male. I was knowledgeable about governance but reluctant to speak up, especially since I attended a small, all-girls school. As I listened to one boy after another confidently asserting this and that to be true, statements that were seldom evidence based, it dawned on me: *"They don't know what they're talking about. No facts, just talk."* Maybe I can hold my own in a bigger world.

By senior year Leslie and I ran the place, or so we thought – she as president of the student body, me as president of the athletic association. That year, I won a trip to New York City after placing first in a city-wide design, sewing and modeling contest. While I was realizing that I was smarter than a lot of boys my age, it was still important in 1959 to master the skills of homemaking.

I enjoyed a #2 academic ranking behind Leslie. Our plan was to head to Wellesley or Smith College in the fall.

Our headmaster threw me a curve ball. Headmaster Lovett told me to apply to easier schools as my SAT's were low. Why did he do that? Why did he choose to value a random test over years of strong performance? Why did he – head of school – encourage me to lower my sights? My response was: *"I'm going to the best college that will have me. And I am only applying to Smith and Wellesley. Does it matter whether I don't test well or am an over-achiever?"*

My confidence was not as bullish as the words I spoke. But once I uttered the words, that would be the plan. No turning back. I refused to apply anywhere else. Wellesley, which was my first choice, turned me down. Smith College, thank God, said *"yes."* Leslie also got into Smith so the team would continue.

On Friday June 10, 1960, 23 of us wearing long white dresses and carrying a dozen red roses walked down the aisle, graduating from the Hillsdale School. Commencement is supposed to be a beginning. But this ceremony looked back in every detail to Eisenhower's 50s.

As Dad often did, when he saw a daughter or pretty girl dressed up for a dance, he whistled as I walked by.

SMITH COLLEGE

"Peggy was the hardest working student I ever taught."

— R. Bruce Carroll, Smith College Professor

N 1840 CATHERINE Brewer became the first American woman to earn a bachelor's degree in the United States, graduating from Wesleyan College in Macon, Georgia. Before that, joining the nunnery or attending a seminary was the only way for a young girl in the United States to get a college education.

A generation later, in 1871, Sophia Smith founded Smith as a private all-girls college designed to educate women to the same level offered by the best men's colleges. To put her idea in the context of the times we need only read the 1873 Supreme Court Bradwell vs Illinois decision. The decision affirmed the lower court's ruling that women had no right to practice law. According to Justice Bradley, the *"[t]he natural and proper timidity and delicacy which belongs to the female sex evidently unfits it for many of the occupations of civil life . . . The paramount destiny and mission of women are to fulfill the noble and benign offices of wife and mother. This is the law of the Creator."* The pedestal rather than chains became our prison.

In September of 1960, mother drove Leslie and me to college. We stopped on the way at a very nice local restaurant in a rambling, old house overlooking Niagara Falls. Arriving for dinner, mother directed us to seats at the bar and announced, *"I am going to teach you two how to drink and handle it."* First rule. Pay your own way. Second rule. Pace yourself. We honored the first but not the second. By the end of the evening Mom was having a great time with the owners who brought up vintage wine from the cellar.

She remained in complete control. We did not. Coming directly out of a sheltered, girls-school environment where dates were rare and drinking only occasional, we found ourselves overindulged, vulnerable and out of control – polite words for drunk. This would not happen again any time soon. Nor would we be as naïve and vulnerable as when we started the trip. Eve had accomplished her goal without saying a word.

Also, she showed us that college should be fun. That her life was a series of parties is a lesson not lost on anyone who knew her.

Smith was a small college, only about 2,500 students, located in western Massachusetts, where in the small picturesque (and liberal) town of Northampton, the Puritan Johnathan Edwards first preached his "Hell, Fire and Damnation" sermons from his pulpit on Main Street.

At the base of the Berkshire Mountains, in New England's "Pioneer Valley," the area is known for its "knowledge" economy and the exquisite fall foliage. Every October, the President of Smith selects an especially gorgeous day and the bells ring at 7:30 am, canceling all classes for the day. It is an idyllic setting and I have fond memories of my years there.

Smith College is perched on the town's highest hill. Most buildings are Georgian brick or English Gothic stone. Large lawns surround the main buildings on the campus College Hall, The Steele Building and Nielson library.

In place of dormitories, Smith has a series of small houses. Each boasted a housemother until the 80's. The houses were equally divided among members of all four classes. Students served dinner on a rotating basis with white tablecloths every evening and a formal tea in the living room on Friday afternoons.

Tyler House, at the end of Green Street overlooking Paradise Pond, became my new home. Our house mother, Ruth Hesse, was charged with keeping us in line – locked in by 10:00 pm on weekdays and midnight on weekends. To me and other sheltered freshmen, this seemed normal. Ironically, a few years later, the little white frame house next door would become the setting for Elizabeth Taylor and Richard Burton in *Who's Afraid of Virginia Woolf?*

Small self-governing houses and extensive extracurricular groups created ample opportunities for participation and leadership. It is often said that if you put four Smith graduates in a room, by the end of the afternoon you'll have a president, vice president, secretary and treasurer.

Smith, in fact all the other Seven Sister colleges, attracted bright, well-educated women whose parents could afford the tuition and who were able to get in. It was all white except for a handful of students from Africa. Many graduated from all-girl high schools located on the east coast. Still stinging from my Headmaster's dire predictions, I was intimidated by the brainpower and polish of my classmates. The first person I encountered in the hall was Nora, a nerdy looking freshman who announced right off that she had scored 1600 on her SATs. Homesick and insecure, I was shaken. My solution was to work.

Smith protected its students in many ways. The graduation rate, as I recall, was very close to 100%. Although not everybody could or should have earned a degree in four years, the college worked hard with strugglers and those considering dropping out.

Our introductory all-class experience occurred in the large,

John H. Greene red brick auditorium on Elm Street. President Mendenhall gave the welcoming speech, challenging us to capitalize on the opportunities before us and to study hard. *Study hard*. Follow the rules. Stay within the lines. Fulfill our potential, then, after graduation, it was the expectation that we would marry – preferably a gentleman graduate of Amherst, Harvard, Yale, Williams or any of the other neighboring male colleges. That was the established pattern of all past generations for the last century of the school. We would put our education to good use in the community and in educating our own children – the boys to lead and the girls to support. Smith taught us so we could teach the next generation.

However, Mendenhall also said that morning that our Smith education could take us anywhere . . . and that's what I remember. Maybe there was a path that was not the supporting role in life's drama.

On that particular sunny September day, we dressed in plaid kilts, white blouses with Peter Pan collars, heather green Shetland sweaters and Capezio flats. Monograms abounded. This was the unofficial uniform that filled our closets. No jeans or sweats could be seen in the auditorium. We were less mature than today's college freshmen – inexperienced, idealistic, excited and hopeful.

Like my high school graduation, there was nothing on that day to suggest that the peace and prosperity or the suburban conventions still in place would explode into the cultural and political shifts which would shape us into something more than our mothers.

Freshman year rolled in with Elvis' "It's Now or Never" and Chubby Checker's "The Twist" which we happily danced to on trips to Williams and Amherst. Smith social life also offered mixers on campus which were a little too stiff, formal and intimidating for a self-conscious, shy Midwestern girl. The only music in our room to be heard was that of rock and roll pioneer Buddy Holly, who had died in a plane crash the year before at age 22. My still devastated southern roommate June played "That'll Be the Day" and "Peggy Sue" constantly. As Jinny described it: "We had so much fun in the simplest of ways such as dress up parties and dances in our rooms."

Having played competitive tennis in high school, I found it disappointing that Smith offered no intercollegiate competition. The college, however, required that we choose three athletic activities during freshman and sophomore years. In addition to field hockey and tennis, I chose skiing and squash – the idea was to learn, not to compete.

Freshman year at Smith, for me, turned on government and politics. I took the required 101 courses in English, history, economics, French and government. Smith professors were generally excellent teachers as the college, unlike many, hired and retained on the basis of teaching skill rather than publishing output. President Mendenhall taught one history section a year. I was lucky to be in his class and when he selected my first test as a good example of B work and distributed it along with the A example to all freshman history students, I knew I could keep up and was inspired to go for the A.

The course that lit up my life was Government 101, taught first semester by Department Chair Leo Weinstein and second semester by a young professor named Bruce Carroll, both from the University of Chicago. We studied Plato, Socrates, Locke and Hobbes, philosophers I found riveting.

There was more than political theory going on just beyond the ivied walls of Smith in 1960. Senator John F. Kennedy from Massachusetts was running against Vice President Richard M. Nixon for president. Kennedy was the first Irish Catholic nominated for president by a major political party since Al Smith in 1928. Smith, who was a friend of my Catholic grandfather, had lost in a landslide defeat. In Massachusetts and around the country many young people mobilized behind the good looking, charismatic candidate and I was among them. Two weeks after arriving on campus, I watched the first ever televised debates, put up posters and was lucky enough, thanks to sister Nancy who worked on the campaign, to obtain tickets to Kennedy's rally in Boston the night before the election. Election night we all stayed up till about six in the morning to catch the first news of his victory.

Thanksgiving vacation came three weeks later. At the last minute, I decided to go to Washington instead of home, writing my parents, *"I'm going to Washington to meet the president-elect."* This news met with skepticism of course. No matter. Nor did the fact that JFK planned to spend Thanksgiving vacation in Palm Beach.

My sister Nancy and her roommate Lynn Paul had a full-on Thanksgiving dinner. Their Georgetown apartment overlooked the back entrance to the Kennedy home. When Nancy spied an ambulance pull in late that night, she said, *"Jackie is going to the hospital to have the baby."* The three of us rallied. We took a large yellow chrysanthemum from the Thanksgiving table, a "Kennedy for President" button and a handwritten note of congratulations. Then we drove to Georgetown Hospital where we waited with the growing number of writers and photographers from the press. There were no other spectators. Mid-way through the night we bought a very inexpensive box of "It's a Boy" cigars and waited for Kennedy, whose Palm Beach bound plane had turned around in mid-air.

When the president-elect arrived, the press pushed me forward, then snapped photos. Not yet trained in security protocol, Kennedy reached out for the box of cigars then pulled back letting a secret service man take the gift on his behalf.

The next morning my parents opened the Cincinnati newspaper to find a headline which read *"Local girl greets President-Elect"* along with an AP wire photograph of Kennedy, me and the floral decorated box of cigars. Dad sent me a telegram that morning: *"I don't know whether to say never underestimate the power of a woman, an Irishman or a Hogan."*

Courtesy of Nancy, I went to Washington D.C. for the inauguration as a junior hostess for the Inaugural Ball. A huge snowstorm hit Washington the night before, and the day itself was frigid. Nevertheless we stood and heard the new president's inspirational words:

"Let the word go forth that the torch has passed to a new generation . . ."

"Ask not what your country can do for you but what you can do for your country."

". . . it will not be accomplished in the first 100 days nor in the life of this administration nor perhaps in the lifetime of those of us on this planet."

That afternoon we went to lunch at the Mayflower Hotel and saw President Harry Truman, his wife Bess and daughter Margaret in the dining room. I walked over to meet him. The President stood up and introduced me to the rest of the table. My shyness was disappearing.

That night at the Inaugural Ball I did the same thing with Robert Frost, poet laureate for the inauguration and resident of Amherst, near Smith. In my bright red ball gown, I went up to his box, put out my hand and said, *"Hello, Mr. Frost I am Peggy Hogan. I am a Smith College freshman. I like your poetry."* He was gracious.

A couple of years later my sister sent me the photograph with Kennedy's signature and best wishes. Nancy worked in the White House after the election. The president walked by one night, looked at the photograph, which was on her desk, and said, *"I remember her. Do you mind if I sign it?"*

Beyond politics and power, which dominated my first year, there was freshman French. With an undiagnosed learning disability, it was impossible for me to hear and speak a foreign language, nor did the course pique my interest. Smith moved me to another class where we read in French, wrote papers and exams in English. This worked.

Toward the end of freshman year Bruce Carroll, my Government 101 professor, asked me to stop by his office. While I was surprised that he even knew my name, having uttered not a single word in class, I found my way to Wright Hall 221 that afternoon where he suggested, *"I think you should sign up for Constitutional Law."* Constitutional was a well-known, highly regarded class taken, I thought, mostly by seniors. That was the moment that turned my self-doubt into confidence. The class itself determined my major as well as lifelong interest in government and politics.

Sophomore summer, Holly Gill, my friend from Bronxville, and I drove to California just to experience both the country and a road trip. Tyler House sponsored an event in the fall, a "toga" party with Yale's Whiffenpoofs. A friend invited me to Dartmouth's winter carnival which was the "model" for John Belushi's Animal House. My sister intervened, and my parents nixed the trip. Also, we experienced in a frightening way how tenuous life can be as Kennedy faced and guided the country through the 13-day Cuban Missile Crisis – the closest the world has come to nuclear holocaust.

Bruce Carroll was one of several excellent teachers from the

University of Chicago's famed school of political science. Leo Weinstein, Gwendolyn Carter and Cecil Kenyon were others. These professors attracted exceptional students. Additionally, President Kennedy, the Cold War and Warren's active, liberal Supreme Court made the study of politics and constitutional law a living experience, taking us well beyond the learnings of a dusty library.

Government studies became my major and the government department became an addictive and exciting home to me. I spent evenings in Wright Hall (later renamed after Weinstein thanks to Leslie Carothers) studying and talking with teachers. Bruce Carroll became a mentor in the true sense of the word, an advisor and trusted friend. I came to love the work and all its challenges.

I worked incredibly hard. In a letter sent to my parent's sophomore year, I said, *"All I do is write papers – four recently – and take exams. I decided if I were to ever do well at Smith, I would have to make a concerted effort to improve. So I contacted Mr. Young, head of the English department who taught my Shakespeare course, and asked him to give me some old exams. I timed myself. Rewrote. I took them again. Mr. Young corrected. Then I repeated the whole process. I am getting better."*

In the spring, I would visit friends of my parents, Jimmy and Mary Kirgan, who owned a 50-foot fishing boat which they kept in West Palm Beach and Bimini. The captain's name was Vic. As a young man, Vic worked for Hemingway in Cuba. Under his direction, and with the luck of the Irish, I caught a 125-pound white marlin and a 300-pound blue within a year. I hung out with the boat people – the captains and fishermen – as much as the fancy owners.

In the fall of my junior year I fell for a guy. Rick Knauft. Rick was a swimmer from Harvard, who roomed with Frank Wood. Wood was a longtime friend from Cincinnati and Nantucket where we vacationed several summers. I spent a lot of time in Cambridge with Rick my last two years at Smith. We talked about marriage after graduation. That was the plan and it would have been the norm in those days. In 1962 the median age for getting married was 20 for women. Several of my high school friends were already married and having babies. All of my high school classmates and a few college classmates would be married within a couple of years after graduation.

After junior year, I became a government department Washington intern. Getting an internship to work for the summer in Washington D.C. was a huge honor. To the best of my knowledge Smith and Yale were among the very few colleges to send students. Smith selected just 12 of us; the Ford Foundation gave scholarships.

Leslie and I went, with four other Smithies, and rented a house in Georgetown. I asked for and received an internship with Congressman John E. Moss' subcommittee on freedom of information, based on my intention to write my senior thesis on executive privilege. At the time, it was a little-known constitutional privilege that presidents used to withhold information from the public. Kennedy used it during the Cuban Missile Crisis in October 1962. It would become Nixon's downfall during Watergate. Trump has taken it to a whole new level.

This was my first real job, and I hoped it would be a challenging one. The initial assignment involved clerical duties like placing orders for supplies, cleaning the closets and similar tasks. I decided the best way to move to higher ground was to do all the work expected to last eight weeks in the first week or two, then ask to do things that would require thinking. The plan worked. My next assignment was compiling a list of every bit of information in the government or beyond relating to freedom of information, executive privilege and the right of the people to know what was going on. The Government Printing Office published the results that fall.

A fast talking, 45-ish, good looking man name Sam Archibald headed the committee. He was a womanizer, a practiced and skilled one. I had been on the job only couple of weeks when Sam invited me for a drink at the Occidental a few blocks from the White House. With a history dating back nearly 50 years, this iconic bar, combined with the easy way Sam chatted with the staffers and congressmen assembled there, was sure to impress any college junior. It did.

Trying to appear nonchalant and sophisticated, I ordered a Cutty Sark scotch and water and became engaged in the heady conversation. I actually thought my boss had interest in my intellectual contributions until we got into the taxi which was to take me back to Georgetown. It was only a 10-minute ride. However, his advances, which I somehow managed to hold off, were permanently imprinted on my young mind. I cried myself to sleep that night but didn't tell anyone.

Over the summer, I had similar experiences with all five other staff members save a newlywed man named Bill from Cornell. Walking to the break room for coffee, any woman ran the risk of feeling a hand or arm where it didn't belong. When beckoned to one of their offices, I never knew who would implant an unwanted slobbery kiss on my mouth or issue a nefarious invite for drinks. Like Sam, the five others were all old, at least to me. All were married, at least on paper.

I learned to avoid being alone in the office at any time and certainly never after dark. Fending off advances became an art form. There were no other tools. The phrase sexual harassment wasn't in the lexicon of 1960. Like all places of power, Congress and its staff was a men's club; and, if we wanted to be there, we had to keep quiet – Smith's place at the table was in the balance. Boys will be boys.

From an August letter to my parents:

"Nancy has been an amazingly good big sister. About three weeks ago she started to arrange "evenings at home dinners" for the six of us. She calls congressmen, reporters and senators to invite them to our house. Next week we are having Congressman Brademas from Indiana and Congressman Ashley of Ohio; the following week, Hubert Humphrey and Sandy Vanocur with Al Otten (Washington reporter for the Wall Street Journal). She also arranged a special White House tour for us last Saturday, also made up a list of all the places we have to see before September 1.

So many exciting things have happened that I don't know quite where to begin. Last Tuesday afternoon I attended a presidential press conference; this afternoon I went to see Congressman Harsha . . . asked him some questions about the happenings of the district, none of which he answered well. I've been going to hearings whenever I get a chance and have heard both Dean Rusk and Bobby Kennedy on the pending civil rights legislation.

I've loved every minute that I've spent in Washington but have not come to any final conclusions about the people here, their politics and their lives. At this point I'm only sure of two things. Washington is impressive and deceptive."

At our "at-home dinners," we always invited two guests – as each would be more likely to accept a stranger's invitation if there was an associate along to enjoy. And if they were complete duds, they could talk to each other. Senators Humphrey and Kefauver accepted our invitation as did Congressmen, reporters and network anchors. With no Martha Stewart experience or skill, I shudder to think about the quality of food and wine that we served. However, we were young, enthralled by government and politics, eager to learn and hopeful about the future and the role we would have in shaping it. Perhaps that was enough for our guests. It was about conversation.

We also invited Supreme Court Justices Goldberg and White. While they declined the dinner invitation (the only ones I remember who declined) Justice Goldberg invited us to have lunch with him in the Court's private dining room. So impressive was the place and its power that I have no recollection of our discussion.

The summer of '63, one hundred years after Lincoln signed the Emancipation Proclamation, I remember listening to President Kennedy addressing the nation in a major June 11 television speech advocating for civil rights legislation as a moral imperative.

Unrest and violence, mostly white violence against peaceful black activists, continued spreading across the south. To move the President and Congress to action, civil rights leaders called for a major march in Washington D.C. which took place on August 28. Jim Crow laws limited opportunities. Voting laws kept many blacks away from voting booths. Union rules closed off economic opportunities. Black-only, White-only signs permeated the South in hotels, restaurants and theaters, even water fountains. With the goal of passing civil rights legislation that would provide the freedom and jobs which the Civil War had failed to achieve, marchers came by the thousands.

I was completely ignorant of racial issues. As photos from kindergarten through college reveal, diversity was a foreign subject to me. No African Americans attended my high school or my church. The only black person I knew personally was

Elizabeth, the maid who worked in our home for $15 per week plus housing.

I had, however, been studying constitutional law and the increasingly liberal Warren court under Professor Carroll. I had attended congressional hearings and listened to the Kennedys. And I remembered my grandfather's struggle as an Irish Catholic.

One of my friends worked at the newly established Civil Rights Commission and he asked me to conduct a survey of march participants. I did all morning until I ran into a man who came from South Africa. This man kept saying, *"Do you understand how amazing this is to have a march like this? It would never be allowed in South Africa. It would never be peaceful."* I spent the rest of the day marching with him, learning all the while about inequality in a place far worse than the U.S. and the perils his people faced standing up to the power of the white man.

Well over 200,000 mostly black people peacefully demonstrated in Washington that day. They demanded congressional action that would take the country further in the continuing battle for fairer treatment and a more even battlefield. People jammed the mall between the Washington Monument and Lincoln Memorial, mixing poor, struggling blacks with black leaders, curious whites, and rich and famous singers and speakers.

Bob Dylan, Joan Baez, Mahalia Jackson, Marian Anderson, Harry Belafonte, Peter, Paul and Mary and Pete Seeger performed. A young John Lewis, Jackie Robinson and Rosa Parks were among those who spoke eloquently about the nation's original sin.

Martin Luther King, Jr. gave what has become one of the most famous speeches in American history, *"I Have a Dream."*

It was a defining moment.

King and other leaders met that evening with President Kennedy and Vice President Johnson. Bobby Kennedy, himself ignorant of racial issues only a few months previously, predicted that a black man would be president within the next 50 years. While it took almost a year, and the death of a president, the march was instrumental in getting the Civil Rights Act of 1964 passed.

A week or so after the march, we packed up our Georgetown town house and prepared for the drive back to Northampton. I promised to give a ride to Smith classmate, Anne Palms from Richmond, Virginia, who planned to meet me in Georgetown late in the afternoon. The day before departing, a college friend asked if a fellow Harvard law student could join us and, of course, I said *"yes."* I didn't know then that he was black.

When I opened the door to our living room that afternoon, the atmosphere was so frigid it could be chiseled. The appalled parents of my southern friend refused to allow Anne to ride in a car with the black man. The Harvard man remained quiet but firm; fully expecting a ride back to Northampton, he refused to budge. It took time and patience, but Anne finally convinced her parents to let the three of us go. The winning argument was that they could not allow me to ride alone with this man.

We hit the road. But an hour or so into Maryland we stopped to get coffee. The three of us sat at the counter. The waitress refused to serve us coffee. My new black friend, who before this had been compliant, had hit a wall, again refusing to budge. It was a breaking point for him. He would not leave.

In the beginning I thought surely the waitress would give us some coffee and we would continue on our journey. Or, we would convince him to let us get on the road. But no.

A trucker walked in. Then another. And another. And another. None of them liked what they saw and none of them left. After about 40 minutes, surrounded by over a dozen truck drivers, I decided that it was time to make a phone call. I walked to the pay telephone booth when a hairy, muscular, southern driver's arm blocked my access to the phone. At the same time, he made clear that his hatred was directed not to my black passenger, but to the white trash who would keep him there.

I thought we would be killed.

Ten minutes later two state troopers walked in. The white southern troopers disliked what they saw as much as the truckers but apparently this was not to be the moment for another racially motivated murder. They ordered us to get in the car and get out of the state. To ensure against racial hostilities exploding into violence, the state troopers, several cars by now, escorted us to the state line. The truckers led the way, passed on the side, followed behind and constantly honked their horns until we crossed into the north.

My sister Nancy and Fred worked at the White House for the first two years of the Kennedy administration. After the Cuban Missile Crisis, the President moved them to the State Department. I called them as soon as I got back to Smith and recounted my experience. The following Monday, Fred arranged for federal law enforcement officers to visit the truck stop, which would never again refuse service. My innocent world crumbled after that trip. I'd seen the prejudice of my own friends' parents, as well as the red-face hatred of the bigoted truckers.

Back at Smith, I focused on work. Honors students had four courses rather than five. A thesis counted for two in the government department. I had a once-a-week seminar – so only one normal course, which Dad found rather appalling. So, I spent lots of time in Cambridge with Rick and at Neilson library.

Professor Bruce Carroll, by now my friend as well as my teacher, was the advisor for my thesis on executive privilege, an extension of my summer work. I applied to law schools – Harvard as a long shot and Georgetown.

Throughout, John F. and Jacqueline Kennedy continued to inspire. So attractive, so articulate, so able to raise the hopes of Americans, especially young people as he:

- Advocated for saving the seashores which Rachael Carson, author of *Silent Spring,* considered the beginning of the environmental movement

- Called for nuclear disarmament around the world, standing up against the Soviets

- Stood for civil rights, including the establishment of a presidential commission on women headed by Eleanor Roosevelt which was a radical new idea

- Offered the challenge of public service by creating the Peace Corps

- Challenged the country to send a man to the moon.

In presenting new ideas, President Kennedy quoted the Bible, Shakespeare and the founding fathers with equal ease. He created in the process phrases that penetrated the American psyche. He did it with such grace and humor that many of us set our sights higher and came to believe that we could do and be anything at all. That goes a long way toward explaining why a few Smith Juniors could invite Congressmen and Supreme Court Justices to dinner, fully expecting them to come.

Then, out of nowhere, comes Harvey Oswald. I was in Tyler House coming down the stairs for a class when a friend at the reception desk screamed, *"Kennedy's been shot."* There are few times in life − − very few − when one remembers exactly the time and place of an occurrence. Kennedy's shooting and Harvey Oswald's are two.

November 22, 1963, was a fault line for my generation.

With tears streaming down my checks, I went immediately to the Smith College chapel. Feelings of anger mixed with hopelessness and loss filled me. Then, like most of the world, we watched the coffin's procession to the Dallas airport, Jackie in her bloodstained pink suit witnessing Lyndon being sworn in. The death was, because of his youth and vigor, a frightening unexpected event, especially to young people.

We had to do something. On Sunday morning, a couple of us drove to Boston just to be closer to the places where Kennedy lived. We were leaving a service at Harvard's chapel when we heard the news about Jack Ruby shooting Oswald.

For days and days, we were glued to the TV. Of the funeral, Mary McGory said, *"He would have liked it. It had that decorum and dash that were his special style."*

With oversight from Professor Carroll, I focused on my thesis written on the subject of executive privilege, for the balance of senior year. It was an obscure subject, investigated only by a few reporters and members of the Freedom of Information Congressional Subcommittee on Public Information. During the Cuban missile crisis, President Kennedy said he had a cold for a period of about two weeks, which he didn't. He also issued misleading press releases. He wanted time and privacy to negotiate with the Russians. Diplomacy requires secrecy to work well and, in times of crisis, like October 1962 when the threat of nuclear war loomed, time can be crucial.

The Constitution doesn't mention executive privilege. The Supreme Court first addressed the subject when Richard Nixon refused to release White House tapes. Presidents dating back to Jefferson have claimed they could refuse to release internal documents and communications to appear in court. I concluded the public's right to know stops short of full disclosure and is limited by national security. Lincoln – faced with civil war and the need to preserve the country – denied habeas corpus, closed newspapers and held back information to save the union, all under the general umbrella of executive privilege. In retrospect, Kennedy's use seems like child's play – such a minor and short-term imposition on the press and public when compared to Nixon's Watergate, Clinton's Lewinsky scandal and Trump's impeachment shut down, constant lies and congressional stiff arms. Privilege taken to a whole new level.

Professor Carroll was a teaching scholar capable of imparting knowledge with the best of professors and inspiring students. That's not what made him special. What made him special was his ability to make young people believe in themselves, believe we could compete with anyone, at any level.

After my graduation ceremony at Smith I said goodbye to a half dozen Tyler House roommates with whom I have remained friends. Rick and I embraced one last time. I would not see him again for over 30 years. I attended his father's funeral but didn't make myself known. The past is the past.

My family helped with the packing. We carefully wrapped my diploma, mementos from weekend trips to Harvard, Yale and Williams, a few of my best college papers, a poster from the 1960 campaign along with the engraved invitation to JFK's inaugural ball and the constitutional law syllabus from freshman year. Then we tossed the trunk out my third-floor window.

As we drove away, I could almost hear Bruce saying, *"Okay, Peggy, you got this. Make a difference."*

PART II
GETTING STARTED

AMERICAN EDUCATION INTERNATIONAL

"She was the architect of a business that provided study abroad programs for American students who were challenged to understand international relationships due to the cold war of the 60s. Ahead of its time."

– Lynn Paul, Early IBM programmer

FOR AS LONG as I can remember, I intended to be an attorney. As my father said in a Cincinnati Magazine article about the Hogan family, *"Becoming a lawyer was almost like getting breakfast in the morning."* Bruce had persuaded Georgetown Law School in Washington D.C. to admit me despite another low score – this time on the LSATs.

Just before graduating from Smith, I got a surprise job offer in Cincinnati from a man named Doug Burke whom I had dated. Working with two other Procter & Gamble brand managers, Doug was considering starting a company that would send students on European travel programs. The idea appealed to me. It would expose American students to other cultures, like Kennedy's 1961 Peace Corps.

Their thought was to have me do the start-up work to determine whether the idea had legs before they left Procter &

Gamble positions. The pay wasn't much but they promised an equity interest if the company got off the ground. Academics had been my focus for so many years that the idea of stepping away for a while was attractive, and it was a learning opportunity.

When Georgetown Law agreed to a one-year deferment, I said *"Yes, I'll do it"* and moved back to Cincinnati. I had no business skills but could do a bit of everything – I was the inexpensive "Jack of all Trades" that they needed.

We developed a name, "World Language Academy," and set up a small office in Cyril's apartment on Hill Street in Mt. Adams, a Cincinnati neighborhood just becoming trendy. I worked alone developing the program. Six months later we had hundreds of students signed up. When the men quit their jobs, they reneged on the promise of equity. However, Cyril presented a non-compete agreement for me to sign. How crazy? Three P&G executives apparently found a 21-year-old with six months experience threatening.

About the same time, I ran into Jimmy Kirgan, the family friend and wealthy Texan whose fishing yacht I frequented during college. Jimmy was large in size with a deep powerful voice, drove only Cadillac El Dorados and lived in a former Ohio governor's house. He knew what I had been doing at the World Language Academy. He thought the field had potential. One night at a party at my parent's home, he said, *"I'll give you $5,000 to write a prospectus."* That would be the equivalent of nearly $50,000 today – a significant amount of money to a newly minted college graduate.

Not knowing what "prospectus" meant, while suspecting it wasn't anything bad, I responded, *"Let me think about that."* Later that night, looking the word up in Webster's, I learned; *"a document describing the major features of a proposed project, business venture, etc., in enough detail so that investors, may evaluate it."*

A prospectus appeared remarkably like a college paper, so I thought, *"I can do that."* It changed the trajectory of my life.

In a call to Jimmy the next morning, I asked him to send the money, made plans to move back to Washington and began launching another company. Less than a year after graduation, I became a CEO.

Even as the 60's were changing, start-ups were rare in America. For men, "the gray flannel suit" way of thinking and dressing still dominated. There weren't any venture capital funds. Entrepreneurs were unusual. And for perspective, people who launched a company often stayed with the same company for life.

In D.C., once again on my own, I set up a small office downtown. My sister Nancy and brother-in-law to-be Fred Dutton helped. Fred agreed to lend his name with its White House and State Department experience as an advisor, providing instant credibility. Lou Beller joined as office manager and secretary. Lynn, Nancy's college roommate and one of IBM's first programmers, and I leased a place in Georgetown.

We called the new enterprise American Education International (AEI). As countries became more connected, American young people needed to think globally. We would take high school students to France and Spain on a first-class university program where they could improve foreign language ability as well as their understanding of other cultures. Memorizing conjugations and reading *Le Petit Prince* began the learning process. The missing link was "motivation."

We set about creating a platform that provided motivational materials – newsletters and 33 LP records designed to capture the attention of teenagers. We included: Charles DeGaulle's address to the U.S. Congress, Winston Churchill broadcast in broken French to the people of France after the Germans invaded, Jacqueline Kennedy's tour of the White House for French radio and the Spanish version of the Beatles as well as Ladybird Johnson's Spanish greeting. AEI provided teachers with materials that were a cross between *Seventeen* and *Sports Illustrated*. Sure, the students would learn something about the language. More importantly, they would become more interested in learning. Shamelessly ignorant of copyright laws, and with access to friends who worked in Congress and Voice of America, we were able to "borrow" the material.

The next challenge was to create a membership organization that would qualify under aviation laws for charter privileges within the airline industry. We discovered that the Department of Education maintained a list of 16,000 French and Spanish teachers. Through a friend, we secured the list and hired a few high school students for $1.00 per hour to type, stuff and mail, offering the teachers motivational teaching aids as well as the opportunity to travel to Europe for free by recruiting eight of their students. Because teachers at the time didn't generally have the opportunity to travel abroad, nearly 1,000 joined the organization. The solicitation piece generated a response rate of 6.25%. The idea struck a nerve. In 1966, only about 1% of Americans had a passport whereas now 40% do.

I had eight months of business experience, spoke only Latin and had never ventured outside the U.S. except to Canadian lakes with my family in the summertime. However, I didn't give any thought to what I didn't know.

After the membership drive, I just got started. I traveled around the U.S. recruiting teachers and giving speeches to parents, asking them to entrust their teenage children to AEI and pay $975 for the privilege. I had no concept of the magnitude of risk involved in taking responsibility for sending a few hundred teenagers to Europe. Just a few years before I was one of them.

My Dad understood the risk. He encouraged me to buy insurance. I called an agent I found in the yellow pages. Confessing my ignorance, I asked him to spend the day teaching me about the industry and, in return, I promised to purchase a policy by day's end.

Dad flew to D.C. also to warn me about Social Security and employer income tax and other funds companies hold back from payroll to send to the government. Write those checks first. It's easy for cash-strapped companies to postpone IRS payment only to find later the money's gone. *"It's a criminal offense with jail as the penalty."*

Strangely, I remained blissfully confident about the venture until flying to France to make summer school arrangements. Getting off the plane in Paris and hearing only the sound of French, I was suddenly petrified. Despite intellectual awareness, the reality of hearing everyone talk in an incomprehensible language shocked me. I took a taxi to the hotel and went immediately to bed, sleeping for a long time.

The next morning, I called my Smith roommate, Randy Fletcher. After Smith and her junior year abroad in Geneva, she landed a job in Paris with IBM. It took time to get through the corporate telephone maze with a French operator not knowing the office where she worked or what she did. But we connected.

Randy proved to be the key to extending hospitality and tour guide expertise. She put me in taxis and on trains to Rennes and Grenoble where we had made university connections. After two weeks I had travelled through France, eaten raw fish and warm croissants, drank cognac at the base of the Eiffel Tower with Randy and signed contracts with universities for four-week teaching programs, dormitory arrangements and weekend excursions. I even learned to love escargot.

Back in the States, the task was travel arrangements. Our guiding principle was always to find the highest quality partner. Given that our program was new and the CEO inexperienced, I decided to work only with skilled people and well-regarded organizations. So, when it came time to make travel arrangements, it would be American Express. Sadly, my contact at American Express looked at me, then at the request to charter a transcontinental jet or two and laughed. The man was not interested.

I had heard that the banking industry was trying to break into the travel business, and so I made an appointment to talk with the newly appointed Director of Travel at Citibank in New York City. This midsized stocky guy, who looked like the banker in Mary Poppins, opened the travel department. As luck would have it, AEI was to be the Bank's first and largest travel customer. We settled on chartering only a major airline – Pan American – as the charters were considered less reliable.

In March 1966, *Mademoiselle* published a "Young Tycoon" issue: "Special! Owning Your Own Business – the How's, the Why's, the Where's" article about working women. It focused on "women bosses," finding seven of us to feature in a national search.

After a few months, 28 teachers signed on, enrolling high school students in the process. It seemed like we were ready. But then it hit me; I had no experience taking care of a single teenager let alone a couple hundred. What if someone got pregnant? What if a teacher misbehaved? What if they actually acted like teenagers? The reality that I had zero first-hand experience with any of these issues suddenly flummoxed me.

As I had done at Smith many times, I called Bruce. It was early

May and we were set to depart next month. The Carrolls had two small children – Tim, 5, and Megan, 3.

"Hi Bruce, what are you and Gail doing this summer?"

"Nothing planned."

"Well, how about an all-expense paid trip to Europe for the family? We can't afford a salary, but the University of Grenoble is on a mountain lake in the Alps. You wouldn't have any specific responsibilities – just be there in case there's a problem."

They agreed, as did Randy and a couple of other College friends, who would be campus directors.

Before taking off, the Chief of Protocol, James Symington from the State Department, agreed to speak to the group of students and their parents from Washington D.C. Leaning against the door of our Georgetown house, Symington advised, *"Be sensitive. Keep a record of your impressions. Write down what you think and why. Keep names and addresses."* And he later added, *"Every one of you will be America over there. But don't let this overwhelm you. Just be more of yourself than you ever were before."* The Evening Star covered the event.

Some 230 students from 20 states departed for Europe on June 27. Three groups of students went to French universities (Tourane, Rennes and Grenoble) and one to the University of Madrid.

From JFK Airport, I watched the PanAm jet lift off for Paris from the observation deck – feeling incredulous, proud, excited and yes, a little apprehensive. I joined them a week later.

On July 8, employees of the major airlines including Pan Am declared a strike. It worried the parents – who started a seemingly endless series of calls – but not me.

The program involved four weeks of intense language instruction at the universities followed by two weeks of travel in the country being visited. Teachers and their students would live in dormitories with other foreign students. Citibank made all the arrangements.

Within a couple weeks, problems surfaced in both Grenoble and Madrid. Fortunately, I was on my way to Europe. In Madrid, a 45-year-old male teacher had been taking the kids away from the University and out for wine in the evenings, which was against the rules. A group from New Orleans recruited by elderly Catholic nuns saw AEI as a way to get close to the Pope, not as an extension of their "in loco parentis" responsibility. The sisters had neither the skill nor interest in the serious business of chaperoning.

In Madrid, the carousing Miami Florida teacher refused to behave despite calls and telegrams. Concerned he simply wouldn't accept a young woman's authority, I wrote and presented a letter which stated, *"The Board has met and unanimously voted to dismiss you effective immediately."* We did not have a Board of Directors. He left Madrid. On short notice, Bruce Carroll found a friend from Middlebury College, Mr. Daly, who was able to fly over immediately and take command of the Madrid program. He was a priest. Well chosen, Bruce.

The high schoolers from New Orleans were behaving like spoiled brats, while the nuns in charge continued to avoid disciplinary oversight. The kids complained about everything. They complained about the food, the dorms, the supervisors, the program. Several were saying they wanted to go back to the States. The Carrolls and I developed a strategy. That night we gathered the kids in a large room where I announced calmly that, *"I, the CEO, have flown from the United States with the express purpose of taking dissatisfied students back home immediately and at AEI's expense. Please raise your hand if you are unhappy and would like to be in that returning group."*

You could hear a pin drop. A little nervous fussing. Then silence. We waited a few more painfully quiet moments before announcing that, *"We are pleased to learn nobody's unhappy. Going forward, we don't expect to hear a single complaint or even a bit of negativity. If we do, there will be consequences."*

It was a high-risk approach. It worked. Teachers and students alike settled down and had a positive experience for the rest of the summer.

The program was successful by most measures. The kids were exposed for the first time to a university atmosphere, learned a little Spanish or French and, as a student from Yorktown said in a Washington Post article, *"had the opportunity to become a real part of French student living."*

Bruce and Gail never worked harder. Nor had I. For a while we felt like a million dollars. New experience. New learning, new horizons, all good, all around. The students had settled down, were learning and having fun.

The airline employees strike, grounding all transcontinental flights of United States carriers, continued. In Washington we had to focus most of the remaining summer on getting the kids back from Europe on-schedule during an airline strike which, as it turned out, lasted longer than our program. We managed to do that by convincing Citibank (which financed several of the major airlines) to find a solution and give our program priority because our children and inexperienced teacher chaperones needed more help than corporate managers and thousands of well-to-do travelers that were marooned across the pond. We convinced them. Rumor had it that Citibank talked Pan Am into painting over one of its planes with a Sabina logo. We'll never know for sure. All I know is that every student came home within 24 hours of their original schedule.

Bruce was 44 at the time. He and his wife Gail oversaw campus directors whose average age was 23. After the trip, Gail described the experience: *"It was a miracle – a miracle that it worked out so well. We were so young and inexperienced."*

Good ending for the kids but not for American Educational International. Time was spent on the strike rather than planning and selling the following year's program. We had to spend all available cash – all profit – on the rescue mission. The bank account was soon empty even though I had stopped my own salary in June. Later, I turned down a $25,000 ($194,000 in today's dollars) buyout offer that would have put me under contract for three years. Three years seemed like an eternity to someone only 23.

I took steps to close the doors. There were a half dozen creditors. Ironically, the largest creditor was American Express. I had applied for a personal card but Amex turned me down because single women, especially young women, couldn't get a credit card in the 60's (or most of the 70's). This turned out to help save me from personal bankruptcy at 23. They were comfortable issuing a card to the new business. The business bank account was empty.

My Dad wrote the letter for me that we sent to American Express and other creditors:

American Education International

1148 PENNSYLVANIA BUILDING • WASHINGTON, D.C.
AREA CODE 202 • 783-2427 • CABLE ADDRESS: LANGUAGE

October 6, 1966

Dear Sir:

Due to a number of relatively recent events beyond our control, such as the prolonged air strike, costs far exceeded the estimates of our operation for the tour year just closed.

We are, therefore, forced to suspend operations. Though I cannot prevent you from taking action, I do want you to know that this company has no assets and there will be no distribution to creditors.

Sincerely,

Margaret M. Hogan
Program Director

Not one creditor followed up. The most difficult part was telling Jimmy Kirgan that we had to close. I would have liked to have paid him back especially since I turned down a buyout offer, but there was no money. It would take a while for me to get the spring back in my step.

Separately, *The Washington Post* had written a story about the company which was to appear on the Sunday, October 2, 1966 front page of the "Style" section.

Since we were closing the doors, and announcing it the next day, most people would have told The Post to pull the story. I didn't. Why not let the article roll and invite all my friends to a party that Sunday in Georgetown? Out with a bang, not a whimper.

"HER CORPORATE IMAGE IS YOUTH" read the headline. The

writer, Nan Randall, described me as "Looking disarmingly like the teenagers who make up her principal clients" with "slim but sturdy shoulders," and a "why not try it attitude." She described the company as "well on its way to success."

The hesitant students left New York dressed formally in blazers and white gloves, nervously practicing their wobbly language skills. They returned dressed with a European flair, carrying guitars and displaying a definite aura of confidence.

The kids described the program as *"fantastic, a marvelous experience."* I particularly relished the comment of one teenager: *"I thought Ann Arbor, Michigan was the whole world. Now, after the summer I am even reading the newspaper."*

After the party, I had to face the hard reality of closing a business down. Beyond creditors, our business partners and associates needed to be notified. There was a lease for the office and copy machine to negotiate, furniture to give away, bank accounts to close, insurance policies to cancel and various government payments to finish up. As euphoric as it is to launch a business together, it is equally devastating to pull it apart. Saddest of all, I notified students who had participated and others who had signed up early for the '67 program. This was a hard and lonely time.

The pain lingered for a while. What stuck permanently was my disregard for caution in favor of action. I would start and figure it out later whether founding a venture fund, taking on real estate projects, or saying, *"I'll come back after the baby to manage my brand."* Now, my favorite way to describe this approach is "start before you are ready," a phrase coined by our friend Jim Anderson, President and CEO of Cincinnati Children's Hospital Medical Center, for 15 years. His words:

"It came up during a discussion with some senior healthcare leaders at a meeting in the UK about how to get started on

various improvement efforts with most grousing about not having all the pieces in place to launch. I was frustrated by the lack of energy to blast through the barriers and just get going on something. So, I told them they should start before they are ready and learn and adjust as they progressed but above all start something."

Closing American Education International was heartbreaking. I was so very young, so passionate about the mission and had worked harder on it than anything I had ever done. I wasn't used to failure and didn't know how to cope with it. About 10 years later, a Chicago radio reporter asked,

"Since your first business failed, would you tell another woman to plow ahead or work for somebody else first and then start a business?"

Without hesitation, I answered, *"I would tell her to plow ahead."*

Applying for a Job

"Tell me again, why it is that we don't hire women for management positions?"

— John E. Pepper, Jr., Brand Manager at the time

O NCE BACK IN Cincinnati, I lived with my parents while looking for a job. The search reinforced my feelings of failure as about a dozen companies turned me down. Mark Twain described Cincinnati as "decades behind the times" but I didn't see much hope in East Coast companies either. The jobs welcoming to women were as teachers, nurses, salesgirls, secretaries and librarians. I did not have the interest or skills for those. And apparently companies didn't want me for anything else.

I slept late in the mornings and drank Scotch in the evenings. I had little cash and was depressed. A slippery downward slope. Bruce Carroll was the one who shook me out of it. *"Stop feeling sorry for yourself."* So, I pulled myself up and re-started the job search.

Dad suggested that I try Procter & Gamble, saying, *"People come from all over the world to work there."* I didn't have much confidence left. However, I decided to take his advice.

A couple of days later, I took a bus downtown and walked into the first-floor office on Sixth Street that was open to those applying for administrative positions. A middle-aged woman stood behind the desk. With cropped, grey hair, wearing a flowered print blouse, a slim skirt and looking like a kindly aunt, she smiled and then asked me to fill out some paperwork. Then she would administer a typing test.

After listening to her directions, I responded that I would fill out the application but would not take the typing test. *"I don't type. All I can do is think. Don't you have a test for that?"*

In 1966, Procter & Gamble, like all Fortune 500 companies, except perhaps IBM, had separate tracks for men and women. Management positions were open to men. Women could be clerks, typists and secretaries. Men were the designated leaders and women their supporters.

The company literature made these distinct roles crystal clear. One brochure said, "Girls are V.I.P.s!" It described the girls as, "people who take dictation, greet visitors, answer telephones, type memos, make appointments, operate a variety of office equipment, track orders – and do many other special projects to help make P&G a successful company. Getting coffee and reporting to one man or a small group of men." Required skills: "typing . . . neatness . . . pleasant personality," while photos pictured the girls helping male managers, sitting at typewriters and leaving the company to go shopping for their managers.

Another recruiting brochure attracting "brand men" for MANAGEMENT CAREERS pictured a close up of an attractive man looking intently into the camera. "Spark plug . . . moving force" the brochure gushed. "The brand man is an exciting important job filled with challenging, ever-changing problems that provide you an excellent opportunity to demonstrate your ability to handle even more important management assignments." A brand of his own.

I was given the brochure written for girls.

However, for some reason that I will never know, this lovely, normally rule-abiding lady, on this particular day, decided to be a rule breaker. She gave me the infamous "M test," the IQ type test that was given to potential hires for management positions which were, as described, all male. I took the test not understanding that it might well launch a change in the way The Procter & Gamble Company as well as other Fortune 500s might hire managers going forward.

I did well. I did well enough that she forwarded the results to Henry Wilson, head of the advertising personnel department. Henry was responsible for bringing brand management candidates to the table. Henry interviewed me a couple of times. Obviously, he faced a dilemma: Is the applicant qualified? IQ test results and the resume with evidence of intellect and leadership said yes. Do we hire women? Policy said no. Policy questions like this were above his pay grade as a staff person.

So, Henry called a line manager to make the decision on my next step — a full day of interviews for a promising candidate or follow convention and show me to the door since women were not welcome in brand work. Instead, Henry made another offer, *"We would like you to have lunch with one of our brand managers. His name is John Pepper."* John would become CEO 28 years later in 1995 and then again, a couple of years later.

I was not nervous. I had already been turned down by several companies including Kroger, Macy's, American Express, a couple of travel agencies and banks. My expectations were low. Fortunately, I did not realize just how big a deal it was to snag a brand "man" interview with The Procter & Gamble Company. To me, it was a hometown company — I had gone to school with daughters of executives. In fact, Mom called Hillsdale Procter & Gamble Tech. I had dated its bachelors and started a company with three of its brand men. My parents were friends with some of the top people.

Unbeknownst to me, The Procter & Gamble Company was one of the most prestigious, powerful and selective companies on the face of the planet. Revenues put it at 27 on Fortune's 500 list. It was routinely cited as an extremely well-managed company.

Its "brand system" – an iconic management structure created in the 40's by future-CEO Neil McElroy – garnered accolades and imitators. Graduates from top colleges and business schools with outstanding records fought to get a place at the table. Before the rise of intense investment banking, consulting and technology, P&G – which also spent more on advertising – faced little competition in attracting the best and brightest new hires.

The odds of me getting a full day interview were so low, there was no reason for concern. As Symington had advised our AEI students, I could just be myself. Pepper was educated at an all-male boarding school and all-male Yale University and trained in the military. There was nothing in his background that suggested he would be open to a woman. He took me to lunch at a well-known local restaurant, the LaNormandie (now Sotto's). He asked questions and listened like few others that I had met. We spent most of our time talking about American Education International.

After lunch, John went into Henry's office and apparently said, *"She's as smart as anyone here, and has a lot more nerve."* He asked for reasons behind the exclusionary policy. Since there were no good answers, his questions changed the corporate landscape.

Decades later, I learned from his son David something that would never appear on John's resume. In John's family, his mother had been the driving force.

I got the day-long interview.

During the interview, I asked an important question: *"Can I be* president?" I never thought to ask if I could go on sales training, the first promotion level, or achieve the coveted brand manager title. The men on the panel answered, *"Yes."* I followed up with another question: *"Could you arrange for me to meet one of the female managers?"* The answers ranged from evasive to polite, but there would be no introductions. There simply were no women managers in the company. In the 1960's virtually no women with ambition could find a place at P&G or other corporate institutions where power was concentrated.

Group Product Manager Al Harris questioned the accuracy of the response rate to my direct mail campaign that we used to sell the summer travel programs. I explained that it was 6.25%. You mean *".006%, right?"* "No. It works out to 6.25%" (which was about 100 times the norm). I did not know it was good. Mr. Sam Pruitt, also a Group Product Manager, asked how I managed to sell parents on sending their kids to Europe with someone so young. When I answered that the sales pitch focused on the "educational" value to the kids, Sam Pruitt said, *"What's so good about education?"* It was such a silly question; I didn't think it deserved an answer. Rather I shot back: *"What's so good about motherhood?"*

Somehow, I was offered the job. The Packaged Soap and Detergent Division, P&G's largest and oldest division, made me a $7,000 start-immediately offer.

P&G was a well-regarded company for good reasons. One of them was brand management. As the marketing brochure explained, a typical brand group "is responsible for the effectiveness of all consumer advertising and promotion of an important national product . . . a brand group normally consisting of a brand man, assistant brand man and brand assistant . . . the group develops and then obtains company approval on ways and means of increasing or extending consumer demand for the

brand . . . the brand man is the spark plug and moving force."
Your own entrepreneurial business with all the advantages of
one of the world's largest companies.

Procter & Gamble offered two other fundamental and
compelling reasons why outstanding men should join:

1. Revenues doubled every 10 years.
2. Promotion is from within.

I presumed those principles would apply to me as well and
accepted the next day.

P&G assigned me to Bold detergent – a new brand based on
the strategy "beyond clean, beyond white, all the way to bright."
I was one of five people on the team – more than normal for a
detergent brand. However, Bold was finishing up the process of
a national expansion and the demands of an expansion brand are
extensive. The brand manager was a man from Kentucky, Gordon
Wade, who graduated from Harvard on a scholarship – brilliant,
excitable and driven. John Beggs was the assistant brand man
and Bill Danner, the brand assistant. Bill had been there just two
or three months longer than I had.

The Procter & Gamble general office was and is a rectangular
gray marble faced building (although now there is a more
interesting extension). It is balanced and hierarchical in its
architecture as well as its office assignments. On the 11th floor
resided all the senior vice-presidents, the group vice presidents,
the company president and the chairman of the board. On the 9th
and 10th floor was the Packaged Soap and Detergent and the Bar
Soap divisions, which were the two oldest and most prestigious
divisions in the company reflecting P&G's beginning as a soap
(and candle) factory. The eighth-floor housed staff groups
including the promotion and marketing services department as
well as media and copy services.

The first floor looked a little like it does today with a reception area and security officer but sans welcoming coffee bar and lounge. There was an employment office where entry-level people could apply (where I had applied) and a medical office where nurses took care of people when they didn't feel well – evidence of the paternalistic attitude that existed at that time.

In the middle on the fifth floor, was the cafeteria. The company had recently changed from a male section and a female section to a gender integrated cafeteria. Given I was excluded from both, it would not matter to me.

I worked on the ninth floor. There were offices along the south wall for the brand men. At the end the advertising manager had a large office and right outside was his personal secretary. Finance people lined the west wall while the sales managers occupied the north. The placement and size of various offices clearly signaled the power and importance of the person who resided within.

All the rest of us operated out of a large open area we called the "Bullpen," featuring a few inexpensive prints and no comfortable chairs. It was grey and could have been a military base. The furniture was metal except in the corner office where wood served as another status symbol. The color palette ranged from grey metal to off white walls.

All the men wore white shirts and dark suits and rep or patterned ties. There was no facial hair. The secretaries wore simple conservative dresses. No pants. Essentially uniforms. The men were Protestant, Republican, East Siders; the women, Catholic, Republican, West Siders. In a repeat of my high school years, I was the only openly Democratic party member. At P&G, it was a remote possibility of having a liberal Democrat in the house, so everyone assumed I was a Republican. Our manager – remembering that I had political activity on my resume – invited me to an event with the then Senator Robert Taft, a well know Republican.

The visual picture was of solidarity and power and discipline.

It soon became clear that a reason why P&G jobs were so coveted was that Procter & Gamble taught and trained by having people do things rather than operate as a graduate school. I worked on promotions. I filled in charts. I colored maps. The most exciting assignment during the first few months was developing a "pole piece" which was the company's word for a product display device. Bold would give away a free lady Schick razor in return for multiple Bold box tops. These were the days when everyone saved box tops for some premium prize.

I nervously went down to meet with Marty Briede, the art director who would help with the project and then I flew to Chicago to meet with the advertising agency, Leo Burnett, which would develop advertising for the campaign. Although my role was essentially a glorified messenger, deferring to the art director and the ad agencies to make decisions, I felt important. I was on a business trip.

After about four months, I realized my work was on the lighter side. I had expected this to be a "thinking" job. Bill Danner, who joined the Bold brand just before me and worked at the neighboring desk, had more substantive, often analytical, assignments.

While I had a real job at an acclaimed company, it was obvious that the company treated me differently. Fortunately, my Dad, a recently appointed federal district judge, advised, *"Don't worry about the past or how others have been treated. Focus on your situation and your future."*

I made an appointment to talk with my boss, who accommodated me promptly. I tried to follow my father's advice and said, *"Gordon, during the interview every man assured me that there were no limits on my upward mobility, but given what I see and am experiencing, that's not the case. It seems women are stuck at the lowest level and my assignments are closer to those of an administrator or secretary than a brand assistant. What's the story?"*

Gordon gave a straight up, straight from Kentucky answer: *"You're right. We haven't promoted any women and I'm not sure Mr. McElroy and Mr. Morgans (chairman and vice chairman) are ready for that. But how about this; we'll give it a try for a year. If you do well and management is ready, we'll get you promoted. If management isn't ready, we'll give you walking papers. Either way, you'll never be sorry for having worked on the fast track at Procter & Gamble for a year."*

I was pleased by that answer.

Gordon then began to give me tougher assignments and I worked hard on them. In fact, the challenge was well beyond my abilities at first. Roughly half of the brand assistants come directly from business school and all the others were top students at prestigious undergraduate colleges, often with military experience. And they had a boy's club — people to talk to, commiserate with and learn from. I was alone. I was sinking fast.

Late one night I looked at the drawers on the sides of my desk, which were both filled to the top with papers needing some action. How could I ever catch up? Only one way came to mind. Emptying both drawers, I took all that paper to the shredder. If it was important, people would follow up. If not, all the better. Amazingly, there was not a single negative repercussion. I was finally up to speed and could handle the work. Even today, every once in a while, I am known to press the "delete all" button on my iPhone to catch up.

Two months later, in August 1967, Gordon called me into his

office to announce: *"Forget all those things I said before. P&G is an equal opportunity employment company. We treat everyone including women the same. If not, I understand Mr. McElroy or Mr. Morgan could be sent to jail?"*

This was not Gordon talking or it clearly hadn't been two months earlier. It was clear that Gordon shared my request with the powers that be in the recent personnel reviews which were formal bi-annual meetings with Vice-Presidents of Advertising, Personnel and the Division. Someone apparently remembered the 1964 Civil Rights Law which prohibited discrimination on the basis of color, religion, national origin or sex. Without sharing information on the legal imperative, the VPs told Gordon to erase his earlier comments (all truthful) and focus on the company's newly created equal treatment policy.

This about face in policy made me brazen. I asked, *"And Gordon, did anyone tell you by whom Mr. McElroy and Mr. Morgan would be sent to jail? My Dad is the presiding federal judge in this part of the country."*

Long after this conversation Gordon would remember and reference that moment, a turning point, by describing me as a feminazi.

I do not believe Dad's judicial position won me a free ride or even a substantive advantage. The company just isn't like that. However, it did serve to alert everyone not previously paying attention that a law had been passed and P&G – a respectful, law abiding company – would give me a fair shot.

Going forward, I began operating as a regular brand assistant, learning to write recommendations, analyses and the famous P&G one-page memo. The standard route for promotion in the marketing department was about a year as a brand assistant. Then if you were deemed to have a future at Procter the next step was sales training. This meant five months in the field selling to mom-and-pops and supermarkets. Roughly half of the brand assistants earned their way there. The rest were turned away.

My chances were less than 50/50 as I simply didn't have the necessary organizational skills. Tom Laco was my Group Product Manager and mentor. He was a Czechoslovakian refugee who came to America when he was six. He looked at people without preconceived notions and, seeing in me an undeveloped spark of talent, moved me to Dreft, a smaller established brand. It was more manageable than an expansion brand. Dreft was marketed as the detergent to use for babies. Pete Field, the Brand Manager was a well-organized administrative type. It was what I needed, and my skill development accelerated.

The bigger hurdle was sales training. If advertising was a boy's club, the sales force at P&G was the Citadel. If tradition wasn't enough to keep women out there were also laws to help. The law in Ohio and other states prohibited a company from requiring a woman to lift more than 20 pounds, paternally protecting the weaker sex. A case of detergent weighed more than that. Salesmen whose job required building store displays of products had to meet physical demands far beyond 20 pounds.

Gordon Wade and Tom Laco, who by now had been promoted to Advertising Manager of the Packed Soap and Detergent Division, spearheaded the recommendation to send me on sales training – albeit to a Cincinnati district location, which management considered safe to facilitate oversight of a woman. I was told not to build displays, not to lift even a case so other salesmen had to back me up. They did not tell me why. Nor did I ask.

Pete Brady, Cincinnati district manager for Packaged Soap & Detergent Sales, gave the assignment to train me to an older gentleman named Al Menke. Al was a slender, fatherly type with thinning grey hair and a big smile. He was a gentleman of the first order and a seasoned salesman nearing retirement. Al trained me according to the book. For example, the first thing to do when entering the supermarket is to check the aisles, record product package facings, look for competitive activity, record out of stocks, look for displays and develop a plan as to what you intend to present to the sales manager. You needed to know if your product had good shelf position with enough shelf space to stand out to shoppers. Intimidated by unfamiliar surroundings and overwhelmed by details, I didn't do as well at the ultimate job of selling soap.

On my first day selling on my own, I had an automobile accident, thus killing my chance of earning a safe driving award, which most salesmen won on a yearly basis. Frantically reaching into the glove compartment for the company policy manual, I found the accident instruction section: "Step 1 – Call the police." Check the first box, Peg, I told myself. I had hit a police car – confirming everyone's worst fears about women drivers.

After a few weeks in the field and continuing to struggle, another salesman reached out. Steve Ferris asked to accompany me on a call as he couldn't figure why my sales performance was so weak. With about 10 years' experience, this handsome 6'4' former Marine walked into the first store with me but stepped to the side to observe. While I was focused on my list of shelves to check and other "to do's," the store manager came by to say hello and ask,

"How's it going? And what can I do for you today?" Truth is I was a novelty. The grocery industry did not see any women selling anything. The store managers were curious. Besides, their training was to be "nice" to the ladies.

I responded with a polite thank you, adding, *"I'll let you know as soon as I am finished checking the shelves."*

Steve had his answer and he didn't mince words: *"Never ever do that again. Getting the attention of a buyer is the hardest hurdle in sales. When you get it, work it."*

Steve quickly and firmly squashed my feeble objections about not taking advantage of being female and skipping all the process steps: *"Are you kidding? This is not about process. It's about getting to home plate. It's about selling. It's about winning."*

I've never forgotten that lesson.

Before the advertising manager announced my promotion to sales training, the women around me — primarily in market research and administrative roles — had placed bets against my ever getting promoted. Many who had worked for the company for a long time had witnessed no progress in the upward mobility of women and had lost faith in that possibility.

Their skepticism was well-founded since Procter & Gamble had never ventured beyond the comfort of male leadership. Why? Maybe because women before me just hadn't directly asked to be considered. Maybe because there had never been a woman behind the secretarial employment desk with the courage to break away or a foresighted brand manager whom personnel asked to solve a dilemma.

When my promotion to sales training was announced, the same small group of P&G women gave me a simple unframed certificate "presented by her friends" acknowledging "The first women being elected to sales training in the 131-year history of The Procter & Gamble Company." A door was creaking open.

The certificate still hangs in my office.

PART III

WORKING FOR PROCTER & GAMBLE

FIRST BRAND MAN

"At Procter & Gamble, Peg was the woman who opened the doors that the rest of us were able to walk through. Her story will help all women trying to navigate a high-powered career and family and do it with class."

– Meg Whitman, Former CEO eBay and Board, The Procter & Gamble Company

AFTER SALES TRAINING, I was assigned to Duz – a premium laundry detergent brand that contained a free different-size drinking glass in different-size packages. In today's age of instant gratification, it's hard to remember the day when some Americans were patient enough to collect a set of glasses over several months by buying box after box of detergent.

The work was challenging. In learning to write my first increased ad spending recommendation, I remember 14 drafts. Fourteen; no exaggeration. Multiple drafts were the norm.

And there was the then-famous one-page memo to master. The one-pager was even more difficult, requiring that it be concise, thorough and accurate on a single sheet of paper. The rationale behind this discipline was centralized control. The CEO approved every move of importance, and to facilitate his ability to oversee every decision, all communication had to be short, clear and concise. I remember recommending 15 years later that we buy Norwich Eaton, the first major acquisition in 20 years at a cost of $371 million. One-page was still the norm.

The format in the memo was:

TO: one's boss
FROM: writer
SUBJECT:

RECOMMENDATION: This is to recommend _____ action at a cost of $_____ The Legal and Promotion & Marketing Services Departments are in agreement.

BACKGROUND: What's needed to understand

BASIS FOR RECOMMENDATION: the purpose is to recommend that Ivory Liquid move to a new advertising campaign. The reasons (evidence) are:

1. _____

2. _____

3. _____

INDICATED ACTION: Next Steps and Timing of Implementation

To this day, I write most notes and documents with the one-page memo format in mind. "This is to thank you for a lovely evening. Food, music, atmosphere and people were all unusually enjoyable. We look forward to getting together again soon."

Raises came frequently. Bosses never said (nor did I inquire) if my starting salary was well below the men. The company just kept giving me more.

I travelled more, mostly to New York City to the advertising agency. Every once in a while, there would be a female copywriter in meetings, but mostly it was "Mad Men of Madison Avenue," who smoked and drank just as portrayed in the TV series.

The Duz assignment was challenging but fairly routine, until we started to expand a new product across the country, and a new set of glassware as we changed sets every few years. I picked the new design. It meant holding introductory sales meetings around the South and Southwest cities where the brand group presented to about 25 salespeople to generate enthusiasm. All of the sales reps were men.

Our fifth stop was Lubbock, Texas, a town of about 200,000 people located on the northwest plains in a county that was dry until 2008. In a Holiday Inn, the brand group set up at about 3:00 pm in the afternoon to practice for the next day's sales meeting. The windowless beige conference room had a green patterned carpet. Joined by four sales managers who brought provisions, the group commenced drinking almost immediately. I did not.

By the time we left for dinner, a couple of the men were drunk; one stocky, dark-haired 45 year-ish unit sales manager in particular. When his flirtatious behavior became noticeably aggressive, District Manager John Cutrer assigned an older gentleman named Tom to escort me to the restaurant. Tom was helping me into the back seat of a dark Chevrolet to take us to dinner when the drunk pulled out a switch blade, threatening, "Get out of the way, she's mine."

I had never before asked for help in the face of flirtatious and aggressive behavior, believing that other men didn't want to hear about such incidents, let alone be dragged into them. The expectation was that women like me should be able to manage alone and in silence. And until that night I had done just that.

Mad Men were nothing new to me and I had developed skills to fend them off even gracefully, but the combination of mad, drunk and armed with a knife exceeded even my abilities.

I was scared and knew that when dinner ended the problem was likely to reoccur.

At dinner, I waited until my brand manager, Skip, got up to go to the men's room. I excused myself as well thinking this could be handled discreetly. Skip was a small boned 5'7" guy.

His response to my request for help: *"I can't do anything. He's bigger than I am."* No help there.

Then I went to John, the district sales manager and his boss, whom I had never met before. *"He behaves like this with anyone who wears a skirt,"* was all he said.

With narrowing options as dinner was ending, I had to find a way. I would not be a victim, not me. That moment I looked over to Larry Plotnick. Larry was the new brand assistant on Duz who had graduated recently from the University of Chicago. As an Assistant Brand Man, I had a higher rank but no authority over Larry. Nevertheless, Larry was formidable physically, and eager to succeed in his new position.

In my firmest, most intimidating voice, I declared, *"Larry, for reasons that are obvious, you will stay at my side until I am locked in my hotel room. If you don't, guaranteed, I will find a reason to get you fired within the next month."* He did and I didn't.

Nothing was spoken again about the incident. Men in the late sixties, even the good guys, ignored the sexual misconduct of their associates or subordinates as they didn't know how to handle such incidents; sadly, some still do not report this behavior today. Men misbehaved because they could. And it was simply accepted. Way too much terrible behavior was excused with "Boys will be boys." There were no laws against sexual harassment. No policies. Not even any expectations.

About five years later I heard P&G fired the unit manager for similar behavior.

In 2018, people criticized Christine Blasey Ford for not being able to call up certain details about the incident with then Supreme Court nominee, Brett Kavanaugh. The coverage in that hearing helped me finally understand why I can remember every detail of my experience that night, including names of everyone present, except the central character. I see his face clearly but cannot recall his name. The mind mercifully blocks out the unimaginable.

I stayed on Duz as an assistant brand manager for about another year. It was hard work. The men were getting used to me and, while lunch invitations were still rare, a few men reached out and became my friend. Social invitations never came during those early years. I felt more comfortable in my role in this predominantly male world. However, I was still a test market that nobody wanted to expand.

A year or so later Mr. Laco called me into his office to announce that the Board of Directors had approved my promotion to Brand Manager of the Bonus Brand. Whenever anyone comments on my career in the press or in conversation, they usually describe me as "P&G's first lady brand manager."

MAD MEN

"Pressure is a privilege."

— *Billie Jean King*

"If you don't like what's being said, change the conversation."

— *Don Draper, Mad Men*

I N THE *MAD Men* TV series, it may be just a coincidence that the name of the 1960's secretary who became a copywriter and then creative director is "Peggy." She lived in the Madison Avenue advertising world of hard drinking, chain smoking, infidelity and sexism. While I often visited that Manhattan world and worked in a toned-down Cincinnati version, there were plenty of similarities.

Like Peggy Olsen, I lived in the crazy creative culture of the 60's. Most men didn't look to women for brainpower in business. It was a time of Marlboro men and martini lunches. There was a lot of smoking and drinking and a history of married men who acted as if they were not. And midway through the decade, drugs entered the scene.

Without corporate leashes, naive wives and the newly approved birth control pill, the place where I now lived was far removed from my earlier years. Its madness contributed to the appeal of getting married, even if the groom fell short of Prince Charming.

It was a blind date at an engagement party for Weezie Egbert, a Hillsdale classmate, and Bill Streng, a young lawyer with the Cincinnati Taft Law firm, where I met Jim Nelson. He was a check-the-box kind of date. Tall, dark, handsome and rich. Graduate of Vanderbilt University and law school, law review, decorated Green Beret Vietnam veteran, clerk for chief judge of the federal court of appeals of the Sixth Circuit and then associate with a prestigious law firm. Just about all my friends were married, many with children so I assumed it must be time for me.

We met right after I started working for Procter & Gamble, when AEI's closing was a fresh memory and there was serious doubt about my making the cut. I had lost much of my self-confidence. Jim and I became engaged in 1967 and married the fall before sales training. By the time the wedding came around, I was apprehensive, but went ahead while secretly making certain there would be no children — even though taking birth control pills without the husband's consent was against convention as well as the law in many states.

Jim viewed himself as "lord and master" of the house. Growing up without a father and spoiled by his older, doting and kindly mother, he had an elevated self-image that years of being an in-charge marine in Vietnam fostered.

Together we bought a beautiful house on top of a hill with a pool and pool house. We were up and comers in the Cincinnati business and legal world. But all was not happy in the house on Signal Hill. Jim's need to be totally in charge ended the honeymoon.

At first his controlling attitude was okay when I was looking for someone solid to lean on. But not as I gained footing at the office, regaining my independence and confidence. He became increasingly abusive. It was verbal put-downs at first, humiliating comments about everything from cooking skills to looks. He morphed into calling me "Piggy" rather than "Peggy." Then physical threats came. He had a gun. Towards the end, he threatened to kill me, then himself. That prompted me to call the police, only to learn that the officer wouldn't take any action.

"Has he done anything yet?"

"No, he threatens. He's locked in the room with a gun right now."

"Well we can't do anything then."

"Do you mean there has to be a shooting before I'll get any help?"

"That's right Ma'am."

I left that night. I had not until then shared a single word about my situation with a friend or family member. I knew of no friend nor family member who had gotten a divorce.

My Dad was an Irish Catholic who didn't believe in divorce. His first comment was, *"I don't know how you stood it so long."* This response surprised me because Jim adored my father and tried hard to please him. Having lost his own father, he clearly wanted to have mine. But I shouldn't have been surprised that my father was not taken in by Jim's attention. Dad always cut to the heart of the matter. It made him a highly respected judge.

Later I learned that as a Green Beret in Vietnam in the early 60's, Jim was in charge of thousands of Montagnard tribes (or mountain-dwellers) and may have participated in wartime atrocities such as the systematic killings of villagers — including women, children and the elderly — that happened in Vietnam and Cambodia. Vietnam had its effects well beyond Southeast Asia, well beyond the soldiers who fought.

To keep him away from our home on Signal Hill, the court issued an order. He fought the divorce. I bought out his interest in the Signal Hill home that we had just purchased and, to manage economically, rented a room to another P&G woman. I withstood the pressure from my attorney and parents to sell the house, saying, *"If necessary, I'll sell memberships in the swim club"* as there was a pool.

With work challenges at P&G, social pressure generally and the divorce, it was all I could do to try and put one foot in front of the other every day.

A few of the men at the office also behaved badly. My immediate boss – with whom I had to travel to a series of Duz sales meetings – asserted that he was trapped in a marriage forced upon him by his wife's long ago claim of pregnancy (good line). He fell in love with me (according to him) without any deliberate provocation on my part. My boss's boss tried – on several occasions – to get me to try marijuana while simultaneously making sexual advances. I repeatedly declined. It is a wonder, particularly in retrospect, that I kept my sanity during this period.

But what could I do? Nothing prohibited a husband from violence against his wife. There was nothing against sexual harassment in the workplace. The prevailing view at the time was "boys will be boys" so society turned a blind eye. It was up to the women to take control and manage . . . or to succumb silently.

All the men my age or older were married with kids, seemingly happy. My continuing one and only P&G woman manager status already brought attention to every challenge. Now, becoming a divorcee magnified my problems. People talked. I tried to focus on the work needing to be done. Mostly, I tried to look forward. Tomorrow would be a better day. People who worked with me during this period now tell how I smoked like a fiend and often came to work with clothes on inside out! Maybe it was an unconscious tactic to make myself less attractive to fend off adorers.

That's when I met Jack Wyant, love of my life. And, while marrying Jim was my biggest mistake, marrying Jack was my best decision. Newly hired into the Packaged Soap and Detergent Division, Jack came to the Bonus office one afternoon just to introduce himself, an unusual show of friendliness. Despite the interruption, I stayed focused on my work as was typical but I took note. At 5'8" with curly blond hair, a slim athletic build and sparkling blue eyes, I thought "cute guy."

He was born in Granville, Ohio, a Norman Rockwell town of 3,000 east of Columbus, Ohio. His parents, Margaret and Jack, were deaf mutes due to childhood illnesses. They were born in the 1920's when there were limited educational opportunities for people with disabilities. Jack attended the Ohio State School for the Deaf. He once signed out of his dorm hitchhiking at the age of 16, all by himself, to California without telling the school or his parents. His curiosity prevailed despite communication skills that were limited to a pencil and small pad of paper.

Margaret and Jack lived the first few years in Granville, Ohio where he grew up and his parents, Honey and Pal, still lived. Pal, as the name suggests, knew no strangers, greeting everyone with, *"Seldom have a bad day,"* while Honey, as her name reveals, was kindness personified.

Jack, Sr. worked for Denison University in the maintenance department where he befriended lots of students and helped out the young coach Woody Hayes' football team. Employers didn't hire persons with this or any disability for management jobs, too often and wrongly describing them as "deaf and dumb." The Americans with Disabilities Act (ADA) would change all that beginning in 1990. This overdue civil rights law addressed legally the needs of people with disabilities for the first time. It prohibited discrimination in employment, public services, public accommodations and telecommunications.

Margaret and Jack, Sr., Jack and his younger sister Rita, moved in the early fifties to Hamilton, Ohio, a small industrial city 30 minutes north of Cincinnati, so Jack, Sr. could get a higher paying factory job and Margaret could be close to her family. He worked on the assembly line of Diebold Safe and Lock Company for over 50 years, missing not a single day of work. After Jack and Rita went to college, two miracle babies were born, Kent and Andrew.

It is hard to imagine doing the same thing for days and weeks, for years and decades in total silence. And yet Jack did it with unfailing dedication and pride. Once I saw him rip a sign language card out of the hand of a deaf man begging for money, angrily signing to him: *"You have eyes. You have legs. You have arms."*

I never saw either of my future in-laws complain, then and across the next 35 years.

The oldest child of adults who cannot hear or speak communicates for his parents with the outside world as soon as he can talk. So, from the age of about three, Jack served as an interpreter at gas stations and grocery stores, on the road getting directions and in the neighborhood. Also, at an early age he worked – delivering newspapers, selling door to door, parking cars, cashiering at the Albers grocery chain (its first male cashier), selling Scott paper products to gas stations and as a lathe operator at a Ford Motor Company plant. Graduating from Garfield High School in 1964 as President of a class of 330, he earned a scholarship to Denison University. His Dad wrote so many letters to the admissions office that the director finally responded ahead of schedule: *"STOP writing. We are admitting your son."*

At Denison, Jack majored in political science and communications. With a devilish grin and a big personality, he was known as "Mad Jack," driving a motorcycle and becoming a fraternity leader in a university dominated by fraternities. As rush chair, then fraternity president, he convinced his Phi Gamma Delta chapter to pledge a black student, a move that generated death threats as well as a serious sustained resistance effort from national headquarters in Washington D.C. The move violated their "white Christian membership bylaws" that were enacted in 1848, almost 120 years earlier. It did not deter Jack.

One year later, at its biannual national convention, the fraternity delegates from 130 Fiji chapters voted 51/49 to eliminate the White Christian clause in the bylaws.

After college Jack started law school at the University of Cincinnati. Midway through the first year, the Army sent a draft notice. After enlisting in officers' candidate school, Jack received an army diagnosis of a chronic kidney abnormality, the problem prompted a discharge after the start of second semester – too late to return to law school.

Through a strange and unexpected series of events, including a job teaching high school English to fill time before returning to law school, Jack received a sales brochure from The World Language Academy – the company I helped start four years earlier. It offered the opportunity to go to Europe in the summer of 1969. Jack responded positively and spent the summer with students in Greece before returning to Cincinnati and applying for a position in brand work. Former P&G brand managers, now executives with the World Language Academy, recommended P&G as the best place to start a career, in recognition of its excellent training and flexibility. A couple years in brand work running your own small business was known to open doors in multiple directions. These guys, Jack Davidson and Gary Tabor, coached Mad Jack on how to write the resume and answer questions.

Jack's entrepreneurial and leadership skills earned him a job offer. Jack started in October 1970 on Thrill liquid detergent in the Packaged Soap and Detergent Division. A few months later, he was moved to Bonus reporting to me.

Bonus was another premium brand – this one with a towel inside – bath, hand or washcloth. While once popular in the South, the business now reflected declining sales. Despite a range of efforts, nothing worked. The concept had simply lost its appeal as customers, even low-income customers in the Deep South, began to move from a collection to an instant gratification mentality.

My analysis suggested the smart move would be to shut down the brand. P&G's Tide had a 40% market share nationally. Research showed that well over half Bonus customers also used Tide. Then it was fair – we reasoned – to assume that if Bonus wasn't available one out of every two customers would switch to Tide. Tide was 3x more profitable so the company profits would be higher.

Without talking to anyone, I excitedly recommended that, instead of continuing to fight a losing battle, we close the brand down and at the same time increase company profits.

It was the right approach. But it didn't fly. Management slapped my wrist for losing sight of my primary responsibility – building the business, no matter the obstacles or other courses of action.

"But even more important than building revenues shouldn't we be working to increase profits for the shareholders?" I asked.

"No, your focus is revenues. Corporate leadership can focus on profits." The powers that be responded.

It didn't make economic sense to me, but it was the way it was. Five or six years later the company finally stopped selling Bonus.

Jack was single. He didn't smoke or drink much. He was respectful, good looking, positive and fun. But when he showed romantic interest, I – near the end of a difficult divorce and putting up with married men acting badly – asked him to back off: *"My life is a mess. You want to stay away."* And so he did, saying, *"I'll be your friend."*

Jack was an important part of efforts to grow sales. Faced with little consumer interest in collecting towels, we decided to promote the brand by showing women how to make clothes out of towels and actually wearing them. It didn't work. The idea, however, showed creativity and became a fun memory. And Jack, who wore a bow tie and vest made of yellow terry cloth towels to Cincinnati's most famous five star restaurant and to multiple sales meetings, proved he was a particularly self-confident man.

Shortly after, Jack earned a promotion to sales training. Instead of waiting for the company to assign him to one of 32 districts, which was the norm, Jack identified the strongest district manager in the country, a man named Karl Maggard, and talked Karl into requesting that Jack be assigned to his Louisville district. Bingo, that's where he went to obtain the best training. It was a complete reversal of authority. Then he asked for an appointment with the Division's Advertising Manager, Tom Laco, to ask for career advice. Nobody did that. Of course, Tom gave Jack the time.

His approach said it all. Jack paid little attention to process or conventional ways of doing things but he could sell. It was evident from the time eight-year-old Jackie sold bars of soap door-to-door to pay his way to the YMCA Camp Campbell Guard. On sales training, his expense accounts were seldom in order nor did he make the 10 calls per day that were required. However, he could talk store managers into big displays, increased facings and buying more product than they had ever done or needed. For failing to cross T's and dot I's, he would come close to getting fired but then do something so impressive he would make headlines. Karl and I would back off.

Jack had been selling in Louisville for a few months. A goal of his was making an initial sale to a chain of variety stores called Dollar General. Despite sales of about $40 million, Dollar General had not bought a single P&G product. Jack came up with a plan and called District Manager Maggard, asking Karl to ride with him to Dollar General headquarters in Scottsville, Kentucky, about three hours south of Louisville for an 8:00 am meeting the next day. While that is generally not what district managers did, Jack convinced Karl and off they went.

Cal Turner, the Dollar General CEO, wasn't "sold" and the two drove the three hours back to Louisville in silence. Jack had, however, listened well to the objections. He stayed up late reading their annual report and developed a new approach. He called Karl early the next morning saying, *"We need to go back."*

"Are you crazy?"

"Probably, Karl, but I think it's worth a shot. I read a lot about their strategy and listened to their objections. I have a plan to convince them to change their mind." Karl acquiesced.

The two drove back and, this time, made the sale, perhaps more because Turner was impressed with their persistence than by the new sales pitch. It was the largest initial product sale in the history of Procter & Gamble.

Jack was definitely different. Everyone else walked the line. No one else dared to make a direct contact with the boss' boss. The prevailing attitude was that people like Mr. Laco are to be respected but should be admired from a distance. Jack believed that Tom held the advertising manager position only because he was older and had been there longer. Rank was determined by the year you were born. And rank alone shouldn't matter.

Things degenerated with my divorce. Jim, a lawyer himself, didn't show up for hearings or respond to complaints. When he became violent, threatening at first to kill himself and then pulling a gun on me, I needed a friend.

Seeking help from my boss wasn't possible as he was part of the problem. Besides, my Procter managers expected me to be strong enough to manage any difficulties on my own. I couldn't reveal weakness. Being embarrassed by the turmoil, I was uncomfortable sharing with my parents. With no women peers, I didn't have girlfriends. Jack became my friend and confidante. In that role, I got to know him, falling in love before we ever held hands.

Perhaps his most unique asset was his solid, well-deserved belief in himself, his judgment, his abilities. While strong women threatened men, Jack intended to partner with a woman rather than dominate. He became my biggest cheerleader. I told him I didn't want to be his friend anymore.

When we started spending time together, he was renting 417 Oregon Street in Mt. Adams with a drop-dead view of the city. He owned a ski boat with a 100-horsepower engine, a sporty VW and a 3-bedroom log cabin on a Kentucky lake. He had four or five maxed-out credit cards. He was quick to go to a party or put a trip together spontaneously. He didn't worry. He pushed the limits of P&G's rigid 8:30 am starting time and had less routine than was typical. But he had a big personality and sales skills that were rare in that environment.

Like his grandfather Pal, Jack never met a stranger and was as at ease with an usher at the ballpark as he was with a CEO or senator. When Jack later worked with Kings Island theme park, which ran the PGA golf tournament, he was paired for a round with Ben Crenshaw. Crenshaw had just won the US Open. I would have been a nervous wreck. Jack who had played maybe two rounds of golf in his life, welcomed the opportunity. *"Ben can give me a few tips."* He is comfortable with himself.

Dean Woodward, the Denison University chaplain, performed the wedding service. A couple months before the wedding Jack and I drove to Granville, the small town where Denison is located, to meet him. I wore a brown and white sleeveless dress, Jackie-O sheath, purchased just for the occasion as I wanted to impress the chaplain. After driving about an hour, I looked down and saw a single black leather shoe, low-heeled to which I said, *"Oh darn, I didn't mean to wear the black shoes."* Half an hour later I crossed my legs and looked down again to see a brown shoe and commented, *"Oh, I'm so glad I wore the brown shoes."*

Dean Woodward immediately noticed "Peg's folly." Over the next few decades whenever we returned to Granville and saw the chaplain, he would comment that I was the only bride he ever met with mismatched shoes.

That spring, Dean Woodward married us in a simple, daytime ceremony on the Denison campus overlook with family and a few close friends.

Jack's sister Rita, an airline stewardess with Capital Airlines, lived in Hawaii. As a wedding present, she gave us two tickets on Capital Airlines, her home on the north shore for a week and an open-air jeep.

Midway over the Pacific, I heard the pilot announce, *"We will be landing in Kahului."* Neither Jack nor I had ever heard of the airport that was announced. The woman next to me was an older lady with gray hair and conservative dress. When I asked, *"Do you mind telling me where we're going?"* An unforgettable look of shock came across her face. All she could say was, *"Oh my God, oh my God, oh my God . . ."*

It turns out we landed in Maui and caught a commuter flight to our destination. Rita (and Jack) viewed it as such an insignificant detail as not worth mentioning. To me, it was pretty shocking – the equivalent of sending a person expecting to arrive in New York City to Boston.

Life would be an adventure.

FIRST BRAND MOM

"Mom is the toughest cookie with the softest heart."

— Missy Wyant Smit, daughter

BETWEEN THE MAD Men and my divorce, 1972 was an "Annus Horribilis," to borrow a descriptive phrase from Queen Elizabeth. 1973 proved to be the best. Shortly before the wedding the company promoted me to brand manager of Cascade, one of the company's most promising brands.

It was a plum assignment, a leading brand with more than 40 percent share of the automatic dishwashing category. Neither my boss nor his boss had experience with it (dishwasher penetration was still low), which meant the people above were less likely to micro-manage. I could be a true entrepreneur and run the business. We set about building Cascade to a 50 percent share position. I was working with top notch people. Sandy Weiner was my group products manager, a prince of a man who came out of manufacturing. He would have become a CEO candidate for the company had he not died too young of cancer. Sandy was the first openly Jewish man I worked with at P&G.

The assistant brand manager was Jack Balousek, a bright guy who had attended Catholic boys' schools and had trepidation about reporting to a woman. He later became CEO of Foote, Cone & Belding, a large advertising agency. Jack and I looked him up in San Francisco about 20 years later and he said: *"Had I not worked for you I never could've become CEO of a major agency with a significant female presence."*

Managing Cascade was fun, perhaps the most fun position I had at Procter. Compton served as the advertising agency for Cascade. The Compton Advertising Agency, now Saatchi & Saatchi, overflowed with talent. The people were able. The business grew.

Early in the year, *Mademoiselle* decided to write an article on females in the workplace entitled the "The Coffee Controversy: Women as Secretary" and "Women as Boss." In answer to specific questions during the interview, I defended P&G's fairness and objectivity.

Is sex a help or a hindrance? "It makes absolutely no difference. It is the skill that counts. Fortunately, Procter & Gamble is evidenced-based. What counts is performance.

My sex may prove to be a help or hindrance for a short time. In other words, people may go in with prejudices which may have occasionally made a difference, sometimes in my favor and sometimes against it. But going in prejudice is short lived."

Would you rather have women or men report to you? "It would make no difference. I want capable people working for me."

What are your responsibilities to your staff? "To train my people to take over my job."

Advice to others? "Be professional. That's especially important for women. One cry per career."

Do you work harder now? "I have always worked hard."

Do men have an advantage? "Of course men have an advantage. That's as it should be. Women are still unproven."

The reporter concluded:

"On the day of the interview she wore red patent heels, natural hose, a gray flannel jumper banded in white at the neck and armhole and a red and white checked blouse. A ring with two diamonds. No earrings. No ornaments. Hair casual, short length, blunt cut. Very little make up. Good teeth, warm smile. Happy person.

I got the impression she would be a good boss. I think she would make every decision just exactly as a good male boss would, totally on the basis of whether it would be good for P&G.

To me she has the most business-oriented mind I've ever encountered in a woman. A pro."

What is shocking in retrospect is the extent to which my comments suggest a level playing field. Naturally, political correctness played a part because not every man at the company behaved perfectly. But relative to a period when few women even got a chance to work in management and there was unchecked harassment as well as personality-based favoritism, I recognized how different Procter & Gamble was. Objective, fair and ethical – ahead of its time.

Years later, I asked Gordon, my first boss, how we had managed to change so many entrenched policies so painlessly, in such a short time. In the beginning policies kept "girls" at the typewriter and there were rules against staying in the building after 6:00 pm, earning a management job, going on sales training, lifting more than 20 pounds, working beyond the five months' pregnancy mark and keeping a brand manager's job vacant.

His response was illuminating.

"You've heard of Jackie Robinson?"

"Of course."

"Well, you were like Robinson – handpicked. We thought you would perform on the field while absorbing the jeers, the distractions, the detractors." Obviously, I am not near the same league as the Hall of Famer, but the comment meant a great deal to me.

About this time, Richard Nixon issued an executive order requiring companies to activate an affirmative action program. The consequence of failing to do so would be loss of military sales which accounted for about five percent of Procter & Gamble volume. In other words, this order put teeth into the 1964 Civil Rights Act as it relates to women, a group which had never been the focus of legislation. Blacks had been the focus.

Management decided that it would make discrimination on the basis of sex as well as affirmative action a major imperative. That fall it was the headline article for the company magazine called Moonbeams. And it would be a highlight of the year-end meetings. Every December, Procter & Gamble brought senior leadership from around the world to Cincinnati for three days of intense meetings.

In June, Tom Laco called me into his office to ask if I would speak on the subject. The company lawyer would open the session by explaining the law and what it required all managers to do, followed by me. The date – December 14, 1973. At the time, I had not shared with P&G the news that our first child would arrive in early January. Company policy required that women leave when five months pregnant and were not permitted to return. I had other ideas, but being a keynote speaker?

I sat across from Mr. Laco thinking and debating in my mind:

"I can't do it. I will be nine months pregnant. Tom doesn't know about the child. The audience will be older and all male. Most other speakers will be VPs. It would be way too difficult. Too embarrassing. No. Just say no. Besides, you dislike public speaking.

Then Tom intervened: *"Peggy, it will be an opportunity. An opportunity to influence P&G leadership."*

His comment made me think again. The company trusted me. Maybe I could do it. Just maybe. Being pregnant – if I could do well – could make a big impact on behalf of progress for women.

I said, *"Yes."*

After agreeing to make the speech, I got nervous. We all had second thoughts, including, I am sure, my bosses when they learned I was expecting. Would my taking the stage nine months pregnant be an effective way to sell senior men – some from countries where women couldn't even drive – on hiring women for management jobs? Most didn't want women anywhere near places of power . . . . especially not a young pregnant girl giving a lecture.

Then, something happened. Billie Jean King, the world's top female tennis player, accepted Bobby Riggs' challenge to a highly publicized tennis match called "Battle of the Sexes." It captured the attention of 50 million television viewers which was the largest TV audience in history.

The match wasn't really about tennis. Bobby Riggs, a cocky, self-proclaimed male chauvinist, intended to put women back in the kitchen. Billie Jean set out to show that women belonged on the playing fields and she put in the work to prove it. She had the courage to take on the pressure. She won. In fact, she won decisively (6-4, 6-3, 6-3) leading the London Sunday Times to call her victory "the drop shot . . . heard around the world."

The match occurred three months before my due date. When I made the decision to stay the course, I was deciding, in my own small way, that going onstage was a way to follow Billie Jean on court. As she said, *pressure is a privilege.*

Even so, walking to the podium in mid-December was frightening under the glare of hundreds of middle aged senior male executives. And while I doubted there would be many instant converts, I tried to come across as well prepared, which I was, thoughtful and intelligent. I stood there as an "example" of an accomplished brand manager and hoped the men would see it that way.

As planned, the company lawyer preceded me, explaining to everyone's chagrin that new laws would force change. After hearing about the "stick," my job was to be the "carrot."

I opened by acknowledging that men in the room had a perfectly good right to be skeptical about bringing women into their workplace. After all, P&G had thrived since World War II under male leadership. The economy did as well. *Father Knows Best* was among the most popular shows. Why change what works?

I then acknowledged that new laws forced the issue and provided a rationale with factual and statistical support as to why women would benefit the company in the end. The simple truth is that females represent 51% of the country's brain power (based on Harvard's IQ test) and over 90% of P&G's consumers. Industrial and medical advances, with long-term effects, provided freedom from ties to the home (prepared foods, washing machines and the pill among them) and exploding education opportunities supplied the tools.

Purposefully, there was nothing in my talk suggesting that

men and women are the same. Rather, I tried to tantalize the audience with the thought that difference would bring new, fresh thinking to the long-established Ivory Tower. They faced a unique opportunity to open doors and give Procter, whose asset is people, a competitive edge.

Regarding my personal situation, I went so far as to claim that I expected to work until the baby – due three weeks later – was born. Nobody believed me, and I was about four months beyond the policy-based departure to home. Over the weekend, we played tennis a couple of times. I woke up early Monday, December 17 – around 5:30 am – and we drove directly to Christ hospital as there was no time between labor pains. While childcare classes predicted 12 or more hours of labor, Dr. Stanley Garber told Jack, *"Young man you'd better hurry."*

Jackie was born at 7:38 am Monday morning. We never saw a labor room. Luck, tennis and genetics – although my sister Nancy said, *"it was the Irish peasant in me."*

The word spread around the P&G world. Flowers and gifts filled my room, including a huge blond elephant from Tom and Barbie Laco. Policy in all countries changed overnight, if not literally, in reality because everyone – including the women – knew that I had worked until the baby was born, continuing to function as a rational, contributing manager. Actions are more effective than words. That small podium became a global stage.

If there were no precedents or guidelines regarding pregnancy, there were obviously none covering how to handle a leave of absence or childcare. The company was open to whatever I suggested. I had saved two weeks' vacation from 1973; putting that together with two weeks of 1974 vacation, I asked for an additional four weeks of unpaid leave.

As Cascade was such an attractive assignment, I also asked that the position of brand manager be left open (an unprecedented move). Other members of the brand group could step up and I would, as needed, run the business from home without pay. I would return in early March to take the brand through the daunting annual process of budget preparation and the famed budget meeting, the most challenging responsibility of the year.

Running the brand from home with no compensation seems, in light of today's generous policies, unfair. But then it was a precedent-setting breakthrough for a tightly managed organization that expected employees to be available 24/7. I recognized it as such and was relieved to hold onto my coveted brand. Real change happens one step at a time.

And that's what happened. I don't know for certain but would suspect that P&G's willingness to change and its near flawless accommodation of pregnancy and maternity leave was among the most advanced in the country. We know Jackie was "the first Procter & Gamble baby." He could well have been the first Fortune 500.

I loved being a mom. Jackie was beautiful and well behaved. Returning to work, however, was emotionally difficult as it is for all mothers. My attitude was, *"Let's give it a try. I love the work. I've got three years before being vested in the profit-sharing program which required 10 years of service. If it works, great; if not, I'll resign."*

By this time, Jack had decided to leave Procter & Gamble. It was not an ideal fit given his entrepreneurial spirit and the heavy organizational responsibilities of a big company. When we married the company moved Jack to the Paper Division, which was even less suited to his talents, than Packaged Soap and Detergent. His first step would be returning to law school, and so he started at Salmon P. Chase College of Law night school in the summer of '73. Being from a family of lawyers, I was delighted by the move, although I never anticipated how full our plates would become.

Nor did I anticipate that circumstances – a husband with a full-time job and night law school literally couldn't help around the house. No time or, to be honest, inclination.

Going back to work worked well. In my absence, the guys stepped up big time. We achieved the targeted 50% share amidst lots of fanfare. All was well.

PART IV

LEADING THE CORPORATION

RULE BREAKER

"Peg Wyant walks us through the early life experiences that instilled the confidence and independence and grit to become one of the top marketing executives of her time. Even after she leaves the corporate world, we see Peg brings her brand of 'true diversity' to every organization she touches."

– Jerry Gramaglia, Former President & COO E*TRADE

AFTER CASCADE HIT the 50 percent share mark, my career prospects bumped up and I moved to Ivory Liquid, an iconic and bigger brand than Cascade. The Ivory stenographer was a young woman named Kathy McNamee, whom we called "Mac," from the western side of the city. An 18-year-old high school graduate, she was so bright that connecting with her was a stroke of good luck that would affect most of the next 45 years.

The men underestimated the brainpower of women generally, particularly at the clerical and administrative levels. As a wife and new mother, I had a need to delegate. This prompted me to access and draw out the talent of those reporting to me, especially Mac. I gave her more responsibility than most others in her position.

I had other good people in the Ivory brand group, including

Dean Butler who founded LensCrafters in 1983; it would become the largest purveyor of eyeglasses in the United States. Another was Jerry Gramaglia who would become a driving force as President and COO of E*TRADE, an innovative trading start up.

An amazing number of top executives from companies around the world started their careers in Cincinnati at P&G. This speaks volumes for the caliber and scope of their training program.

Advertised on the basis of its mildness to hands as well as its economic benefits, we put Ivory Liquid on a growth trajectory despite new light duty liquid competition and some unexpected advertising support challenges from the Federal Communications Commission.

My next career move in the typical P&G progression would be the position of brand promotion manager which actually meant group products manager with three or more brands under the same leader. While there was an opening expected, there was also serious competition for the spot, especially from Steve Donovan, a very competent brand manager who was on the same timing track as me.

I was pregnant again. However, I had not announced the pregnancy officially and decided not to. If the executives knew, two opposite outcomes seemed equally possible. I could get the nod, to avoid the appearance of discrimination, or my associate might be promoted, reflecting the company's desire to avoid the GPM going on leave. I would never really know. "Silence is a virtue" as my Dad noted frequently at the dinner table. In the courtroom on a bench in front of him, Dad kept a handwritten sign on a folded piece of cardboard from a dry-cleaning shirt insert: "Keep your damn trap shut."

Jack left P&G in May 1975 for a position working for Bill Price, head of marketing for Kings Island, a relatively new amusement park located just outside Cincinnati owned by Taft Broadcasting.

He was mid-way through night law school. The move was a great one for Jack. His boss, Bill Price, became and remains Jack's best friend and the company CEO, Charlie Mechem, his mentor. Jack was in his element. The theme park business is all about fun.

I received the promotion to Group Products Manager, ahead of Steve, in August 1975 but he moved up soon thereafter and shortly after that I told Sandy Weiner that I was pregnant. Sandy was a leader in the tradition of Pepper and Laco, and he reacted in a supportive fashion. Some of the smaller minded men were less generous. Now I had three brands — Gain, Era and Ivory Liquid. Our daughter Missy joined the family December 7. I worked until the day Missy was born, which was a Sunday.

I now had two beautiful babies and a promotion I coveted.

I had everything but time. That scarcity — time pressure — helped me develop a management style that worked for me. Be decisive. Simplify. Delegate, delegate, delegate. Don't sweat the small stuff. Worry about the downside. The upside takes care of itself. Be tough to be kind. Terminate quickly. Develop the promising people as they are the future. Look ahead, always think long-term.

When Missy arrived, I was struggling with more responsibilities at work, just getting started at the new management level. Missy, like Jackie, arrived at about 7:30 am after only a couple hours of labor. This time with two children under two, I did not engage in any brand work while on leave. Blessed with another good baby, I took three months off. Unfortunately, this time, I returned to myriad problems at work.

Gain was the challenge. In 1967, the company put Gain in test market as a new enzyme detergent and it grew to annual sales of about 10 million cases. Enzymes provided superior stain removal, but with Gain's success, P&G worried that Tide, the long-time market leader and cash cow, would suffer. Management panicked.

It added enzymes to Tide – and changed its advertising. Tide was now the most effective cleaning and stain removal detergent. Gain with micro enzymes and a claim that it "treats stains like dirt" lost its raison d'être and slid into a painful decline.

Returning to work in March, there was a serious risk that P&G would fire me – for good reason. There was no chance of stopping the slide and turning the brand around by traveling down the conventional path of analysis, written recommendations, long waits for approvals and permission to execute. That process would take a year or more.

If we were going to save the brand, we would need to change its course dramatically and now. I made an appointment with Sandy Weiner, the PS&D Advertising Manager, to ask his agreement to a 90-day period during which the brand group would have absolute freedom to take any and all actions with the product, the packaging and the advertising. Giving me, and the brand manager, complete control. To understand how revolutionary this request was, imagine a top-down managed company where every decision – even changing a single line of copy on the package – required the agreement of the Executive Committee which met every Tuesday at 10:00 am on the hallowed 11th floor.

Once more, to enhance the probability of success, I requested the assignment of the brand manager of my choice – Tom Herskovits. It was a bold request given that Tom was #1 in the division hit parade of brand managers.

If we had a shot at turning this ship – the barge actually – around, we needed power, control and top talent. And no bureaucratic entanglements. Amazingly, Weiner agreed.

First – the strategy. We would have to develop a new vision. Gain would lose on the basis of stain removal. Tide now owned that. We would have to rely on a new idea. Delving into consumer research we discovered an attribute we could work with.

Consumers liked Gain's smell. The smell was hard to describe. Research and Development ("R&D") people wrote: "Technical Overtones: Orange, lemon and blossoms with a modern fruity, green twist. Undertones: White floral jasmine with a hint of woody amber." That language would not sell soap.

Elusive and lingering. Reminiscent of clothes hanging on the clothesline. That was closer to consumer language.

If we could convince people that the brand's fragrance made clothes smell noticeably better, maybe fragrance could be the back door to success. We could also claim fragrance as proof of cleanliness. This approach seemed plausible. Consumers talked about the lemony lime smell with woodsy hints. It would be unprecedented to try and sell a laundry product on the basis of fragrance but that's all we had. We redesigned the package – which was already bright green – as well as the product, intensifying the perfume, adding speckles as evidence to the consumer of fragrance.

Our New York-based advertising agency was Doyle, Dane, Burnbach- new to Gain, new to Procter & Gamble. On the street Doyle, Dane had the reputation for being the ultimate creative shop. Procter had a reputation for killing creativity by getting overly involved and niggling the details.

Bob Levenson, creative director, and his team came to Cincinnati. Attempting to solicit the most ingenious advertising copy, I said, *"Whatever you recommend we will produce."* Two weeks later Bob came back with a storyboard. It pictured a frog that, after being washed in Gain, smelled so good that a beautiful princess kissed the frog which transformed instantly into a handsome prince. It was the worst commercial we had ever seen but true to my word I said, *"Produce it."* Two weeks later, Bob presented the film. It was as terrible as we knew that it would be. After one viewing, I said: *"Scrap it."*

Mr. Lotspeich, Vice President of Advertising, asked for a viewing. I refused. But, I did ask for the frog costume – the only time I ever requested a prop and for years wore it on Halloween, trick or treating with our children.

Then we told the agency to take another crack at it. Having proven to the creatives we would give them the license they deserved, we got results. They brought us an advertising storyboard showing people walking through the woods smelling the "outdoor freshness" of Gained washed clothes. It was distinctive and persuasive.

Tom Herskovits proved to be the talented manager I had hoped he would be. Creativity, vision and risk taking were sweet spots of mine. While Tom didn't lack for these attributes, his real skill was drive and the organizational ability to get all of these changes in the marketplace. We were an effective team.

Ninety days after our commandeering authority, Gain had a new strategy, new package, new product and new advertising. The brand stabilized. In today's instant gratification world this might not seem special, but given that the ordinary timeframe for such changes would have been about two years it really was impressive.

Decades later, I was shocked to discover in a P&G annual report that Gain had become one of the company's highly touted $1 billion brands and still operated on the basis of our outdoor freshness strategy. Cheer, Dash, Bold, Salvo, Era other detergent competitors at Procter are now all gone. Tide the king and Gain the upstart were, 50 years later, the surviving two powerhouses.

Work became easier after that. I had three rock-star brand managers: Tom Herskovits, Dean Butler and Mitch Wienick. Mac handled secretarial work as well as administrative follow-up with brand managers. She managed the workflow. I managed the brand managers. I delegated to the brand managers. I didn't micromanage or niggle their memos.

But I did manage to complicate things. Working with Tom I had been impressed. A Hungarian Jew, his mother survived the Holocaust as well as the subsequent communist takeover of Hungary. Tom and his sister, Judy, witnessed the murder of their Dad at the border when trying to escape. Their mother, Mamala, was taken off to prison. After reuniting in Israel several years later, the family immigrated to America, landing in Brooklyn. Tom, at age 10, speaking neither English nor Hebrew, started his education in the first grade of a Hebrew School. He caught up quickly, graduating from Syracuse University and Business School on age appropriate timing, with a perfect academic record. P&G recruited him from Syracuse. Tom rose quickly at the company. Competitors sought him as well.

I decided he – focused, disciplined and brilliant – was the perfect match for Rita, Jack's sister – fun and bubbly, with the most compelling and likeable personality. Company personnel reviews were serious happenings. The group product manager (me in this case) presents recommendations for their people to the advertising manager, vice presidents of the division and vice-presidents of personnel and advertising. In the review following our positive Gain experience, these serious senior men were debating, *"What assignment would be effective in keeping Tom with the Company for the long term?"* I listened to their meanderings for a while. Then I interrupted the conversation: *"What Tom needs is a wife and two kids. I'll fix that."* They didn't know what to say.

Following the review, I introduced Tom and Rita to each other. There was pushback initially. He's Jewish. She's Christian. He lived in Cincinnati. She flies all over the world as an airline attendant. It took nearly a year to get them together. But then, trapped on the

23rd floor of the Plaza, on their first real date during the July 13, 1977 New York blackout, that was it. They married the following summer with the reception at our home. We kept Tom at Procter for a couple of subsequent positions before he left the company. But 44 years and two children later, the marriage magic lives. If not for P&G, Tom and Rita and their family would not be.

When they started to date, I had to tell my boss, Sandy Weiner. As such complicated romantic relations weren't the norm, I was a little fearful about his reaction. Everything I did seemed to be "out of the ordinary," requiring a people or policy change (The company moved Jack out of Packaged Soap when we married). Sandy's simple response: *"How many more Wyants are there?"*

Rescuing Gain, plus learning to manage a group of brands, proved time consuming, taking me away from home and children more than ever. That spring, George Lucas released Star Wars, the epic space movie which quickly became a global pop culture phenomenon. I was eager to take Jackie along with Rob Roy, our next-door neighbor's youngest son, to see the show. I believe it was our son's first movie. From the opening moment: "a long time ago in a galaxy far, far away" through to Luke Skywalker's victorious flight in the Millennium Falcon spaceship against the evil imperial agent Darth Vader, Jackie was mesmerized, as was most of America. No surprise, he asked Santa for one thing that Christmas: Luke's Millennium Falcon spaceship.

I started shopping later than most moms. Pregnant with our third child, working harder than ever, plus being Mom to a two and four-year-old, I seemed to always be a step or two behind in both worlds. I went to K-Mart, Toys R Us (both out of business now) and local toy stores. I called FAO Schwarz in New York City as well as outlets in other cities. I snuck into back rooms. No luck. There were none for sale anywhere at all. That was no excuse for letting Jackie down. I refused to permit Santa to disappoint.

Thinking outside the box, it seemed that following the normal mom roads wouldn't lead to finding the illusive prize. Maybe, by applying business skills, there could possibly be a successful ending. So, I began thinking – where in the world would there be a Millennium Falcon? George Lucas! Of course. So, we called his studio in Los Angeles.

Working my way to a production assistant who asked, *"Who is this, anyway?"* *"I'm Peg Wyant, an executive with The Procter & Gamble Company."* The lady on the phone asked, *"Let me check"* and a few minutes later asked where to send the spaceship. Jackie got his dream present and I got for free!

Timmy, our third child, arrived on December 19, 1977. With a millennium falcon in hand and a new baby brother to love we all – especially Jackie – had a special Christmas.

MANAGING THE PLAYROOM AND BOARDROOM

"Life is like riding a bicycle. To keep your balance, you must keep moving."

– Albert Einstein

IN 1981 SMITH College celebrated the 100th anniversary of the Alumni Association in a centennial symposium entitled "Decisions by Women." By the early 80's women's changing roles were bubbling up in discussions. The pedestal or the executive office.

Smith asked seven graduates to speak at the public library's cultural center in Chicago with Jill Ker Conway, Smith's President, to provide a historical perspective on women's work as well as introduce and moderate the subsequent debate. As women were just beginning to enter higher management, while many continued to follow traditional paths, Smith titled the symposium, "Decisions by Women." Invited speakers included a young doctor, a community volunteer, a publisher and Pulitzer Prize winner, a federal judge and Barbara Bush as civic leaders. Smith described me as "business executive and mom."

Jack, always proud and supportive, took the two older children who were then ages 7 and 5. They sat in the front row and listened as intently as could be expected.

None of the women on stage and few, if any, in the audience were following my path – simultaneously pursuing a business career and mothering three children, so Smith asked me to speak on: *"Making It Work in The Playroom and in the Boardroom."*

To provide historical context, I reviewed the depression and World War II, explaining that after those events the country, the economy and the spirit of America boomed – such that having a stay-at-home wife became a status symbol.

> *"In 1960, we had over 20 million children under five, a sign of hope and confidence. Nine out of 10 of these mothers stayed home. When Kennedy announced that "the torch has passed to a new generation," we all thought he meant a new generation of young men. But it was the women who were changing. The percent of working moms now has swelled to 40%.*
>
> *These waters – dual careers – are uncharted and the outcome is at risk as our most important societal function – raising the next generation – is being delegated by moms (and dads) to people we hire.*
>
> *Even so, the right thing to do is move forward. More and more women have the freedom, education and desire to get off the pedestal and contribute to a broader world."*

I gave advice as to how to make it work. This consisted largely of applying business skills to the home:

- *SET GOALS – as two 60-hour jobs can't fit into a 168-hour week. One has to think like the Red Queen in Alice in Wonderland: "I dare say, Alice, you haven't had much practice. When I was your age I always did it for half an hour a day. Why sometimes I believed in as many as six impossible things before breakfast."*

- *PRIORITIZE – there are daily conflicts between kids and work. Make choices and be flexible.*

- *GIVE THINGS UP AS YOU GO – such as girlfriends and parties. When Jackie was 1½, I also gave up tennis.*

- *ORGANIZE AND DEVELOP SUPPORT SYSTEMS – paying to get things done around the house frees time to spend with the husband and kids.*

- *HAVE A POSITIVE ATTITUDE – the key to happiness.*

- *BUILD ON STRENGTHS – it is the best avenue to productivity.*

- *TAKE RISKS – which means accepting failure, which is after all the only way we really learn.*

- *BE CREATIVE – old ways don't work anymore.*

I also addressed the value of taking home skills to the office. Often, the workplace atmosphere bordered on a marine boot camp. Was that the best way to get the best out of people?

"Why couldn't you stop and explain things more clearly? Why do promotions for individuals with different responsibilities have to come at the same time? How can I improve when your only comment on my memo is "garbage"? Why does the Vice President's question have to be answered by tomorrow morning?

Must everybody really work until 10:00 pm during budget season? Is 8:30 am the right starting time for everybody? Can't you teach me your shortcuts?

"Won't the organization be a better place to work when it goes co-ed?"

Although pundits at the time focused on the similarities between men and women, I chose to address the differences as well:

"We are not equal; we are different. And it doesn't matter whether the causes are social or biological. Men are more authoritative, aggressive and logical. Women are more caring, emotional and intuitive. Men are more practical; women are more visionary. Although this is an over-simplification, the point is the two sexes bring distinct experiences and attributes to the table. If we are true to our basic characteristics there can and will be synergistic and potentially superior results."

"I see many examples of women trying to be "tough as men." If women try to imitate the worst characteristics of the boardroom, we will all end up simply being more capitalistic. If men don't put greater energy into the family we run the risk of letting the family fall apart . . . And perhaps society along with it."

The talk in 1981 never mentioned "life work balance" as I didn't think of it that way. Running a business and raising a family bleed together, often in messy ways that defy the idea of balance. The principles which lead to success in both fields are the same – hard work, love and striving for excellence.

Great-Grandmother, Momgee, center, raising her eight Edwards children as a widow, circa 1895

"Ladies, it's up to us."

Ohio's Crusading Attorney General, Grandfather Timothy S. Hogan, 1912

Engagement portraits of my parents, Eve Roberts and Tim Hogan, 1933

Grandmother Margaret Roberts and Great-Aunt Alice Edwards, Advocates for the Vote, 1910

Peggy in a pram, 1943

Nancy, Evalon and Peggy, 1943

Mom and Peggy, Lake Worth, Florida, 1944

Lt. Colonel Timothy S. Hogan, Berlin, Germany, 1945

Peggy learning to ride, 1948

"Once in the woods, there is no turning back."

Peggy and Timmy on the farm, 1949

Terrace Park Dancers, 1951

Timmy, Peggy and Nancy, 1953

Peggy, 1955

Terrace Park Cheerleaders, 1955

Peggy's Graduation, Hillsdale (Seven Hills School), 1960

Peggy, Tim and Nancy, 1961

"You can do ANYTHING."

Post marked YOUTH

TEEN OF THE WEEK

Peggy Hogan Scores With Racket, Needle

PEGGY HOGAN
...and the audience cheered

The fashion judges and audience ooooohed and aaaahed when Peggy Hogan opened her satin trench coat to show the applique of roses.

The tennis crowd ooooohed and aaaahed when Peggy Hogan ran to the left, swung and bounced the ball just out of her rival's reach.

outdo 40 other high school girls.

"It's a nice climax to those 3 a. m. sewing sessions," she laughed.

Peggy, junior girls' champion of the Cincinnati Tennis Club, will play tennis every day this summer "to see if I can become good enough to be a profes-

Peggy, first prize winner of Macy's design and sewing competition, at Waldorf Astoria NYC, courtesy of *Vogue*, 1960

Peggy modeling for Macy's design and sewing competition, *Cincinnati Post*, 1960

The Evening Star

WASHINGTON, D.C., FRIDAY, NOVEMBER 25, 1960—48 PAGES

10 Cents

6-Pound Son Born to Kennedys

Thank you note from Jacqueline and President-Elect John F. Kennedy upon birth of John-John, 1960

Peggy and President-Elect John F. Kennedy, Washington, D.C., *The Evening Star*, 1960

"Make a difference."

"For Peggy,
With thanks
and best wishes,
John F. Kennedy"

Chris during tenure as White House Staff member with Peg under JFK's portrait, White House Holiday Party, 2013

Yale Whiffenpoffs at Smith College, 1962

President John F. Kennedy
Inaugural Program, 1961

Tyler House classmates, Smith College, 1962

Peg in 2019 with Smith Professor
R. Bruce Carroll– Advisor,
Mentor and Friend for 59 years

Peggy and Leslie Carothers, Government Interns,
Washington, D.C., *Cincinnati Enquirer*, 1963

Captain Vic, Peggy and Jimmy Kirgan who
financed American Education International, 1963

Stuart Simington, Chief of Protocol, addressing
AEI students, *Evening Star*, June 21, 1966

Peggy in Paris, France with American Education International, 1966

*"Start before
you're ready."*

Peggy in the *Washington Post*
Sunday, October 2, 1966

YOUNG EXECUTIVE: With office walls appropriately   study-abroad service for high-school students is
decorated with travel posters, 33-year-old Peggy Hansen's   launched toward success.

Her Corporate Image Is Youth

ONE RED
SHOE | Peg Wyant

Procter & Gamble
Bullpen, 1966

"Mad Men will always be with us... so will Peggy Olson."

"Tell me again, why is it that we don't hire women?"

John E. Pepper, Jr., 1966

"All I can do is think. Don't you have a test for that?"

Peggy Hogan, 1966

P&G recruitment brochure for Men:
"Be the spark-plug and moving force; Exciting and important job; Challenging ever changing problems; Looked to for leadership; Be resourceful and creative."

P&G recruitment brochure for Women:
"You Bet P&G Girls are V.I.P.s!; Décor is attractive, office is close to shopping. The girls are the people who take dictation, greet visitors, answer telephones and type memos."

P&G Year-end Sales Meeting, 1968, Peggy dressed in a red suit

"You see more clearly from the outside looking in than from the middle of the pack."

Greetings

Be it hereby known to all that

Mary Margaret Hogan

being the first woman elected to

Sales Training

in the 131 year history of the

Procter & Gamble Company

Soap Divisions

is presented this document by

her friends

this 19th day of September, 1968

in commemoration

of this significant occasion.

1st woman in P&G's 131-year history sent to sales training, 1968

Peggy marries Jack Wyant at Denison University Overlook, May 19, 1973
Best Man, Bill Canfield; Maid of Honor, Rita Wyant and Denison Chaplain Dean Woodward

"Don't defer."

Jack Wyant and Peggy Hogan
dressed in Bonus towels,
P&G *Moonbeams Magazine*, 1971

**Affirmative Action
...What's
That?**

*"Peggy, an Advertising Brand Manager,
holds a traditionally male position,"*
P&G *Moonbeams Magazine*, 1973

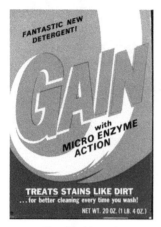

Troubled brand

Princess and the Frog
commercial, 1976

The Gain Turnaround

"Break the rules."

First female Group Products Manager, *Money Magazine*, 1976

"Insist upon love."

First Brand Mom Peggy with
Jackie, 1974

Peggy, Jackie and Jack featured in "The Irrepressible Hogans" cover story, *Cincinnati Magazine*, 1975

Peggy, inside playhouse, and the Houseful of Values Team, 1979

*"If it's impossible,
give it to Peg."*

Houseful of Values Certificate, 1979

Turning nickles into (Olympic) gold

First Charity Driven Promotion, 1980

Grand Opening of College Football Hall of Fame, Missy, Jack and Jackie, 1978

"Cap'n Crunch and Chaos"

Peggy dropping rice over Rita at her wedding to Tom Herskovits, July 2, 1978

Missy and Jackie
Palm Beach, Florida 1979

Timmy, Missy and Jackie vacation with Prices
Sanibel Beach, Florida, 1979

The growing Wyant Family, Cincinnati, 1976

Missy, Peggy and Jackie,
Washington, D.C., 1977

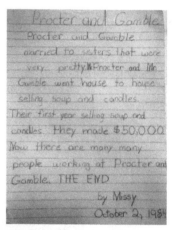

Procter and Gamble

Procter and Gamble married to sisters that were very pretty. Mr Procter and Mr Gamble went house to house selling soup and candles. Their first year selling soup and candles they made $50,000. Now there are many many people working at Procter and Gamble. THE END

by Missy
October 2, 1984

Story by Missy, 1984

"First P&G family."

Artwork by Jackie, 1980, who would later work in Brand Management at P&G

The Laundry Basket Baby
Missy and Chris, 1982

"Committed to excellence and doing the right thing."

John G. Smale, President,
The Procter & Gamble Company, 1979

"Figuring out what P&G should be in the next Millennium."

"Food Match: Nutrition versus Taste"
Peggy, who coined the term "junk food" in 1972, fighting for nutrition against entire Food Management team's focus on taste, 1983

Sketch of Peggy, *Cincinnati Enquirer,* 1983

Empowering P&G Executives
Tom Laco, John Smale,
John Pepper and Ed Artzt

"Managing the Playroom and the Boardroom."

Handling the homefront

- Hire the best people and lots of them for childcare, cleaning, cooking.

- Delegate.

- Set priorities and review regularly along with other family members.

- Make project lists and backup plans. Develop backup plans to backup plans.

- Select the best schools.

- Ask yourself, "Can I afford to work full time?"

- Lower your standards for unimportant things.

- Stop feeling guilty about a messy house.

- Bury the TV. Try conversation.

- Schedule family time. If it's not on your calendar, it won't happen.

- Get your husband to handle 50% of the work (be prepared to live with lots less).

- Be flexible. It's less stressful.

- Pamper yourself. In the family room, you're irreplaceable.

- Aim for the stars.

Tips for getting to the boardroom

- Hire the best people.

- Delegate.

- Set priorities along with managers and subordinates and review them regularly.

- If a project becomes unnecessary, drop it.

- Focus on the three most important goals.

- Be decisive.

- Make it simple and short.

- Speak up–no matter what the consequences.

- Work hard, work smart.

- Find a mentor, a role model, a friend.

- If the system limits rather than expands productivity, challenge it.

- Be patient. Systems change slowly.

- Never give up. Find a more creative solution.

- Climb the ladder or use the stairs–both get to the top.

Presentation for Smith College 100th anniversary, Chicago, 1981

MULTI-TASKING MOM

Jack and Peggy coaching Hyde Park All-Stars baseball team
(Jackie 2nd row, third from left), 1981

Timmy's birthday party, 1984

Timmy, Chris, Missy and Jackie, 1982

Jackie and Timmy, 1985

Peggy coaching Missy's Hyde Park All-Stars
baseball team, 1986

"Family first."

Timmy, Jackie, Peggy, Jack, Chris and Missy
family portrait, 1982

YPO Family weekend,
Brown County, Indiana, 1984

Full-time mom, 1985

Family RV trip to
Grand Canyon, 1987

*"Don't brake;
accelerate."*

Jackie's 16th birthday party, 1989

Jack and Peggy wedding anniversary

Changing the Rules
of Marketing

"I don't think anyone wants to be one of a hundred colors in a box."

— Peggy Olson, Mad Men

WITH THE GAIN laundry detergent brand stabilized and showing signs of growth, pressure at work subsided somewhat while increasing on the home front. Jack left the comfort of the King's Island marketing department, accepting the position to design, build and manage the National Football College Hall of Fame. Although he was still in night law school until June of '77, building the Hall was more demanding and took more energy and travel than the marketing role had.

Meanwhile, challenges with childcare continued to be significant. With so few higher income working women, childcare as we know it now just didn't exist. In our first few years of parenthood, we had two or three different women helping out, which worried Jack and me.

We hired a young woman from Austria whom immigration stopped at the border and deported. We hired a Jamaican woman who hated the isolation of Signal Hill where we lived and returned home. We hired an ultra-strict woman named Rose with experience. She stayed awhile. Cultural clashes ensued.

At one point, I told John Pepper, now our Division Vice President, that if I couldn't solve the problem by the fall, when Mary Martin, a UC student getting an associate degree in education went back to school, I would have to leave the company. He immediately called his wife Francie, while I sat in his office, and suggested she send their nanny whom they had brought from the Philippines to our house. An amazing gesture on his part. However, I could hear Francie's "no" through the phone . . . no uncertain terms. John then suggested I take a month or so off to solve the problem. I did and we did.

Jack's position as a Taft Broadcasting General Manager took time, especially with the approaching Football Hall of Fame grand opening. Jack coached and took the kids on special trips. He was engaged in all their sports – softball, tennis, squash and soccer. While a great father, he provided – like his peers – little help with the day-to-day practicalities such as homework, doctors' appointments, carpools and discipline.

To truly lighten the load, one has to "take responsibility" for jobs needing to be handled. Help on occasion is simply not enough. Happily, more men take that responsibility seriously now.

At the office I enjoyed a strong group. Mac, my secretary, able brand managers – Tom, Dean and Mitch especially – and good leaders in the management above. It was not auto-pilot but close. I delegated more than most of my peers. Delegating by pushing power downward lets people grow. I didn't sweat the small stuff. I didn't worry about healthy situations or when business was on an upward trajectory. I worried only about downside risks. That's where focus is needed.

I was quicker to fire poor performing brand assistants than

anyone on record. In my judgement, everyone hired by a company of Procter's caliber was talented. If someone wasn't pulling their weight, it wasn't a fit. They knew it. I knew it. The sooner we could help them get to a place that suited their skills and personality, the better.

After Timmy was born, I took nearly six months off and tried my best to make it work. Then, Mary Martin graduated from the University of Cincinnati with an Associate degree in Education and started working for us full time. It was a blessing. A joyful personality, she kept love and laughter in the house.

More women came into P&G marketing. They would bring their challenges to me. I tried to help smooth the road. The changing P&G culture made it pretty easy. There were, of course, some rotten apples among the men. We worked around them, and eventually, they were fired. Our ability to hire and train women wasn't good when we started in 1974 but was getting better.

My parents helped. Throughout Jack's law school and beyond, the kids and I had dinner at their place two or three times a week. Dad picked them up for choir practice and sports practice.

Three children are generally considered the "mommy breaking point," as demands and stress increase exponentially, but not time or Mom's hands. So, with Timmy, it became clear that, while I could handle the demands of half a dozen brands – about $2 billion in today's dollars in revenue – I did not want nor could I handle (without messing up the kids) the next level up: the Advertising Manager job. Besides, it didn't seem to me to offer a substantively new challenge, just more brands.

In Fortune 500 companies at that time, flexibility did not really exist. In a line management position, the manager had a number of defined responsibilities and the company dictated the "what and when" as well as the processes, procedures and patterns by which people got things done. There were daily sales reports, top management meetings Tuesday at 10am, annual budget meetings with a strict schedule leading up to the final presentation.

Although it was hard for me to acknowledge, especially after all those speeches about "how to make the Boardroom and Bedroom work," I was finally in over my head. I first asked if I could have a more flexible line position – maybe three or four brands rather than five along with a three- or four-day work week. Senior management put down that idea pretty quickly (now 70% of employees have flexible work schedules).

Then I thought of "retiring." John Pepper suggested that an alternative first step – a test market if you will – would be to move from line management where profit responsibility lies to staff which provides support to line and offers less pressure, more flexibility.

That's the route I took. I asked to transfer to Promotion and Marketing Services. The General Manager, Bob Wehling, had just moved there from a Bar Soap and Household Cleaning Products line management position. Few highly regarded men had made such a move. Most considered "staff" to be out to pasture. I wanted to work for him and that's the assignment the company gave me.

The 8th floor where Promotion and Marketing Services managers resided was directly below the 9th floor home of the powerful company leading Packaged Soap and Detergent Division. A few steps made a world of difference. Line managers had responsibility for meeting revenue and profit expectations and all of the related pressures that they entail.

Staff has none of that. People typically arrived at 8:30 a.m. and left at 4:30 p.m. without a briefcase. The position of Promotion and Marketing Services Manager involved responding to the operating division requests for help in the promotion arena –

such as coupons and premiums. Brands took responsibility for making promotions pay out.

However, right about when I moved to the eighth floor, Bob Wehling challenged me to do something not done before. Each brand operated on its own as if it were an independent company. If Tide put a coupon in Sunday's paper or sponsored a mail-in, Tide acted alone even though Ivory liquid might be paying for exactly the same thing. And, as if to magnify the independent notion, every division (there were five divisions) was totally isolated from the others. Each had its own marketing group. Each had a separate sales force. No sharing. No efficiencies. Brands weren't fully accessing the power of Procter & Gamble, which was generally considered to be the mightiest consumer force in the grocery store.

There was corporate interest in experimenting with having brands and divisions work more closely together. And shortly after moving downstairs I was tasked with trying to help make something happen.

A theme emerged from my research pretty quickly: Houseful of Values was a tagline consumers understood. The HOV promotion would be on products all around the house. It was simple and clear. Beyond saving money via price-off coupons on perhaps a half dozen products, the hope was to bring it all together by offering a premium free in return for collecting and submitting proofs of purchase from the various brands.

The premium would have to be unique and compelling. The premium department, our in-house experts, suggested the ubiquitous Fischer Price plastic house – which fit strategically with the concept but would cost a lot to ship and was available everywhere. Other suggestions were equally boring. Nothing compelling. In the midst of the search I went home one evening to find our five-year-old son Jackie playing with the cardboard

Pampers shipping container and Crayola markers. He was drawing a gingerbread house on the case for him and his sister Missy to play in. Bingo.

It was an 'aha' moment. I said, *"Keep going Jackie."* And he did, creating a child's rendition of the Hansel and Gretel cottage. Children would relate. The next morning, I packed up the Pampers container and took it to Art Department Director Marty Briede saying, *"This is what we need to make."* He thought I was crazy. I also asked him to use the design for the die cut Sunday coupon insert and the in-store display piece.

Meanwhile, we engaged brand managers and sales managers from several Divisions, selling them on the idea of working together to save money and increase the impact of promotion dollars rather than continuing territorial boundaries. Meetings. Lunches. Memos.

Cascade and Tide agreed. Then Pampers, Crest and Ivory liquid. Duncan Hines, Pringles and Downy. In the end, 15 brands from four Divisions participated. Consumers who purchased and sent to P&G proofs from 40 of these products received a "free" child's playhouse.

P&G policy required approval by the Administrative Committee – the company's ultimate authority – for expenditures over $5 million. This event was expected to cost in excess of $50 million. But since each brand had its own approved promotion budget and would spend less than the threshold amount, I sought permission from no one. Nor did any brand.

Bob Goldstein, Senior Vice President of Marketing, under whom this project fell, recognized the lack of top-management approval shortly before the launch and long after the opportunity to stop or influence it had passed. He could have, should have, taken the project to the Administrative Committee. I had gone out of my way to keep HOV under his radar.

Now all Bob could do was listen. He called me up to the 11th floor to discuss what was about to happen. He was visibly worried. In a company that required that every aspect of everything be vetted and tested, it was an unprecedented "togetherness" approach with a completely unknown, never-manufactured-before premium. Without taking the "just do it" road, we never would have gotten to the market so quickly.

Bob was not happy. I was unapologetic. He and I had never connected. With three sons – no daughters – that was perhaps not surprising. He was similarly skeptical when Mac suggested she job share with another secretary – a completely novel idea at the time. But we managed to launch that model, too.

The promotion launched in early September. Surprisingly, 15 brands and the four sales forces worked well together. The idea of a "big impact event" excited store managers. And the "playhouse" generated unprecedented consumer enthusiasm. Moms saw the opportunity to get a fun, high-impact toy for their kids at no cost other than buying a few good products – which the trade discounted to generate store traffic.

Thousands and thousands of moms collected box tops anticipating a unique Christmas present. The magic ingredient was the playhouse which only a child's imagination could've created. It was cozy, kid-sized, maybe three feet by five feet. It was colorful with a red door and shutters, bright blue shrubs, happy flowers lining its base and a quirky striped awning protruding from the window.

I don't remember how many women bought 40 products to get an item only available through P&G. The promotion was so popular it changed the price of cardboard worldwide. We had to use the "power" of The Procter & Gamble Company to get all the cardboard needed.

Having inadvertently put the company in the role of Santa

Claus, we could not disappoint. Consequently, to every family who fulfilled the requirements and sent proofs received by December 20 we were able to deliver a Playhouse. Pre-Amazon, that was a feat.

Business went through the roof. Quickest payout in history. I suspect there is no way a man in my position would have watched and listened to the creative work of a five-year-old, let alone insisted that experienced Art and Premium Department executives copy virtually every line and color of his concept. To a mom (and now perhaps to dads, as well), the power of a kid's imagination could prove to be magic.

That spring, Bob Wehling presented an award from the four sales departments that had worked together on the promotion. It was a certificate which read:

"WHEN SOMETHING SEEMS IMPOSSIBLE, GIVE IT TO PEG WYANT."

And attitudes changed. Instead of fighting the concept of working together, the brands clamored for another group promotion. The 1980 Olympics were around the corner. We launched a similar promotion around the Olympics. But instead of collecting box tops for a special premium, we promised to give two cents to the Olympics for every P&G product coupon redeemed. To the best of my knowledge, using the power of a nonprofit to motivate purchase was another concept new to P&G as well as the grocery industry. One I firmly believe was probably more likely to have been conceived by a woman than a man. It worked, not as well as Houseful of Values, but well.

The following year the Company asked us to do it again. The challenge was that the Olympics are a once-every four years event. But I had heard of Special Olympics from my days in D.C. and my sister's work with the Kennedys.

Burr Robinson in my group flew to Washington to talk with Eunice Kennedy Shriver about partnering with the 10-year-old and still somewhat obscure Special Olympics. She agreed. We repeated the couponing idea, marketing it heavily. It worked for P&G brands. It made "Special Olympics" a household word. That was even more important than the money we raised.

Meanwhile Jackie, Missy and Tim continued to play in their playhouse and for years thereafter Pampers featured it in their catalogue.

The value of diversity is that it brings people with different characteristics together and people with different characteristics think differently. Diversity of thought, when brought into the tent, makes everyone think and progress happens.

Planning
P&G's Future

"Peg could see the future."

— *Susan Steinhardt, member of John Smale's secret task*
force team

N January 1979, John Smale asked to see me. A Canadian by
birth, John was the revered 51-year-old President of Procter &
Gamble. As a young brand manager, he had diligently worked
to win the American Dental Association endorsement for a fairly
new, struggling cavity-fighting brand named Crest, tripling the
brand's market share and creating an enduring market leader.
It was the first endorsement ever from the American Dental
Association and among the first for the company, establishing an
innovative marketing approach for P&G brands.

John graduated from Miami University in Oxford, Ohio where
he met Phyllis, the strong-willed red head who would be the love
of his life as well as his rock. He credited her – smart, independent
and dedicated to family – as the compelling reason he could
become a corporate leader.

According to Company lore, John paid his way through
college in part by writing, publishing and selling pamphlets
called "Party 'Em Up" and "Party 'Em Up More" to fraternities and

sororities around the country. John's personality belied that of a partying frat guy. The personality that we knew was hardworking, disciplined and reserved. The dichotomy reminded me of Jack's grandfather Pal whose sayings included: "whiskey is made to be sold not to drink." What "Party 'Em Up" actually revealed was the seeds of a marketing genius.

I first met John around 1969 when he transferred from Vice President of the Toilet Goods Division to VP of Packaged Soap & Detergents. As a fairly green assistant brand manager, I was called up with my boss Dick Egan to the executive floor on eleven to meet with Mr. Smale. As we went up on the special elevator that was reserved for the top floor only, Brand Manager Dick warned me: *"John is serious. He won't smile so don't take it personally."*

While appreciating the heads up, I thought he would be warmer than that. And he was.

When John became VP of Packaged Soap, it started his long-term working partnership and lifetime friendship with Tom Laco, my initial mentor and the Advertising Manager who reported to him. Tom had the big personality; John, the vision. Tom was the motivator; John, the thinker. It was a pairing that Smale and Pepper would later repeat.

Tom and John, along with John Pepper, supported the policy changes that diversity required. They were the change-makers, also the advocates who helped clear the path for my career and others who were different and who colored outside the lines.

Back in 1979, the top floor differed from all the rest. The ceiling was high, and the pale green carpet, plush. We waited before the large Rookwood pottery rendition of the company's moon and stars symbol, the only artistic statement on the entire floor (excepting a few John Ruthven bird prints). It was eerily quiet and foreboding. Even though I had by then been there many times before, I was nervous. He was after all, the "President." I was alone.

When the receptionist announced, *"Mr. Smale will see you now,"* I found my way back to the large corner office.

After customary courtesies, John made a remarkable statement. *"I'm looking for someone to help me figure out what Procter & Gamble should be in the next millennium."*

Did I hear that right? The next millennium was 21 years – an entire generation away. John always took the long view, but this seemed astounding. What CEO thinks like that?

John had been President since 1974 and certainly knew he would be Chief Executive Officer in a couple of years when Ed Harness retired. He knew P&G stock had been declining and prospects for a reversal if the company stayed the course were slim.

John took the time to talk about what he believed fundamental to Procter & Gamble – character, people and growth. This philosophy was ingrained in its DNA. P&G's health depended on growth (doubling volume every 10 years which we all knew) because only with growth would talent have the opportunities needed to grow. Under stagnant circumstances, the most able people simply would not stay.

In the seventies, the company built revenues but, unfortunately, failed to deliver the requisite seeds for real growth. It seemed to lose a competitive edge and its skill in moving forward. The company bought Clorox Chemical Company in 1957, prompting the Federal Trade Commission to claim that it might "lessen competition." In 1969, the Supreme Court agreed, forcing a divestiture in a settlement with the FTC. The Clorox settlement prohibited acquisition of products sold in the grocery store. Research and internal development efforts hadn't produced promising new entries. In the seventies, we failed to open a single new category of business. Bounce, a fabric softening extension of the Downy business, was the only successful new brand. Rely Tampons, which was introduced in 1975, would be recalled in 1980.

Test market success rates had reached all-time lows – far lower than the 50% historic standard. Our new product success rate had dropped from 67% in 1946-55 to 50% in 1956-65 to 42% in 1966-75. The number of new brand tests had dropped from 40 in the 1956-65 period to 19 in 1966-75 – cut in half whereas it needed to double. Even expanded brands, like Hidden Magic hair spray and Wondra hand lotion, did not fare well.

Later that morning, Bob Wehling explained that John intended to interview several people to find an individual who could help him – all older and more striped than I was at age 37. While fascinated and flattered to be in the hunt, I assumed the prospect of getting an offer was slim, commenting to Bob that it wouldn't work anyway. I had recently left line management for a staff job which would allow me to spend more time with our three children. Reporting to the President didn't fit my plan.

Bob called a few days later to tell me that John was giving me consideration for the position. While again flattered, I clarified that, "I have to consider my family first and the pressure of reporting to the President directly would be too much pressure." Besides, I already had a full-time job in Promotion & Marketing Services as we had just finished Houseful of Values and were being challenged to develop a new promotion.

Again, I said *"no."*

The next week, I was asked to rethink. When Bob reminded me that there were 66,000 people employed by Procter, virtually all of whom would give their right arm for the opportunity to work directly with John Smale, I said, *"Great. Let him get any one of those people."*

But he didn't. He called me back into his office asking, *"How can we make this work?"*

"I don't mind the challenge or working hard. It's the day-to-day pressure of being on call. If it snows and our nanny can't get up the hill, what do I do? I can't promise to be here at 8:00 am or even 9:00 am under those circumstances. I have to be home by 6:00 pm and there are events that take priority, like teacher conferences and coaching baseball."

It may have been my imagination, but I recall noticing a slight smile. He understood. He agreed. It would start as a part time responsibility. He would not interfere with my life at home. Of course, it's not the guy who sits on the top of the mountain who worries about the little things. It is the people who are trying to get there. Besides, he, too, valued family.

Looking back, I suspect my saying "no" to such a golden opportunity moved me to the front of the line. Independent thinking would be critical. There are always a lot of "yes" men in executive ranks. The independence demonstrated by Bonus, the Gain turn-around and launching Houseful of Values probably helped as well.

We shook hands and we got to work. I suggested to John that it would be helpful to me, since history teaches us all, to take the first few weeks to analyze the past to try and determine what made Procter & Gamble successful. I asked to start in the archives.

"I know that Procter & Gamble can make toothpaste and IBM cannot. I know that IBM can make computers and Procter & Gamble cannot. I don't know why. Studying the past should reveal the skills behind our successes and help us develop a plan for going forward." John agreed.

I ventured into the archives which at the time was a windowless back room on the first floor about where the coffee shop is today.

There was a lot of learning that came from those days of retrieving dusty material from cardboard boxes and later from the multiple conversations with older men from the research and product development side of the business. As disorganized as the archives were, historic papers revealed nuggets that would prove valuable in developing a plan for the future.

I learned that P&G grew over the years by buying its competitors, scooping up all kinds of little soap manufacturers. Acquisitions were a more significant driver than most of us realized. We bought companies as well as technologies, like the original patents behind Cascade and Tide. I learned that often efficacy – "Like improved cleaning" was not the only key to success. Rather it could just as well be something seemingly less important. Flavor masking fluoride helped make Crest a viable toothpaste. Covering the bad smelling ingredients in Cascade gave the brand a huge advantage over its competitors -so much so that the company tested Cascade with its chemical smell so that competitors wouldn't know about the masking fragrance and copy the technology until the Cascade product with the fragrance was already on shelves.

I learned that Procter was an innovator but it didn't necessarily characterize any one Division nor even any particular discipline. The ability to forge new paths resided in the minds of a few brilliant men like Dick Bryerly, Vic Mills, Bob Duncan and John Smale who were responsible for Tide, Pampers and Crest. Dick quietly persisted with neither support nor dollars for nearly a decade to bring Tide to the market.

An analysis of success factors delivered surprising results. Technological advance mattered, but what mattered most was not spending, competition or market size but the existence of a product champion, a man (all there was then) who saw a consumer need and simply refused to let go. A few creative men championed the products that made Procter & Gamble the great company it became after World War II.

Also, innovation went far beyond products and performance, permeating advertising, promotion and sales examples: Launching a market research department. Creating the radio show Ma Perkins. Advertising (the first TV ad) on a Cincinnati Reds baseball game in the 40s. Inventing soap operas. These put P&G on the map.

Learning that the company took real risks suggested that the careful, test-driven, cautious approach we had come to demand – testing efficacy, product aesthetics, package graphics, copy and every imaginable detail – wasn't always the pattern of the past.

Could the isolated, self-congratulatory bureaucratic "Ivory Tower" be a 70's invention created by nearly 30 years of success?

Richard Deupree and Neil McElroy made the decision to invest the $25 million capital required to expand Tide when company annual sales were below $500 million. They knew Lever would be poised to mimic the breakthrough technology should the company test market. The risk of expanding without significant consumer feedback was huge. According to the book *Rising Tide*, they also bypassed brand, shipping and advertising tests. When he understood the magnitude of the cleaning breakthrough provided by synthetic detergents, Chairman Deupree said: *"Crank her up, full speed ahead."* It was unheard of for a company as careful as P&G normally is.

The archives also revealed how we lost our way. In the 40's and 50's we focused on entering new markets. We did it by developing new brands and acquiring companies – Charmin paper, Duncan Hines and Jif, as well as technologies. In the 60's we implemented the strategic focus on growing revenues with multiple expansions, marketing dollars and innovations like TV soap operas. Aided by a booming U. S. economy, we focused on building the business and rewarding shareholders. The acquisitions fueled internal development and synergistic effects.

Annual reports originally were simple letters. A couple of pages written from the CEOs to stockholders in the corporation – short, focused and clear.

In the 70's, outside events prompted the company to stray from a laser focus on business to a range of peripheral issues such as the environment, employment policies, pricing/wage policies and government regulations. Examples include phosphate issues driven by residents of Long Island (small piece of geography), employment issues consequent to the 1964 Civil Rights act and various affirmative action executive orders, inflation and price controls. These were not the reasons people bought stock. Shareholders are interested in the revenue and profit growth and expect the best of companies to achieve that in whatever environment the company must operate. Had P&G lost sight of the fundamentals?

As John had warned, there were few promising test markets in the works. Had the culture stripped away our ability to even think out of the box?

On April 27, 1979, after researching the archives and interviewing as many of the older players as could be found, I proposed an approach. We would start with a broad-based assessment of all major categories, everything sold through grocery channels. The first task would be to determine total manufacturers' sales in each and every category distributed via grocery stores. To be classified as "of interest," a product line would require some technical expertise (no commodities) and meet ethical standards (no cigarettes or alcohol). A senior analyst named Bob Pipes joined me to help gather facts.

At the same time, Bob Wehling and I developed and

recommended criteria against which to measure each category. These criteria were disarmingly obvious:

1. U.S. market size of $50 million and growth
2. Consumer need unmet
3. Requiring technical and marketing skill
4. Warehouse distribution
5. Profitable

We went through the supermarket and identified the markets meeting the agreed-upon criteria, dividing them into food and non-food. John asked that we start with food, given its large size.

The next step – July of 1979 – was to begin assessing research and development leads and skills. John wanted answers to the questions: *"Did we have the capability to win? Could we succeed by ourselves or did we need to go outside by buying another company?"* To help answer the question, we needed R&D expertise added to our small group. Geoff Place, Head of Product Development, designated two very senior product development managers, Hoyt Chauld and Les Frommes. Les took the lead.

Les, a late 50's British citizen with a brilliant mind (#1 in his class of Oxford) and soft English manners was crucial to our success. He guided me through the maze of patents and projects as well as headstrong Ph.D. personalities at our long-term research center.

Miami Valley Labs (MVL) was located near the bucolic college town of Oxford, Ohio, where Miami University is located. Charlie Broaddus who headed MVL reported directly to the P&G Chairman, Harry Tecklenburg, bypassing the President and avoiding any commercial controls. It was designed as a group of "mad scientists" who researched what they wanted in hopes that freedom to explore, combined with brilliant minds, would lead to successful inventions.

John Smale was not welcome on the premises. They would work unencumbered by marketing assessments – out would come profitable brands. After all, isn't that what Dick Bryerly had done for a decade with Tide? And Bob Duncan as head of the "Explorers Club" in the 40's and 50's, the group responsible for so many of the innovations which led to the company's explosive growth in the 1950's and 1960's.

Without a highly respected R&D man by my side, I could never have procured a security pass, let alone gotten any attention at MVL. All these scientists knew was that I was on some sort secret assignment for Smale. That said, I was a young woman, far less threatening in their domain than a typical general office, older male executive.

Charlie set up a series of product development reviews for Les and me. During these sessions, various scientists showed us projects on which they were working, in some cases, for years and years. We heard about Olestra, the calorie-free non-digestible oil that was intended to replace high calorie Crisco shortening and Puritan oil and, in the process, help solve America's growing obesity problem.

We heard about a meat analog, a plant-based meat substitute that constituted an early version of "the impossible burger." Designed for frozen main meals (plant product tasted better frozen than meat), we concluded consumers should be offered both meat and vegetarian options.

We tasted a cookie that never became stale. It stayed fresher because it had a crusty, top sheet-like surrounding the cookie, similar to Pampers, and was developed by the same researcher. We saw products with the potential to solve hospital-related infections and early attempts to keep skin looking young. Also, there were over-the-counter (OTC) and a few Rx drugs in the early stages.

What soon became clear was that most of the work – while perhaps scientifically laudable achievements – had been under development for years and was being pursued without commercial direction or firm deadlines or cost parameters. These were Ph.D., R&D deep thinkers. No women among them. Their explorations were being done with no eye to what might be acceptable, let alone profitable, from a consumer standpoint. Pure research.

Two examples would be Coldsnap and a carbonated beverage substitute. Similar to Duncan Hines for cakes, Coldsnap was a dessert mix for making ice cream at home. We asked why consumers would buy a mix when every convenience and grocery store around the corner offered multiple selections of reasonably priced, ready-to-serve, high-quality options. They had no good answer.

Apparently, MVL had never even asked that question.

Also, we saw a prototype carbonated beverage that could be used to attack Coke and Pepsi and give us entry into the fast growing and huge carbonated market. Their miracle product could go directly to grocery stores without the diversion of a bottling plant which was a detour Procter wanted to skip. The delivery vehicle was a paper cup which had a tin disk about a half inch from the bottom covering and containing little brown pellets. Adding tap water magically released the flavoring and bubbles which turned water into a carbonated beverage.

It was an engineering feat perhaps but a disaster from a consumer acceptance standpoint. Regrettably during the presentation, I couldn't help but break into laughter. All I could think of was cat litter. Who on earth would drink cat litter?

It was becoming evident that the company had lost its ability to develop internally new products capable of taking us successfully into new categories and doubling the business over the next decade. We would have to make acquisitions. Joint ventures, licensing and other new approaches were also recommended. Fortunately, Terri Schmeltzer and Steve Barrett, and later Susan Steinhart, had joined our group to help with market research and financial analysis.

The line managers in some divisions were not helpful as they resented outsiders, even though we were insiders, looking over their shoulders. Most, however, cooperated with indifference. One, the Senior Vice President of Food, Chuck Jarvie, called me into his large corner office to clarify that no one from his division would provide any information or otherwise cooperate in any way. The pharaoh had spoken. Maybe he thought he could intimidate a girl. I didn't feel it appropriate to "complain" to the Company President. Too small a matter to take up his time. Rather, I decided to work through another channel – R&D via Geoff and Les. They were happy to provide what we needed.

We finished the food review in the fall. The markets we recommended mostly related to providing healthier options, a place where we saw real and growing consumer needs, e.g. orange and apple juice; juice flavored water; carbonated drinks as marketed as well as with healthy additives like vitamins and juice; convenient main meals with analog as well as meat; water – plain old bottled water.

We then turned to non-food. The same challenges became evident – work on products such as pharmaceuticals had dragged on for years. Many areas of focus had too little commercial value. Internal development simply wouldn't be adequate. However, all the presentations as well as fact-gathering did serve to point us in clear directions. We were beginning to see that unmet consumer needs in both food and non-food arenas were clearest in health.

On July 23, 1980 – I wrote John: "The task force is not certain that

Management shares our conviction regarding the overwhelming importance of health . . . which is not simply attractive, it seems essential . . . the only way to meet our corporate goal."

After about a year, our group had three major recommendations, all of which would require buying one or more big companies:

1. Healthcare . . . OTC drugs, nutritious foods and home diagnostics

2. Beauty Care . . . skin care, cosmetics and fragrances

3. Beverages . . . orange juice, lightly flavored fruit drinks and bottled water.

Having identified categories, we put together two books – one food and beverage and one non-food – and distributed them to the Group-Vice Presidents. We met in a large 11th floor conference room to review. John wanted their buy-in. Ahead of the meetings, VP Gerry Dirven asked me to explain the process; I wrote an explanatory memo. John Pepper requested a meeting where he probed our approach in his typically inquisitive manner and, as expected, asked penetrating questions.

No other VP got involved. Truth of the matter is that many were more administrators than leaders. So caught in the day-to-day they had little sense of the future.

John became CEO in 1981. We moved the Company first into beverages, buying Citrus Hill Orange Juice that December and then Orange Crush. Both facilitated the strategy which was to capture a large share of the huge beverage industry.

The particular acquisitions also opened a back door into carbonated beverages by providing the opportunity to develop lightly flavored natural fruit drinks like the French drink Orangina and by entering the bottled water industry whose only real consumer entry at that time was Perrier. Sales of both Orangina and Perrier were roughly only about $25 million each, so they fell short of the minimum $50 million revenue threshold.

Because of the competition scene, I believed – Les Frommes and Geoff Place as well – that it would be extremely difficult to win with a cola entry. Consumers couldn't even tell the difference between Coke and Pepsi in a blind test although they thought they could. Competition was entrenched and dominant. Plus, they owned the bottling plants which controlled distribution.

Healthier options seemed like the way to enter this market. If our selling proposition was "health is the idea," how could entrenched and dominant competitors whose drinks were filled with chemicals, preservatives and sugar defend? It was the mother instinct in me that anchored my conviction. Jackie and Missy were playing on sports teams. The portable drinks parents brought for half-time treats all had 12 teaspoons of sugar. Water, in the eyes of a Mom, offered a better answer.

Once we made the beverage acquisitions, John turned the development over to the line manager in charge. Dick Nicolosi, the newly appointed GM for Orange Crush, turned his attention exclusively to cola. He ignored bottled water, fruit drinks and even turned down the opportunity to buy Gatorade which was then a minor brand with huge potential.

Because John was inclined to return control to the divisions once a move had been made, he let Dick run. Big mistake. Frankly, it was the only big one that I saw John make. These two acquisitions proved unsuccessful. They didn't need to be.

Bottled water is now a $200 billion market. Had P&G started early and captured even 20% of the industry, it would have been able to achieve its corporate goal of doubling revenues every decade.

Our primary initiative and #1 recommendation was healthcare through pharmaceuticals – OTC then Rx. Procter's annual sales were nearly $10 billion. With the long-standing goal of doubling the business every 10 years, it was the only market big enough (excepting water) to make doubling possible. Consumer attitudes, changing government regulations, an aging population and our product development (analytical measurement) and marketing skills (advertising then was not a factor in drugs because of legal restrictions that were being eased), all pointed to a high likelihood of success. Procter had not only a history in healthcare (cleanliness is the first step) but a bright future. Coming from the Toilet Goods division (Scope and Safeguard were over-the-counter drugs) and having been the champion of Crest, John was pre-disposed to favor healthcare products – they represented the potential to meet concrete and lasting consumer needs.

Les and I wrote John Smale that healthcare, starting with OTC drugs and eventually moving to prescription medication, Rx, nutritious foods and home diagnostics, such as pregnancy tests, was the answer. With $10 billion in company sales, the challenge for P&G was to become a $40 billion company within 20 years – $80 billion by 2020. We recommended healthcare as the only way to meet that goal. It is simple math. The market:

- large at $200 and $600 million U.S. and worldwide respectively and growing 12-13%/year

- profitable with 9-13% margins, 12-27% Return On Investment

- recession proof and of significance

- moving up because of consumer trends which includes aging, disease prevention, home diagnostics and self-care

- matches our strengths including the move to advertising particularly as we anticipated that prescription drugs

would be advertised rather than sold through doctors
only

- OTC, over-the-counter healthcare products were sold in
  the grocery and chain stores where Procter was already
  a dominant player. We knew how to sell these stores and
  we could advertise the products. Consumers typically
  start with the lowest cost option to cure their ills.

The initial acquisition target was Norwich-Eaton. We purchased
Norwich Eaton in March 1982 for $371 million. The company
became available and offered exactly the type of products we
sought. There were well known brand names such as Pepto-
Bismol, Chloraseptic, Aleve – all in categories that were large
and growing. Norwich also owned a smattering of Rx brands.
Again, the move evidenced John's leadership as he made the
acquisition of Norwich, as he had with Citrus Hill, without support
from the Vice-President in charge.

The next market we targeted was beauty care with a focus
on skin as a logical extension of P&G's history in face soaps like
Camay, Ivory and other personal care brands. Besides, our most
recent entry into hand cream, Wondra, failed to perform well.

We approached Richardson-Vicks (ironically John's first job in
sales before P&G was with Vicks), a family-controlled company;
their primary skin care brand was Oil of Olay. Richardson
also offered NyQuil, Vicks cold remedies and Clearasil acne
medication. Not only were these well known, highly regarded
branded products, the company had an approach to business
that was similar to P&G's and an attractive foundation globally.

When they said no, John backed off as he was not about to
launch an unfriendly takeover. In 1985 when Lever Brothers
went that route, the Richardson family came back to Procter &
Gamble, the white knight with compatible culture and consumer

philosophies, and sold in a merger worth about $1.2 billion. We also recommended buying Noxell, another family owned company in Hunt Valley, Maryland. P&G acquired Noxell in 1989. The skin care business is now one of the Company's most important markets.

The Norwich acquisition happened in March 1982, just two months before our son Chris was born. It was a career highlight. We were now poised to start building a major pharmaceutical business. I felt comfortable taking a year off – I'd earned it. One will note that my maternity leaves had progressed from weeks to a year. This time – for the first time – paid leave of eight weeks was in place. And now there is paid leave for all employees for all new family additions.

After returning from childcare leave, the next challenge was continuing to investigate global possibilities. People called Ed Artzt, President of P&G's International division, the "Prince of Darkness." His reputation was tough, egotistical, negative, hard to work for and a street fighter trope. I found all that to be true.

In the first meeting, I asked for a list of what products were sold in what countries. No such list existed. Business was run on a country by country basis. An overview, for example, of the global coffee or the personal care business wasn't available. However, it was easy to conclude that the global expansion of successful U.S. brands like Pampers and Crest and Head and Shoulders presented huge potential. When the Richardson-Vick purchase occurred, the company provided a global footprint to build upon.

Also, our small group looked at competition and took the "corporate view" whereas up to then everything was brand and country based. We saw – and could see because we were free of day-to-day responsibilities – other moves with potential. We recommended line extensions, value brands, pushing decisions down, experimenting with venture and joint ventures/licensing.

It is clear that not everything we did proved successful. The beverage acquisitions didn't work. I like to think they could have if we had gone the water, juice and vitamin route. But beverages would have been a stretch for P&G given competition in the bottling system. Some others such as home diagnostics were simply too far ahead of their time to become viable.

As I have reflected on why John asked me to help, I believe being an independent thinker was certainly a factor. He knew about Bonus, Gain and Houseful of Values. Maybe equally important was that I was a woman, an outsider to the boy's club that had always been Procter & Gamble. Outsiders bring fresh thinking. Nobody even thinks to tell us what to think because we are often not part of the in-group. According to Richard Brodhead, retired President of Duke University:

> "In this country, those who have stopped thinking are typically those who have stopped interacting with people who might make them think; namely people who do not already think more or less the same as they do."

In 1973, the year John Smale became President, the stock hit a high of $120 per share ($1.59 dividend) and then began a slide that would see it fall to $84 ($1.20) or nearly 30%. By early 1979 when he launched the search for an answer to the question "What should Procter be in the next millennium?" the company and John were in trouble.

Naturally, there were extenuating circumstance for below par performance – the Middle East oil crisis, inflation and price controls, outside issues to contend with such as environmental pressure and phosphate laws as well as affirmative action and having to pull Rely Tampons off the shelves because of toxic shock claims. But the underlying fault lay within the company. No one area shoulders all the blame. Research and Development failed to develop new, differentiated products, marketing was unable to build volume against strong competition, emerging generic house brands cut sharply into sales, maturing brands and managers who had begun to doubt that the best of the best worked at P&G.

The price continued to decline, dropping to $62 ($.90) per share by the early 80s. I am sure John was disappointed but in none of our meetings did he once mention the stock, let alone any concern about the price. He affixed his stare only on the future.

The resurgence of P&G started in 1982 and then there were an unprecedented four stock splits in the next 15 years. It hit $473 ($37) by 2000 – six times the value in 1979 when we started. Revenue had doubled every five years during this period – twice our long-term corporate goal.

And we were ready to build new healthcare and beauty businesses, as well as expand globally. The re-organization of Research and Development was underway. Acquisitions – on which John spent less than $3 billion – had come back as a viable tool. The road going forward would be fraught with a few failures and false starts. But the company was alive again.

By the dawn of the next millennium, thanks primarily to John Smale's vision and leadership, Procter & Gamble had become a new company.

WHY I LEFT

"If you bungle raising your children, I don't think whatever else you do will matter very much."

— Jacqueline Kennedy Onassis

A YEAR AFTER Chris was born I returned to work continuing the special assignment with John Smale, but resigned a few months later despite pressure from management as well as the few other women at the company who now held influential positions. "You can't quit. You are the pioneer." But I did.

"Why did you leave?" is the question most frequently asked of my Procter & Gamble career.

It's complicated.

I had climbed the ladder and, after 16 years, reached rarified air for women — or men, for that matter. I had made a difference. In his book, *What Really Matters*, retired CEO Pepper would write:

"People often ask me, 'What is the single, most positive change you have seen in Procter & Gamble over the course of your career?' My answer: the dramatically increased diversity of our employees . . ."

Sometime in the fall of 1981, years after son Timmy was born, we had given the bassinet, baby bed, strollers and multiple car seats to our nanny Mary Martin to take to her church. We thought we were out of the baby business. Calls to retrieve – if only for a couple years – were met with *"So sorry, but everything's gone."*

Chris was born shortly after Procter purchased Norwich-Eaton, our first major acquisition in decades, and a week before our planned move from Signal Hill to our new home on Grandin Road. None of the baby items had been replaced.

Coming home from the hospital, we found life with a new baby and an 8, 6 and 4-year-old, on top of last-minute packing, hectic at best. Additionally, the renovation of our new home was close to being finished but not quite. The contractor raced to beat Chris' birth, but his two-weeks'-early arrival threw a wrench into the schedule. No time.

The morning we moved, Jack left town on a business trip and the rest of us needed to find a place for Chris to travel and live. One of the kids opened the door to the master closet, revealing a Kelly green, plastic laundry basket. My grandmother once explained that *"in the old days, moms made baby beds by putting a pillow in a dresser drawer."* Bingo! The laundry basket would be the baby's new bed.

And so, Chris came to be known as "the laundry basket baby." The basket was his bed. It was not exactly a stroller, but we used it that way, carrying him that summer in it from our new home to the nearby pool where there were some very fancy lace prams and strollers. It was his play pen. In addition, strapped into a car's front seat by a seat belt, it served as his car seat. Today's mothers are doubtlessly freaking out (me too in retrospect) and rightly so. But to this day Chris is well adjusted, calm, flexible and able to take things in stride. Laundry basket influence?

After a few months, my mother noticed his little foot had slipped through the lattice. She predicted he would be a hunchback if left in the basket, and went out and bought a real bed, car seat and stroller.

The laundry basket story tells far more than how a hassled mother of four coped with her to-do list. I was trying desperately to make both lives work but it wasn't happening – not with four children.

Demands of P&G and the pull of the home were both strong forces which could easily be full-time jobs. I could do it all. But, if all at once, I could not do it all well.

In 1973 when Jackie was born and company policy said, "stay home," that would have been a comfortable road to take. The fact is, I came back. The move constituted an experiment. And it would be misleading if I said there was certainty and confidence associated with my decision.

Being a working mom worked for me. Not perfectly, but it worked. Being a pioneer meant walking down the road not taken. I loved being a pathfinder but – maybe because I couldn't share the challenges with other women – there was not a day that went by that I didn't feel guilty about something. Mostly I felt guilty about the kids. Among my good friends, only two, Trish Smitson and my sister-in-law Patty Hogan, were working moms. Both were lawyers.

Meanwhile, Jack enjoyed increasing success.

At Kings Island, Jack and Bill Price had become 'best buddy' selling machines. While live music filled the park, they introduced big stars to boost attendance in the evenings ($5 at 5:00 pm), notably country singers Conway Twitty and Loretta Lynn. Eager to fill the Park, Jack authorized the opening event (without Bill's approval) and having little concern for detail, advertised before the star agreed to the deal and signed the contract. The event sold out.

They brought stuntman Evel Knievel to the Park in October 1975 to make his longest ever jump – over 14 Greyhound buses, – it became the highest rated show on ABC's Wide World of Sports for years. Then, the frick 'n frack twins decided to give America its 200th birthday party on July 4, 1976. They talked a network into a 24-hour national TV special – broadcast from Kings Island. The Great American Celebration. They brought the College Football Hall of Fame from NYC to King's Island. Five years in the themed amusement park business was a magical time, especially for our children. It was part of the adventures Jack had promised me.

Then, an opportunity came Jack's way that was too good to be true. It was to be the CEO of a startup enterprise called Home Entertainment Network which, for the first time, would broadcast just released movies to people's homes. This was a new technological feat which was a precursor to cable and Netflix streaming. Boxes leased and attached to TVs would unscramble signals. Cable would ultimately kill the business, but meanwhile there would be a few years to create an enterprise, build a going concern and learn the art of entrepreneurship. It did all those things for Jack.

He started by renting a trailer and buying office supplies, then by hiring a few people: Peggy Burke, fresh out of UC's School for Design (DAAP) who designed and wrote the TV guide marketing piece and Chris McCleary. When negotiating to purchase a TV channel for TV tower space in Chicago with Clint Murchison, Jack went to the men's room and told the smart young guy who carried his Murchisons' briefcase: *"Chris McCleary, you're on the wrong team."* They still work together 40 years later. Jack also hired Bill Price, who moved to Chicago with his wife Mary Beth – whom I worked with at P&G – to open and operate the Chicago station.

He negotiated a multi-million-dollar loan to purchase boxes and service vans from Key Bank. Dean Meiszer, the 24-year-old assistant loan officer, admonished him: *"Don't access the line of credit until next Monday."* Jack paid no attention and started selling. Today, Jack and Dean are founding directors of a startup bank of which Dean is CEO.

On the Wednesday before Thanksgiving, Jack called a Chevrolet car salesman, Gary Greever, and ordered 50 white vans to be delivered the following Saturday. When Gary pushed back on the timing, given that it was a holiday, Jack stood firm. Gary found a way to deliver. We have been buying cars from him ever since. It was a wild, crazy, fast ride.

This talented team built a fast-growing three-city business in a couple of years. Then, because cable was closing in, the group sold Home Entertainment Network for a profit.

Jack's next venture was to purchase Nutrition Technology Corporation (NTC). The company invented and manufactured nutritional drinks, Slim Fast being one, and high fiber products. Given his position as CEO of a company that grew from $800,000 in revenues to $20 million in two years, he travelled frequently and faced a demanding schedule.

Given Jack's focus and our active children, it had become difficult – let's say impossible – for me personally to do a good job with both work and home responsibilities. We spared little expense regarding private schools as well as household and nanny help. When arriving home earlier in my career, I quickly changed clothes, rushing out again for a 6:00 pm tennis match, watching one-year old Jackie started to cry, and that stayed in my head throughout the match. This wasn't fair. It would be my final tennis match until the children grew into the game and could play as well. If I chose to stick with a career, given husbands of the day were focused almost entirely on work, taking little responsibility for the home front, I would have to make tough choices.

I had backed off parties, volunteer work, symphonies and opera (Jack didn't mind the latter). I had given up girlfriends and sports (regrettably) long ago. Our vacations were all-in, all family, all the time together trips.

Having successful men take on household responsibilities wasn't in the cards. The men might help occasionally but taking on responsibility – no way. I actually defended that position when P&G put me on TV shows and podiums defending our women-only approach to dishwashing and laundering. Feminists wanted companies like Procter to show men doing household tasks. I argued that the purpose of advertising was to sell by reflecting society, not to try and change it. When I first passed on what was arguably the most important and exciting position in the company, a reason I gave to John Smale was that I couldn't promise to be there in the morning as the nanny might not show up. Looking back, it seems shocking that neither John nor Jack nor I ever thought that, on those rare occasions, a husband might fill in.

Years later, Chris, in elementary school, would write a perceptive poem:

Oh Dad, oh Dad, oh Dad,
You make me feel so sad.
You go to the grocery once a year,
Come home and say:
'Look what I did, dear.'

I became pregnant with the fourth, due June 15, 1982. Already exhausted, I told Bob Wehling, my administrative boss as well as the head of personnel, that my last day would be May 14. Only then I learned that recently announced maternity policy called for working until two weeks before the expected delivery date. Amazingly, the answer to my request for an early leave was "no," even though all three previous children had come two to three weeks early. Three test markets.

A staff doctor re-affirmed the policy telling me I couldn't leave for another two weeks. My response was: *"Just watch me."* Then I called Dr. Garber, my longtime (though now retired) doctor, who accommodated my request by changing the delivery date.

Chris arrived as Dr. Garber and I predicted – two weeks early, on May 30. The company paid for an eight-week leave.

Jack, who by then was CEO of Nutrition Technology Corporation, managed a company growing exponentially. Money had never motivated me – at least not as the primary driver – but it seemed that we would never again need my income to live well.

The kids were getting older. They needed me at home more than when they were little. One day, as I drove down our driveway to go to work, five-year-old Timmy followed, running as fast as he could with tears streaming down his face – his tears touched my soul.

At the same time, I recognized that my work with John Smale had come to an end. We had identified health and beauty care as areas of growth as well as nutrition . . . water included . . . and launched dialogue with Richardson-Vicks (Olay). We had gotten the company back into the business of growing through acquisition with Citrus Hill and Orange Crush as well as targeted companies with billions of revenues. We had launched line extensions as a new way of doing business and set the globe as our expansion geography. We had started pushing authority down in the organization as well as advanced creative ways to approach growth.

For five years I had operated as a secret agent for the CEO. P&G never bestowed the appropriate title, Vice-President of Strategic Planning and Acquisition that the work should have earner, nor the dollars that would have carried with it. However, I had worked in rarified air, directly with John Smale, a man of rare character and vision. I had helped put plans in place for taking P&G to the next millennium. Also, we had pioneered diversity. We had made a difference.

But I would be lying if I didn't say that I was really disappointed. Somewhere deep down I'd been nourishing a dream of being the first female Vice President at Procter & Gamble. I thought I had deserved it.

So, when Timmy ran down the drive, tear stained, one August morning, I went back home for a while to console him, then went to work. That was the day I closed the door mentally on a big chapter in my life.

Even so, I asked John Smale and Tom Laco to move me back to line management to run a division. They – Tom was the messenger – said no. It was the first time I had come up against a glass ceiling. Tom explained that running a division would be too hard for me to handle along with family, including four kids, and the inflexible demands of a top line management position. Today, that reason wouldn't fly, but then it did. There were now other women in the pipeline so shooting me down didn't foreclose another woman from making the cut. As Justice Ruth Bader Ginsberg argued the pedestal is also a cage.

The decision – it would be too challenging – should have been mine. However, these men, whom I had worked with for 16 years, weren't acting as bosses. They were acting as mentors and friends, almost fathers, trying to do the right thing. And I understood.

Was I just challenging the system? Was I being a rebel one more time – seeing if I could rewrite the rules? Would I actually have gone back to handle the demands of managing a division? Would I have been happy as Vice President?

We will never know.

On my last day, Tom and John called me up to the 11th floor. They wanted to wish me well. They also took the opportunity to share new childcare policies, including plans to build a childcare facility close to the General office: *"This is all because of you, Peggy."*

Then, to their complete surprise – mostly John's – I gave each a hug and a goodbye kiss. We had blazed trails together in a way that would not happen again. In closing the door, I turned back, saying: *"Thank you."* And then I added, *"This is the first and last time there will be a farewell like this. Going forward, the relationship with women will be all business."*

There were stock options to turn back. The Company's stock was still in a funk. It hadn't yet grown in value enough to make my options worth anything. But given the plans in place, I knew explosive growth was in the works and those options would soon be worth millions. The company cut off my access to the employee stock purchase plan as well as Moonbeams, the corporate magazine.

There was no going-away party. I simply walked out the door, down 5th Street, all alone, just like the day I first applied.

A few years earlier, Jack and I had visited the home of a former P&G Vice President and advertising pioneer named Oliver Gale. Procter President Neil McElroy had recruited Gale to work with him on public relations when McElroy served as Secretary of Defense under Eisenhower. When the Soviet Union launched Sputnik into orbit, it suggested that the Soviets were ahead of the United States in missile development.

McElroy did not believe that the Sputnik success represented a major change in the world's military balance. However, he acknowledged a public opinion problem. As Gale had pioneered one of the first internal public relation departments on the corporate scene, he was the perfect recruit. He served throughout McElroy's term of service.

After leaving Washington D.C. in 1960, Gale started his own

PR firm rather than returning to P&G. It was an unusual move as successful executives simply did not leave The Procter & Gamble Company. For that matter neither did the factory employees.

It was years after when we met Mr. Gale. Jack and I were looking to move to Hyde Park and when he put his white pillared Tara-like home on the market, we made an appointment to tour. He was a tall, white haired and distinguished Harvard graduate who looked and acted like a southern gentleman.

After we toured his home, Mr. Gale invited us to have a drink in the library. Having recently lost his wife, he was lonely and we, knowing his reputation and his loss, were eager to spend some time with him. Halfway into my drink, I worked up enough courage to ask why he –a legend – decided to leave P&G.

Mr. Gale sipped his scotch, looked around and asked, *"Do you have a favorite book?"* I said, *"Yes. Gone with the Wind. I've read my dog-eared copy several times."*

After pausing, Mr. Gale shared his story: *"Well, for me, Procter & Gamble is like a favorite book. I have read and re-read it and it will always stand alone as my most admired and loved book. But one day, I came home and realized that there is a whole library out there."* The conversation stuck. I left P&G in search of more great books.

Les Frommes, my strategic planning partner, retired from P&G and in the spring returned with his wife to England. He sent me a treasured letter:

"It will come as no surprise to you to know that I regard you as one of the few truly impressive people I have met. When I have a problem, I frequently ask myself 'what would Peggy do?' I don't always do it as what is in character for you is not necessarily in character for me. But it defines a

place on the map which stands for clear thinking, boldness and integrity. I hope you find an avenue for your intellect and for your energy which satisfies you and provides the kind of leadership society needs in so many important areas."

PART V

MULTI-TASKING MOM

CAP'N CRUNCH
AND CHAOS

"When you opened the door to the Wyant home, you never knew what would be going on, but you always knew something was going on."

— Amy Kattman, babysitter

"Chaos couched in pure love. There was no better champion for children. At the Wyant house we had a chance to be teenagers."

*— Anna Binkley Kennedy, daughter of best friend Bonnie,
my partner in crazy adventures*

A S THE WELL-ORDERED world of The Procter & Gamble Company faded into the distance, I would find a new place on the map for my energy and intellect. It was called home and it was different in almost every imaginable way from the attire to the noise level. My skills, however, were sadly lacking.

I was not and am not the chef my Mother was nor the scratch cook of my grandmother's era. Having grown up in comfortable circumstances, I never learned to clean – not really. I was qualified to serve as a Seven Hills School Trustee (which I was at the time) but far less to be a class parent.

At this point, friends to help navigate would have been helpful. Yet my friends and professional colleagues were clueless men.

We lived in a spacious English manor house built in 1929 at 2386 Grandin Road. The original owner named it Lilybanks in honor of hundreds of day lilies which blossomed in the spring. During career years, we had lots of help, Mary the Nanny, Lucille the cleaning lady, Arthur the gardener and babysitters, notably Amy Bulger and Anna Cunningham who lived in the neighborhood. This was the way I was able to manage it all given the demands of P&G.

Now most of those helping hands were gone. How prophetic were my words to Tom Laco when he asked me as female employees started having children: *"Why are we losing so many of the women?"*

I told him: *"Because being a mom is a harder job than running a brand."*

Tom was incredulous and insulted by the suggestion that his wife Barbara had a more challenging position than he did. He, nevertheless, listened. Today, P&G's TV advertising campaign titled "thank you, mom" describes the job as the "most difficult" in the world.

P&G is, by-and-large, a quiet, controlled and rational place. Competent people execute logical, well developed and agreed-upon plans. There are experts to call upon for help. There's civility and respect. And, if an outlier surfaces, we fire him.

The home falls at the opposite end of the spectrum. It is sometimes illogical, always noisy, unpredictable, crazy fun. No experts at your beck and call. And if a child goes over the line, firing isn't an option.

Daughter Missy nailed it after she and her husband, Yvo Smit, had children: *"Mom, I used to put you on a pedestal for all your pioneering achievements in business. Now, I realize, in going back to work you were just smarter than everyone, sooner than everyone."*

The family has always been close, with a clear focus on church, school and sports. Both of our parents lived nearby. Eve and Judge had us to dinner at least twice week. Grandma and Grandpa visited. And we frequently drove to Granville, Ohio, where Denison University is located to see Honey and Pal, a place he called "the village of knowledge." He greeted everyone with "seldom have a bad day" or "fine, fine, everyday you're alive is a good day."

In the 80's, it was popular to talk about the importance of "quality time" with children. We never adhered to that. We believed it was all about "time" period. We spent lots of time together.

We went to the Episcopal Church of the Redeemer. Jackie served as an acolyte while his siblings sang in the choir. My Dad drove them to practices. Mother was also a parishioner.

All four attended Seven Hills School, from Montessori through high school graduation. Seven Hills resulted from the merger of Hillsdale, which I attended, with the elementary school Lotspeisch and Doherty, under headmaster Peter Briggs. It is a private school with high standards. We emphasized the importance of academics and working hard – just being the best you can be. There was structure – sort of – but no forced hovering. I helped with homework and was the disciplinarian; Jack was captain of fun. Decades later, that dynamic would be reversed with Missy and Yvo.

Our home was boisterous with people around, all over the place, all of the time. It was partially the location (across the street from the Cincinnati Country Club in Hyde Park), but mostly the team of four, all personable and cool. Jack, a people person, brought family, colleagues and neighbors. As our babysitter Amy reminded me: "I'd open the door never knowing what would be going on – but always there was something going on."

We left the key under the front door mat for the entire 30 years that we lived at 2337 Grandin Road. There was one burglary. We learned during the trial that the thief was a young man named T-bone, who with his buddies, stole two cars from our driveway. And yes, the keys were in both ignitions. We are, for better or worse, trusting folks.

Anna, another frequent babysitter, noted how nice the children were – seldom fighting. Really? She must have only come on the good days, certainly not the afternoon when Missy smashed Jackie's head into the windshield, shattering the glass but fortunately not his head.

Three boys and a tomboy make for raucous times. That was part of their growing up. Once when things got completely out of hand, we drew up a contract – one of the many business skills brought home – wherein the "brothers of the Wyant household" promised not to spaz, fight, kill or otherwise misbehave.

Our oldest is Jackie: smart, athletic, handsome and full of energy. He is also a natural leader with a quick, strategic mind who set the course and the pace for the other three children from the beginning.

When he was a toddler, my sister Nancy sent me *"The Plug-In Drug,"* a book about children and television. Its well-articulated thesis encouraged parents to keep children away from TV screens. While Sesame Street, as the prime example, seemed "educational," the book laid out why TV encouraged passivity. Passivity overcame any teaching value it might have. That's not the way children learn.

From the onset the Wyant policy was the same my parents had employed – one show per week per child. The book reinforced its importance. For a while, we successfully held to that standard. Rule breakers were required to write, "I will not watch TV" one hundred times.

TV during the week is Bad!
I will not watch TV during week I will not watch TV during the week I will not watch TV during the week. I will not watch TV during the week. I will not watch TV during the week. I will not watch TV during the week. I will not watch TV during the week. I will not watch TV during the week. I will not watch TV during the week. I will not watch TV during the week. I will not watch TV during the week. I will not watch TV during the week.

But as the kids got older, it became difficult to enforce. Each of the four kids would select a program – Missy liked Fame, the boys liked sports or Cosby. Me, dramas. Jack, news. Not only do news and sports go on for hours there is also the problem of events like the U.S. Tennis Open, Wimbledon, March Madness and the Olympics.

Managing the policy became stressful. The apparent solution was to get rid of the TV. During one of Jack's business trips, I announced to the children that we were going to a funeral. We buried the TV in our back yard. Problem solved. (After they all went to college, I found a small TV hooked up in Jackie's closet on the third floor.) The challenge of how to manage "screens" continues.

Jackie started playing baseball as the team's youngest when he was six. First time at bat, he hit an infield pop-up that was caught. Not realizing that a fly ball means "you're out," he ran the bases as fast as he possibly could. He thought he'd hit a home run. The older kids laughed.

Coach Neal Smyth intercepted Jackie when he touched home plate, leading him toward third and away from snickering kids. I heard Neal enthusiastically say: *"Terrific running Jackie."* The kid was bursting with pride. Then Neal continued: *"There's just one thing . . ."* Jackie left the field feeling like a million dollars. The "Hyde Park All Stars" (the name was self-fulfilling) went on to win championships for several years with Jackie as pitcher and his Dad as sponsor and coach, and me as the first base coach, always motioning them on to second to turn a single into a double. An all-round athlete, he excelled at all the sports he tried. I think it started with the confidence he gained the day of the pop-up fly.

Sports (driven by both of us but mostly Jack) became a part of every family member's everyday life. At the Cincinnati Country Club, Don Mills, the squash and tennis coach, brought them into clinics – Timmy at 2½. They played on school teams as well. Jack and I coached their soccer and baseball teams.

Our second child and only girl is Missy, born two years after her older brother. She brings sunshine and smiles to everyone she touches. Fearless from the get-go, she jumped at 1½ enthusiastically into our pool before she learned to swim (Jackie at 3½, who also couldn't swim, managed to pull her to safety). Her infectious personality draws friends. The "life is a banquet" philosophy of my mother and Jack's sister Rita lives on in Missy. Her personality and infectious laugh light up a room.

She, a born athlete like Jackie, was also the pitcher on her elementary school baseball team, once querying, *"I don't understand how someone can miss catching the ball."* We named her team "The All-Stars," as we had her older brother's team, and they went undefeated for several years. Our friend Neal was the baseball coach while I kept stats – using my secretary and P&G computers – and co-coached. We won the championship so many times that some competitive teams forced us to break the girls up.

Like the doting father he was, Jack called her "princess." And, like most second children, she was a pleaser.

Showing early entrepreneurial spirit, Missy started a summer camp that she named Camp Rainbow, recruiting a dozen little kids. It was a learning experience as well as a liability risk that many parents in our position would have avoided. I became head counselor. Meanwhile Jackie worked in landscaping.

The introspective one was Timmy. Always thinking and acting with purpose, Timmy, whose soccer team I coached, had no tolerance for first and second grade teammates who picked the proverbial daisies on the soccer field. Purposeful marked his pursuits.

Tim also had from the get-go an inborn sense of justice. At age 2½, Timmy sat down on the top of our backyard hill, because he asked me to carry him down to the pool. Arms full with lunch baskets, I said no. He, considering my stand unjust, stayed there by himself for over an hour. Children that age don't do that.

Often, he would take stands against parental or school decisions with which he disagreed. Although he was an honor roll student, he refused to attend a high school cum laude dinner arguing that it was wrong to reward A students when a C student might have worked as hard.

In middle school during the early nineties, when there were few environmentalists, he committed himself to the environment. Creating a company called "Save the Planet," he wrote to Jack and me as heads of our respective businesses as well as managers of our 2337 Grandin Road home, imploring us to take the steps necessary to recycle, including re-modeling our home and office kitchens to accommodate multiple trash cans. To save water, he refused to flush the toilet. Parts of the house reflected the odor. Only when I said to Jack, *"One of the two of us has to move out,"* was Tim forced to modify his behavior. Instead of flushing, he did his business in the backyard for several months.

I never understood my father – whom lawyers and friends described as having an inborn sense of justice – until I met my son, Tim. Like Dad, he gravitated from a young age, and for a lifetime, to service.

Jackie, Missy and Timmy were born two years apart. Then there was a 4½-year gap. Christopher (nicknamed as noted, "Keefer" and "Toeball") had enviable good looks – marked by a full head of golden blond curls. In the early years, he was so quiet and shy that we worried, until we realized there was so much chatter at the dinner table, he didn't have a chance to be heard.

His experiences differed from those of the oldest three who did all the same things at virtually the same time. Chris stood a bit apart. Bonnie Binkley, my best friend during those years, became his champion. Bonnie and I would sometimes take the boys – Chris and her son Nick – out of school on Fridays for special adventures. Since each was the youngest in the family and we had traveled down this road before, we had the audacity to believe that time with the moms trumped school. We could teach them new and exciting things and do it better.

I had much more time to spend with Chris one-on-one – not really working full-time since he was born – than I had with the older children. Together, we learned to play golf, went to plays and cooked meals (he grilled). We spent time at the pool. Our happy-go-lucky last child spent days on end there.

In the early years, before Chris, Jack and I were so busy with life, we forgot about vacations. Frustrated, I announced one day that we needed to go away somewhere, anywhere, for a few days – even though there wasn't much time. I was tired. Jack suggested we check into the Cincinnati Country Club. A travel agent friend suggested French Lick, an historic Indiana hotel dating back to the 1800s in the manner of gilded age resorts. Beyond the mineral springs that made it famous, French Lick offered tennis, golf, swimming, horseback riding and nature walks. We piled in the car and headed west.

The kids were 3, 5 and 7, and excited that Thursday afternoon as we set off on a new adventure. When we entered the lobby, the old place was clearly past its prime – bumpy upholstered furniture and worn-down carpet with the smell that only comes after being trod upon for decades. Feeling deflated, I said to Jack: *"This place is seedy, we should go."* To that, he responded: *"The kids don't know it's seedy."*

We had a wonderful time. There were even unexpected benefits to vacationing in a place so old and tired. Our three could race down near isolated hallways to our room, key in hand, feeling freer than ever. All of us could play golf, no need to worry about children damaging rock hard ground with spotty patches of grass. The horses were old and tired.

After that, we started going to Cumberland Lake every summer – living on a houseboat and skiing sometimes all day on that beautiful Kentucky lake. 24/7 togetherness. Jack had kept his boat for over 20 years and finally we put it to use. After Chris was born, we took our 12-year-old babysitter Amy. On the way we stopped at the supermarket to stock up. I – a working girl – was thinking through what we needed when Amy interrupted with: *"hot dogs Monday, breakfast for dinner Tuesday, hamburgers Wednesday. I think I've got the gist of it. Why don't you go to the car?"*

There is one special cliff on the lake . . . perhaps 50 feet high. Dare devils climb up a rocky slope to the top and, those with courage, inch their way to the rocky edge and jump while people waiting in the 30 or so boats below cheer. My husband and all the children made numerous jumps.

Along the way, we bought a minivan, the ultimate mom car. It was a grey and purple hand-me-down from the Prices. We took road trips. And we always took the time to stop for a historic site or special learning experience.

We went to see the play Tecumseh in Chillicothe, Ohio, in a rustic outdoor amphitheater where horses galloped across the landscape and Native Americans held up scalps, dripping with the blood of white folks they killed. It was scary for the little ones. Then we pitched our own tent and slept in a friend's parents' back yard. While coyotes howled and pictures of Shawnee's warriors danced in our heads, we cuddled.

On the way to Cumberland Lake over the years we stopped to see other outdoor dramas – Blue Jacket the Indian chief, Abraham Lincoln and Daniel Boone, Frontiersman. Other trips incorporated Gettysburg battlefields, the Boston Tea Party Ship, Concord and Lexington, Big Sur, Hearst Castle, Independence Hall and the Liberty Bell, Congress, the Supreme Court and the White House.

In Cincinnati, we made our own history. With Bonnie, we took the kids to Paris (a street). Later, Chris and Nick dressed as French Presidents Charles de Gaulle and François Mitterrand, and drove in small cars down the *Champs-Élysées*. There was a picnic in Lytle Park, at the foot of the Lincoln statue, on Presidents Day while someone read the Gettysburg address. Then we snuck into one of Cincinnati's nicest hotels, changed into swimsuits in the bathrooms and enjoyed a swim.

Every March during spring vacation in the 80's, my parents rented a house in Sea Island . . . a dream place for kids. They participated in all the activities, which were run as contests, including ping pong, shuffleboard, tennis and sandcastle building. A Wyant almost always won. (News flash – Sea Island still runs the activities but has eliminated the competitive aspect. No winners. No losers. Not so much fun.)

Our favorite trip was an RV trip from Colorado to the Grand Canyon. It included Zion and Bryce Canyon, 35 Colorado Springs, a dude ranch and rafting down the Grand Canyon. Years later, Jack, Jr. and his wife Amelia adapted and expanded the idea, taking their three boys on RV trips on both coasts.

We celebrated just about everything. Birthdays and anniversaries and graduations, for sure. Accomplishments as well. We didn't give every player on our team a trophy but we hosted parties and tried to acknowledge their unique contributions with certificates ranging from MVP to most fun. We – mostly the children themselves – created birthday party themes and all the trappings. Jackie would build an obstacle course for the younger ones, a water park, an Indian outpost.

Anne and Allen Zaring, whose children were a little older than ours, showed us the way regarding family celebrations. Putting each child in the center of a party gives them confidence.

Looking back, I try to remember what we did well and where we might have fallen down in raising the kids. We made some good choices – going to church every Sunday (we tried) so they would have a spiritual foundation, sending them to the best schools even though we struggled financially to do so, and opening the door to athletics, particularly the game of squash.

Personally, I reflect on how tough I was at critical moments. Was I too tough? Not long ago Yvo, my Dutch son-in-law said: *"Kind is not a word I would use to describe you."* The words stung, but Yvo was right. The first words people use to describe me are smart, strong, competitive, fair. Kind doesn't rise to the top.

At work and at home, I have always believed that you've got to be tough to be kind. It's why I didn't have trouble firing aspiring brand managers. Everyone has talent. If a person's talent is ill suited for a particular position, it quickly becomes evident. The sooner one moves on to find a fit, the better.

Jackie was in the fifth grade and paying little attention to school when, one day, I abruptly stopped the car in Hyde Park at the corner of Paxton and Observatory. On the left stood Hyde Park School, which, at that time, was a public elementary school, and across the street was a gas station. In a frustrated voice, I said *"Jackie, why don't we take you out of Seven Hills and send you here? It's free. It's easy. There's no homework. You and I can stop fighting about grades. After graduating you can walk across the street and get a job at the gas station."*

In middle school, Missy became a little concerned about her weight. Not mincing words, I agreed that "Boys don't like fat girls." Right then we commenced going to diet counselors and trainers for information. We packed up and travelled to a health spa that summer. Missy was 12. Other guests were generally 50 plus. We still go to spas – a favorite time together.

We spent our time with the children. Early on, we decided that, for us, the amount of time mattered more than quality time. It's why we scrunched together in houseboats and RVs. It's why I left The Procter & Gamble Company.

We wanted to expose our children to all kinds of people and opportunities. We were particularly pleased one evening to bring Missy to the opening of a new building, as we were seated next to Neil Armstrong. After dinner and, in her words, copious glasses of white wine, over comes this bubbly blond with an outstretched hand enthusiastically exclaiming *"so nice to meet you, Mr. Glenn"* then turning to her right added *"pleased to see you as well Mrs. Glenn."*

Always the self-effacing gentleman, Neil with a kindly smile replied: *"Missy, the pleasure is mine."* On another occasion, our friend Charlie Mechem witnessed a stranger say to Neil: *"oh my heavens, you have the same name as the famous astronaut"* Armstrong responded: *"yes, I do."*

Upon graduation from high school, we invited some teachers and coaches who had had a strong impact on each child to join us for dinner at the Maisonnette, Cincinnati's famous five-star restaurant. Timmy gave a talk at his graduation dinner, thanked Susan Marrs, his college counselor, for helping him get into Harvard. He thanked Mr. Turansky, the school's riveting history teacher (a socialist among upper income kids) for *"his never-ending pursuit of knowledge and ultimate concern with the less fortunate."*

He thanked Don Mills *"for giving me and my siblings squash, something to identify myself by. For being a second father. For managing the perfect balance of knowing when to demand more time and effort, and when to let me go."*

Then, turning to Jack and me, he said: *"I am grateful to you because your children have been your primary focus, and because you have always been there for us giving love, opportunity, pride, morals, discipline. You encourage us and give us compliments as if on a crusade to make sure we feel good about ourselves . . . also you have taught us by example."*

The "Boardroom and Playroom" speech that I had first delivered in the early 80's addressed the way to bring business skills home. It left the impression that the Wyant house ran like a well-oiled machine. Set priorities. Delegate. Organize. Develop a system and backups. I prefer to recall it that way. I also prefer to remember our culinary fare as healthy (which it was), consistent with the mandates outlined in my recommendations to the CEO about nutrition and health. But, when I asked Missy to describe growing up at 2337 Grandin, she instantly responded: *"Cap'n Crunch and Chaos."*

One of the boys said, *"It's not fair to say there was never food in the house, we just didn't know what to expect."*

At the August 2008 rehearsal dinner for Jack, Jr. and his fiancée, Amelia Julian, my brother-in-law, Tom Herskovits, of Gain fame, gave an insightful toast about being a Wyant:

My name is Tom Herskovits and I have been married to a Wyant longer than any person in this room with the exception of Peg. I feel a responsibility to let you, Amelia, know what you are in for. I will say that you could talk to Peg, but she is finally marrying off her eldest, so I do not think she is an objective and reliable source on this issue of what it is like to be married to a Wyant.

There are three primary things that I would highlight in the experience of being married to a Wyant. First, is communication. Wyants are communicators. They are the only ones that do not need a Bluetooth with their smart phones – it is built into their ears. They call you, they call each other and they will call all of your family too, anytime, anywhere and about anything. Amelia, I suggest that you do as I did, buy stock in the phone company.

The second area, and this is serious, is that Wyants go to everything. We are talking about kindergarten graduation, parents' day at elementary school, basketball games, dancing recitals, high school graduation, etc. etc. Now there are about 12 Wyants with a lot more on the way. So, if you figure 18 events per person, you are talking about 300 events, or about one fifth of your life over the next five years. And don't think you are protected being in Philadelphia – the farther the event the more likely they are to show up.

Third is this energy. The energizer bunny has nothing on a Wyant. Parties that last till 4 am, seven-day trips in three days and on and on. And you would think that over the years they would wear out, but they don't. They just keep on ticking.

Loyal, family oriented, all good looking and smart, they produce fabulous off-springs and they attract brilliant great looking mates. The one thing you can count on is that they will make your life fun and exciting."

SQUASH

"This sport is steeped in the principles of sportsmanship and fair play! Winning is a goal, losing is a part of sport, but how you treat these two imposters shows the essence of the person. The Wyant children are beacons of fair play."

– Coach Paul Assaiante, USA National Coach and Trinity Men's Squash Head Coach

N 1977, WE joined the Cincinnati County Club. Actually, Jack became the member as it was virtually all men only, except widows. Joining cost $2,750. I thought it was too expensive; Jack was all in. The Club offered social activities, which we passed on. Mostly, it offered sports – golf, swimming, tennis, paddle tennis and squash – into which we became immersed. Coach Don Mills and the game of squash would change our lives.

The sport itself is typically played by two players in a four-walled court with a small, hollow rubber ball. The players strike the ball with their badminton-looking racquet, hitting onto the playable surfaces until someone misses or hits out of bounds.

First played in 1837 at the Harrow School in England and still grounded in education, the British military took it around the world as the commonwealth spread. Relatively fast growing and healthy (Forbes named it "the healthiest sport"), it has also been traditionally elitist; you will find squash courts at all the top colleges and clubs while companies like Rolex and wealth managers target advertising to the players.

There are two other appealing aspects of this highly competitive sport. First, it is like golf, a "gentleman's sport," in the best sense of that word, with character-building rules requiring players to give their opponents ample space as well as calling their own faults. Second, the key to winning is persistence and grit, even above skill. If the player gives it everything, simply refusing to give up, then you can almost always get to the ball. It's like life.

Jack fell for squash immediately, winning the Club's C level championship in 1979. When he started going from the airport after business trips directly to the squash courts, I felt compelled to beat 'em or join him. We started playing as a family.

We signed our children up for both tennis and squash clinics with Coach Mills. Some of ours were younger than the other kids, but I didn't want them at home with a nanny all day. They walked with the nanny from our home to the Club, starting as young as 2½.

Don was one of those rare coaches who drew young people in with passion and skill, then kept them engaged with discipline, vision and values. A native of Philadelphia, a hotbed of squash, he earned all-state honors in three sports. At Trinity College, he captained the squash team, and, after graduating, married Judy and came to Cincinnati courtesy of a management job with Macy's. Don continued competing in squash and, over the decades, won over 30 national and world titles in singles and doubles. He set an example of excellence.

One day Coach suggested Jackie focus on squash. Showing, like his father, an instantaneous love of the game, Jackie started taking lessons and training. Missy, Tim and Chris followed.

The Cincinnati kids had a challenging everyday work schedule.

They met at the courts at 6:00 am, before school, to drill, run the hills or practice. A huge hill on the golf course called Big Bertha was the most challenging. After, Don took them to breakfast, then school. Back after school most days for lessons and play. Then, many weekends were consumed with tournaments.

The junior squash circuit turned out to be demanding as well. On numerous Friday mornings throughout fall and winter, we'd all go off to the airport, flying back late Sunday night. Mills insisted that the children dress in blue sports coats, Oxford shirts and khakis for the boys; nice dresses for Missy and Libby Eynon, who were the only girls competing. Don thought that appearance effected attitude and confidence. His players developed both. Many of the tournaments were played in top universities, including the Ivies. The players came to believe they belonged there.

Our oldest became a skilled and even-tempered competitor. Tough and consistent, he seemed to win every match that was within his grasp. By the age of 12, he ranked number two in the nation behind Harrison Mullin, a young man from Brooklyn Heights. Jackie and Harrison joined forces on the doubles court, winning two national tournaments. And Jackie was a steady fighter, winning a memorable match in a tournament at the University of Pennsylvania by staving off nine match points.

It took Missy awhile to gain the confidence of her brothers even though she moved to a top five group rather quickly. During play, she would look back and up, seeking approval and encouragement from a coach or a parent. That remained a pattern throughout college. In the final intercollegiate tournament, she lost the first game 9-0 of her pivotal match against Harvard. She looked up. Then finally it clicked and looked within herself. She won.

Chasing his older siblings, Tim talked us into tagging along to a tournament in Washington D.C. when he was only seven. "Please, please can I go? I've already packed and I don't take up much room." We agreed but set expectations. "Tim, this is a national tournament and the opponents will be older and stronger than you. You will not win a match, likely not a game and maybe not even a single point."

When we got to Washington, we found that Timmy had been given a bye on the first match, thanks to his older siblings, whose squash records had already given the Wyant name a bit of an aura. He next played an opponent that may never have played a match and could barely hit the ball. He won handily.

On to the semis where Tim met his match. The opponent was a good Washingtonian player named David Moss, who instead of playing to win – as quickly as possible would have been the approach of most 10-year old's – played so that Timmy had to lose, hitting the ball to him time and again until Timmy missed or hit out of bounds.

He honed his squash skills and confidence that weekend. For years afterwards when our children faced a weaker opponent, we would start to make a suggestion only to find each ahead of us: "I know. I need to play a David Moss." Dave and Jackie went on to be Princeton roommates and close friends.

Trying to catch his older siblings, Timmy, who was small in stature, worked hard. Before a national match at Princeton, I asked if he was nervous about playing a guy name Mike Sabatini – tall, hefty and mature beyond his years and nicknamed "The Giant." Timmy answered, *"No, everyone's a giant to me."*

By age 12, Tim appeared to be on track to become national champion. Then along came a talented, bigger, stronger competitor named Dave McNeely who beat Timmy in a February match. Timmy behaved perfectly on the court but broke down in tears after losing once, then again. Seeing that Timmy had become too wrapped up in results and too emotionally entangled, Don decided to take him off the court for a few days in the critical month before nationals. Coaches rarely get the chance to see one of their players win the nationals. Obviously, Don put the possibility of a national championship at risk. In the end, after time to pull himself together, Timmy won.

As a high school sophomore, Jackie complained that "all I have time for is squash and school." Jack and I couldn't have been more pleased that our teenage son felt that way. He also commented the first time he made honor roll, "it wasn't even hard. All you need to do, like squash, is put in the time."

The "Mills Kids" excelled. Among the 30 or so serious tournament kids Don coached and traveled with, virtually all went to top Ivy League schools. Many became MVPs and national champions, individually or as members of national championship teams. Admittedly squash is a small sport. Even so, Coach's percentage of success developing young champions is impressive.

Jackie, Missy and Timmy became highly ranked players (1 to 5 in their best years), often getting to finals. Princeton's Bob Callahan recruited Jackie, who won Ivy League Rookie of the Year as well as first team all-American honors. Missy and Timmy at Princeton and Harvard earned the same accolades.

Chris earned a top 10 ranking as a junior. Senior year, he was named Yale's most valuable player. Most "youngest of four," whose older siblings brought home trophies and graduated from highly regarded colleges, would not try to follow in their footsteps, let alone excel as Chris did.

I played with the kids until they could beat me, about age nine, and never developed beyond that level. About 20 years ago, I announced that I, too, was going for a national title (not many women my age play). Despite some incredulity, I jumped into the arena and at the next U.S. championship tournament at Yale, all six Wyants played.

Back home, over the next few years, I played a couple times a week and managed to capture a couple of B level titles.

Jackie called one day to say: *"All the brothers are fighting over you."*

"Over me?"

"Yes. The national mixed doubles are coming up and we all three want to be your partner." What a gift that was.

Jack, Jr. and I played. Because he's a pro, we played at the "pro" level. All our opponents played a "nice" game against Jackie's Mom. The highlight for me was, of course, the mother-son dynamic. A close second was that one of my serves, which soared high above his reach, dropping directly in the left back corner, aced John White, former world #1. After John whiffed, he looked towards me and said: *"You're going to tell everyone about this, aren't you?"* I replied, *"Yes, I am."*

Jack played in the Father-Son Nationals with both Tim and Jack, Jr. over the years. In 2010, Jack and Jack, Jr. won.

U.S. Squash also sponsors a national tournament called the Century where ages of the two competitors have to add up to 100. In 2008, Tim and I played, getting – thanks to Tim – to the semifinals. An article about the semifinal match appeared in Squash Magazine.

"The guy is all over the court – front, back, sides, middle – hitting low reverse corners, floating lobs and hard cross-courts to the left wall, aiming to get it passed an opponent with graying hair and probably 30 years his senior. Who whips his racquet behind his back and takes a stab at the ball, nicking but not hitting it true. His head dips down. 'Sorry, Mom,' he calls out.

But his mother isn't in the gallery above the court, watching as I am. She is on the court with her son, playing the right wall in the mixed doubles semifinal match of the U.S. Century Doubles Tournament. While her son is bounding all over the court showing remarkable athleticism, her forte is experience and patience; she knows when the ball is hers and while she doesn't hit it hard, she knows where she needs to put it, steadily hitting the ball deep into the back-left corner."

We made the semi-finals of the Century Nationals, thanks to Tim.

Jack, Jr. would go on to become the Director of Squash of the University of Pennsylvania. Tim would become Executive Director of the Squash and Education Alliance (SEA) with programs across the U.S. and abroad that bring the game and education to economically challenged inner city children. Chris and Missy serve on the boards of Metro Squash in Chicago and Squash Drive in the San Francisco area.

We've all benefited so much from the game. We've learned. We've travelled. We've met friends. We've partied. We've experienced heart-stopping moments, painful losses and ecstatic wins. To give something back to the game the family decided to start an urban squash program in Cincinnati. Sadly, Cincinnati didn't present the opportunity to partner with a university like Columbia, Fordham, Chicago or Yale as happened in many cities, as our local colleges didn't offer the sport. We had to look for a place to build courts and classrooms of our own.

After a 10-year search, Emanuel Community Center (ECC) in Over-the-Rhine, came onto our radar. When broker John Frank called, Tim, Jack and I were in Washington Park at a Camp Nati (grandparent camp, short for Cincinnati) outing when we learned about the potential opportunity. We hopped up from our family picnic and talked our way through the receptionist to tour the place on our own.

The center began in 1837 as part of the Nast Trinity community outreach program to serve the German immigrants then coming in droves. They were "hard working, but non-observant and unruly." And they drank a lot of beer. So, for 176 years the organization served the community, spiritually through Church, and socially via the Center which was built in the twenties and attached via a secret passageway. In the face of changing neighborhood needs and lingering debt following a renovation, ECC was forced a sale.

The potential fit with ECC was evident. We could convert the old gym where Ezzard Charles and Aaron Pryor trained and developed into world champion boxers to squash courts. Classrooms were already in place. The balance of the building lent itself to rentable office space which would help support the non-profit. A good business model. We would buy, renovate and fill the space with aspiring student-athletes.

On the cover of Coach Mill's junior squash brochure when we first met was: *"Excellence is achieved. It is not stumbled onto in the course of amusing oneself. It is built upon discipline, tenacity and purpose."*

Economically-challenged people growing up in the urban core would learn the game of squash. Hopefully they would also learn a Mills truism: *"The biggest weakness of most squash players is thinking they cannot get to the ball. With persistence, you can almost always get to the ball."*

"Figure it out."

Timmy

Family Turkey Trot, 2000

Jackie

Cliff jumping

Limbo contest,
surprise anniversary party

Missy

Grampa signing with family, Greece, 1995

Jack with Chris

Jackie Wyant, 1984
1st Place National Squash Doubles
2nd Place National Squash Singles

Jack, Jr. and Jack Wyant, 2010
1st Place National Father/
Son Squash Doubles Century
Division Championships

Peg and Tim Wyant with Austin Schiff, Executive Director
Cincinnati Squash Academy opening, *Cincinnati Enquirer*, 2014

Coach Don Mills

"Excellence is achieved, not stumbled upon."

Wyant boys playing family doubles

#DONTDEFER #BETTERTOGETHER
University of Pennsylvania President Amy Gutmann
with Jack, Director of Squash and Coach

"If you never give up, you can almost always get to the ball."

Tim Wyant, right, squash doubles tournament, Merion Cricket Club, Haverford, Pennsylvania

Cincinnati Squash Academy sportsmanship

Cincinnati Mayor John Cranley visits the CSA squash courts, 2014

New Cincinnati Squash Academy squash courts

Rachael Parker, Academic Director, Cincinnati Squash Academy classroom, 2015

NEW VENTURES

"Step outside of your comfort zone."

Smith Alumnae Quarterly Magazine, 2006

Founding Partner, Isabella Capital

Consultant to Fortune 500 CEOs

CAPEZIO

Bristol-Myers Squibb

LENSCRAFTERS

Kimberly-Clark

Camp Nati painting by Allen Zaring

Be in Charge
PEG WYANT
Walking in New York several years ago, Peg Wyant suddenly collapsed. She later learned that one of her lungs collapsed. After 3 days in the hospital, Peg came home to Cincinnati with a renewed focus on her health.

An avid exerciser and squash champion, Peg has expanded her health focus to helping others. A 10-year Mercy Health Partners board member, she championed policies that turned Mercy Hospitals into a completely smoke-free environment effective January 1, 2007. The policy means that hospital staff, patients and visitors cannot smoke anywhere on hospital premises – not even in their cars.

Winning the Trifecta at Chris's graduation; Tim (Harvard), Missy (Princeton), Chris (Yale) and Jackie (Princeton)

Award for making Cincinnati smoke-free

GRANDIN
PROPERTIES
NEW SPACES CLASSIC PLACES™

A selection of Grandin's properties

Peebles, Hyde Park Square

Weston Flats, Hyde Park

ECC, Over-The-Rhine

Grandin, O'Bryonville

Hogan Building, Over-The-Rhine

Kemper Lane, Eden Park

Kathy Meier, COO

Missy Wyant Smit, Top SF Agent

Peggy Wyant, CEO

"Girl Power."

Jack, Sr., Jack, Jr. and Peg during construction

Acquiring, renovating and managing historic properties in best-of-class urban neighborhoods

LA TOSCA
EDWARDS AND OBSERVATORY
HAS BEEN PLACED ON THE
NATIONAL REGISTER
OF HISTORIC PLACES
BY THE UNITED STATES
DEPARTMENT OF THE INTERIOR
1915

THE
STRIETMANN
CENTER

A SPACE
WHERE
CREATIVITY
CAN
BREATHE

Inside The Strietmann Center, 2020

The Strietmann Center, 2020
Grandin's most ambitious project to date and site of Oscar-winning film *Carol*

CLUBS AND NETWORKS

President George W. Bush, first Opening Day
Wyants partnered with new Castellini Reds
ownership group, 2006

Wyants and Zarings discussing Women's
Capital Club

Dancing with Cincinnati Reds'
Hall of Famer Johnny Bench

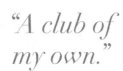

"A club of my own."

Wyants—first investors in FC
Cincinnati, 2016

P&G Alumni Network celebration with Bill and Mary Beth Price
and Tom and Rita Herskovits, 2005

Peg Wyant started her career with Procter & Gamble in the 1960s, when a woman in the management ranks was rare in corporate America. THE ENQUIRER/AMANDA DAVIDSON

Confident woman around mad men
Wyant changed corporate makeup of P&G

Helping launch P&G Alumni
Network

POLITICS IS HABIT FORMING

Ohio Crusading Attorney General
Grandfather Timothy S. Hogan, 1910

Timothy S. Hogan, 1938

"Be informed and involved."

Sister Nancy, Kennedy's White
House Cabinet Room, 1961

Peg, participant at the '63 Civil
Rights March on Washington,
with Congressman John Lewis
in 2018, a speaker at 1963 event

At the height of Watergate,
Peggy, Senator Ted Kennedy
and Jack, 1974

Judge Hogan, featured in "The
Irrepressible Hogans" cover
story, *Cincinnati Magazine*, 1975

Patty campaigning for husband Tim Hogan running for Clermont
County Commissioner, featured in "The Irrepressible Hogans"
cover story, *Cincinnati Magazine*, 1975

Peg and Senator Hillary Clinton, 2003

Peg and President George H. Bush, 2008

Kathy Meier, President Bill Clinton and Peg, 2005

Chris Wyant, Ohio Campaign Manager; Candidate Hillary Clinton and Peg, 2016

"Expect to be President."

Hillary Clinton and Chris Wyant, Ohio campaign, 2016

Chris and President Obama, Oval Office, 2010

Peggy's 70th Birthday, Cincinnati, Ohio

Peggy with Finny, Johnny and Charlie, Camp Nati

Jack, Sr., 2019 (Peg skied too)

Finny Smit and Johnny Wyant

Reva and Sachin Wyant, 2020

Henry Wyant, 2020

Palmer Smit

Owen Wyant

Sam Wyant, 2012

"Looking forward."

Jack and Peggy with Charlie, Sam, Finn, Johnny and Palmer,
David Herskovits wedding, Palm Beach, 2018

Kathryn Herskovits with Amelia, Meeta, Charlie, Sachin, Johnny and Sam Wyant, New York, 2020

Celebrating in Cinque Terre, Italy, 2019

Lauren, Henry, Owen and Chris Wyant, Chicago, 2020

Biking with Tim Wyant and family, Governors Island, New York, 2019

The Wyant Family as of December 2019

"We know a famous guy," Missy showing off Tim's cover 2020 at the 25th Anniversary Jubilee, 2020

The gang of four at the Grand Opening of the University of Pennsylvania's new squash center, 2019

Peg and Jack, Baltic cruise, 2019

Peggy with Missy—best girlfriends

ACKNOWLEDGEMENTS

Judge's fish

"Start and end with the truth."

Sachin proofreading a draft of *One Red Shoe*

Finny, editor, and Palmer, artist, *One Red Shoe*

"I'm so excited to read your book, Peggy."

BRAIN DEAD

"I am not afraid of storms, for I am learning how to sail my ship."

– Louisa May Alcott, author

"Turn your wounds into wisdom."

– Oprah Winfrey

1988 WAS A tough year. Dad had suffered from cancer for 15 years. The judge still presided in his courtroom, but cancer was finally winning. Mom's sister, Aunt Ruth, with whom they shared a two-family house, died of a brain tumor.

Then Jack's company, Nutrition Technology Corporation, ran into trouble. This often happens with serial entrepreneurs. Thompson Medical, which sold Slimfast, a diet product Jack's company invented, suddenly stopped ordering and revenues fell from $20 million to a few hundred thousand.

It had become clear that we needed to leave 2386 Grandin, as we no longer needed nor could we afford it. We discussed the move openly with the children. Besides, living in a mansion isn't the best idea for young people anyway. As Dad would say, *"keep it simple"* and *"it's only money, honey."*

It took over a year, but we found 2337 Grandin Road – just two doors down and across the street. Built in 1899 by the then governor of Ohio, it was a wedding present for his son George Hoadly and Guinevere. George and his teenage bride moved into 2337; she lived there as a young widow with her in-laws and stayed until her 90's when a greedy nephew forced her to move to the Scarlett Oaks retirement home.

The Spanish revival home, designed by Elzner & Anderson, was the architect's first experiment with concrete. Four years later the firm built the 16-story Ingalls Building in downtown Cincinnati, the world's first concrete reinforced skyscraper. We like to think that the lineage of tall buildings and city lights traces back to our basement.

When the nephew sold it in a private auction, we prevailed and closed on a $355,000 contract March 1, 1988. Untouched since being built and unoccupied, it would need all new mechanics and a major renovation. But condition and location made it a terrific buy.

There was the turmoil of moving into a not-quite-renovated home, money pressure from four children with private tuitions and squash lessons and tournament travel bills, and trying to spend time with Mom, whose health was starting to slide but whose strength of character and independence persevered. It was during this same period when Timmy first became an environmental activist and Jackie turned 16. The others struggled in school. Those events presented challenges of their own.

Jack merged Nutrition Technology Corporation with a Long Island company called Frookies. The completely wacky Richard Worth owned it. Jack became COO. Richard was a crazy visionary who wore gym shoes and T-shirts decades before Steve Jobs made them stylish. He was certifiably nuts – calling store managers to announce that a truckload of product was being delivered ("I know you don't want it but it's being delivered anyway") and once driving me over winding Long Island backroads in his red

Corvette convertible at 100 mph while refusing to slow down or let me out.

Sugarless, juice-sweetened Frookies and NTC's high fiber Fibbers – both cookies with personality – were harbingers of the natural health food industry that would grow exponentially in the future. But not just yet.

Jack commuted to New York weekly, leaving me during the week to manage three teenagers and an eight-year-old as a single mom. When Jack returned to Cincinnati late on Fridays, he brought with him – uncharacteristically – the cutthroat qualities of a badly behaved New Yorker. By Monday, he would be a nice Midwesterner again.

After months of this, I took a stand: "*Jack, I don't care what the economic consequences are, you have got to come home.*"

Had leaving P&G been the wrong decision? While I seldom look back (the devil lurks there) I couldn't help but re-hash this decision. I wasn't sure.

Regardless, I was leaning too heavily on the children, looking to their successes in the classroom or on the courts as my successes. I had to get back to work to find myself again as well as to make money. What I was about to learn was that many people, particularly men, thought that women who spend full time on being a mother have lost their ability to think, let alone function in the business world. They were deemed brain dead.

There didn't seem to be any business opportunities for me.

Procter & Gamble was one of the largest companies in the world and frequently listed by Forbes as its "most admired." As its lone female executive among a handful of corporate women in high positions around the country, and a pioneer in the new field of strategic planning, I had become known in business circles. Besides, Procter & Gamble graduates peppered the leadership ranks of companies around the country.

Clearly, the employment solution was consulting. After leaving Procter, I had done strategic planning work for Fortune 500 CEO's, including Bruce Gelb of Bristol-Myers, and John Bryan of Sara Lee. My references and track record were exemplary. Plus, the work with John Smale was now public. Skincare and healthcare acquisitions were making a difference. The stock was soaring.

The resource to use for getting business would be the Procter & Gamble alumni booklet. It was published every other year listing several hundred former managers – many of whom I knew – who had gone on to work for other companies. I wrote a letter to each of those listed – a few hundred – saying, "I'm back. I'm ready to work."

There was not a single reply.

Pablum. Diapers. Carpools. Class mom. Shopping. Cleaning. Reading stories. Baths. Coaching. Playdates. Cooking. Walking to school. Finding a Disney Band-Aid. Hospital runs. Hugs. Teaching a kid to ride a bike or kick a ball or do the right thing. Saying no. Making costumes or a birthday cake. Tears. Matches. Soccer games. Helping him learn something new. Encouraging her to work harder. Losing a grandparent. Holding hands. Being there.

Sadly, these are not resume builders.

Time at home with kids may be the most important time we spend, but it's hard to measure outside the home. No pay. No value.

Discouraged, I asked my long-time champion, Tom Laco, who still served as Vice Chair of Procter & Gamble's Board, to lunch. We went to the Queen City Club where I shared the current state of affairs and my desire to get back to work.

Maybe I secretly hoped he would suggest I come back, although I knew that leaving THE world's best enterprise revealed such bad judgement that its executives could never in those days understand. At the very least, I assumed he would use his vast and powerful network to get me started.

Tom suggested that I do "volunteer work." It will, he added, "get you back in circulation."

I was incredulous. Tom Laco was my original champion and longtime mentor. He knew my talents and potential as well as anyone. What did he not grasp? Why could he not relate? Did he not understand I needed money – did men still not think of women as wage-earners? He meant well. But I was crushed, sitting in the dining room of Cincinnati's premier men's club and facing the suggestion that I give away my time in order to prove my worth. If Jack were at this table, would Tom be suggesting volunteer work?

Far more painful than the disappointment of that lunch was Dad's declining health. Somehow, we expect our parents to be there forever. I did. They hold back the waves. But in 1989, the father, that I loved and admired so, died, followed two years later by the mother who pushed and inspired me.

During the last few days of Dad's life, I thought about the little and big things he and Mom had done. Married as the Depression launched, Mom said in an interview with Jackie when he was in high school, *"We learned how to make fun out of nothing – games, roller skates, cards: Some of the best time of our lives."*

Dad made breakfast every morning while Mom slept in. Describing it as "breakfast" is a compliment. Jell-O and cold biscuits are an example of one of Dad's meals. My mother did little cooking while I was growing up but later in life, she became a gourmet chef. There were countless evenings, especially when Jack travelled, that I hauled the kids to their place on Eileen Drive for dinner.

I remember Dad saying to a wealthy client on an estate

planning call – *"I helped you ruin your children. I refuse to help you ruin your grandchildren."* When my parents sold the farm where I grew up, most of the money went into an educational trust for the grandchildren. It paid tuition for all nine. *"Education never hurt anyone,"* he would say. *"Money did."* He was pleased to see us leave the mega mansion behind.

And, while it's not fair to say his socks never matched, they often didn't. What is true is that he was the federal judge whose decisions were seldom appealed and, when appealed, reversed fewer times than any other judge in the country. In 25 years on the bench, he never used a gavel.

I think he was proud of my accomplishments, but his expressed emotion centered on how hard I worked . . . too hard. He would have been more comfortable had I spent more time on the pedestal.

Mom's health was declining as well. She suffered from high blood pressure and an identified aneurism, but decided against an operation which carried risks of debilitating damage. A disability of any sort would not have suited her personality.

Not long after Dad passed, I was having a drink with her at the breakfast table where Mom and Dad would have bourbon and water every single night when she announced: *"I had a dream last night. I dreamed your father was up there flying around with another angel. It's time for me to go."*

A couple months later, I took coffee and a St. Patrick's Day sweet over to her place. As soon as I opened the door, I knew she was gone. No music. No TV. No talk. Mom was never, ever surrounded by silence.

According to Pal, they were now in the lands of the "sky pilot."

I miss her. I miss the big personality and the commanding voice saying: *"Peggy, you can do that."*

It was a difficult time. Financially challenged, mothering three teenagers and a younger child, being told to do "volunteer work," moving into an unfinished house and living as a single parent while the husband traveled weekly to Brooklyn Heights, my confidence, and perhaps my competence as well, felt like they were slipping away.

Again, I had to ask myself, in leaving The Procter & Gamble Company, had I made the right decision? The children seemed headed in the right direction, which was our priority. But where could I go?

Not long after, Wellesley College asked First Lady Barbara Bush (a fellow Smith alum) to give the commencement address. By 1990, accomplished women at top colleges increasingly expected to have professional careers. Wellesley students protested against Barbara's selection, concerned that her status related to her husband rather than to her own accomplishments.

Despite student objections and the ensuing press uproar, Barbara went ahead with the commencement address. After making the case for diversity, she called upon graduates to make three choices – get involved in something bigger than yourself, have fun and value the human connection. Her last comment spoke to me:

"The third choice that must not be missed is to cherish your human connections: your relationships with family and friends. For several years, you've had impressed upon you the importance to your career of dedication and hard work. And, of course, that's true. But as important as your obligations as a doctor, a lawyer, a business leader will be, you are a human being first. And those human connections – with spouses, with children, with friends – are the most important investments you will ever make. At the end of your life, you will never regret not having passed one more test,

winning one more verdict, or not closing one more deal. You will regret time not spent with a husband, a child, a friend, or a parent."

The decision to leave P&G was the right one. Nothing trumps family and friends.

Barbara Bush closed her speech with a spontaneous twist.

"And who knows? Somewhere out in this audience may even be someone who will one day follow in my footsteps, and preside over the White House as the President's spouse," **and then she said,** *"I wish him well!"*

PART VI

NEW VENTURES

I Can Do That

"I'm convinced that about half of what separates the successful entrepreneurs from the non-successful ones is pure perseverance."

— Steve Jobs, Founder of Apple

BEING STONEWALLED BY all the companies I solicited for consulting work was depressing. The sad feelings which followed AEI's closing after college resurfaced, while "volunteer work" rattled endlessly around in my head.

Sure, it had been years away from executive responsibilities, from the hustle and bustle of business, but that didn't mean I couldn't think. I kept reminding myself: "All I can do is think."

In fact, managing a home, with its built-in conflicts and contradictions, where there are few experts to lean on, where emotion sometimes trumps rational behavior, requires skill. There are no lawyers to resolve conflicts or art directors to design environments or human resource experts to help understand and develop husbands and children. No assistants to help carry the load and keep all the balls in the air. No professionals to coach, guide and teach organization and help reduce stress and clutter. No boss to set priorities. A multi-tasking mom has to handle it all.

What to do?

As Dad would have suggested, *"keep it simple."* One choice was to forget what Amelia Earhart once said that I had long admired: *"No borders. Just horizons."* The borders were closing in. I could hear the naysayers. I could spend the rest of my life doing volunteer work and playing golf. But that wasn't me.

The other was to do what I had always done – find a way to move forward and figure it out. I still believed in me, and happily so did Jack.

What I decided to do was to say "Yes" to any and every opportunity that came my way. I would say "Yes, I can do that." Experience and know-how would be lacking. I would simply have to jump in and, through trial and error, make it work.

Laurie Maguire had recently moved to Cincinnati from Louisville because Merrill Lynch transferred her husband C.H. Their children enrolled at Seven Hills and were the same ages as ours.

In Louisville, there was a successful retail operation which sold high quality children's clothes – second hand – in four big sales a year. Laurie had an interest in starting a similar operation here. When she asked, *"Would you like to partner?"* I said, *"Yes, I can do that."*

We found a space, sent postcards asking for kids' clothes on consignment and set a Spring Saturday for our first sale. Our "brand name" would be KIDS KLOSET. As I sat on the floor labeling little boys' pants, I remember thinking: "I don't know what God intended for me, but it's not this."

After the one and only sale, we closed "Kids Kloset." Laurie mentioned she wanted to get her real estate license. I had conflicting reactions. First, I viewed real estate agents with little admiration, as I (wrongly) thought of myself as intellectually superior. Second, I hadn't taken a test in over 20 years. Getting a license required passing the state exam. There was a real possibility of my failing based on my college SAT experience. I was very nervous. Nevertheless, my response was: "I can do that."

We studied together for about eight weeks. The course was hardly riveting. However, being back in class was a positive and learning something new is always intriguing. We drove to Columbus in late October and both passed the exam, becoming partners with a company called Sibcy Cline. Laurie was the better agent as she is organized, bright and service oriented. As a native Cincinnatian, my role became rainmaker.

The first year, we each made about $30,000 – a credible start. While we stayed together for another couple years, my growing interest was in real estate investing. My friend Laurie stayed the course.

Over the years, I had come to learn that I was the "go-to gal" for executives with a wife or daughter who wanted to take on a business challenge. John Smale's daughter Cathy had started a business in Richmond where her husband Rob Caldemeyer was attending medical school. John had asked me to give her some advice. "Happy to help." After that, we would talk every once in a while, about Cathy and her progress. On those occasions, John's business mask always gave way to warm demeanor.

Around 1980, Jack and I were having dinner on the porch at the Cincinnati Country Club when we saw John and Phyllis Smale. I asked about Cathy. Uncharacteristically, John had a negative response, *"She's not so well. She is home with two small children and frustrated with the life that brings. She has this crazy idea. She wants to renovate houses."*

I said, *"I can do that. Have Cathy call me."* I had renovated and sold one house already. In fact, the purchase price of the inaugural property was $170,000. After a $50,000 upgrade which took six weeks, we sold it at a party for a $50,000 profit without even listing it.

Cathy and I started looking for a Hyde Park house to renovate. We found one on Westside Street, three blocks from Hyde Park Square. As it was in an estate, we were able to buy at a good price. The landscaping was overgrown, the house nearly hidden by a tall evergreen. It needed new bathrooms and a new kitchen. Cathy has a great eye, so we made creative additions like painting diamond squares on the attic floor, which turned a formerly unusable storage room into a playroom.

My brother Tim, a real estate appraiser, had taught me a little about real estate. First, location, location, location. Second, you make your money when you buy, not when you sell. And third, properties are like buses. If you miss one, another comes around shortly thereafter, so don't overpay. Those principles helped us make money.

John pushed us to develop a financial model that could be applied again and again. We did. Based on resale price, the target purchase price was 50%, renovation 20%, carrying cost 10% and profit 20%. It worked. We renovated and sold a half dozen houses profitably.

If one didn't move in the first six weeks, we lowered the price and moved on, whereas the temptation is to hold on (hope springs eternal) or even raise the price to offset interest, taxes and other carrying costs.

By the way, in neither the partnership with Laurie nor with Cathy did we write anything down. No contract. To the best of my recollection, there was never a conflict or disagreement. We got along. We made money. We had fun. We brought homes up to date and families to better places.

Of course, that's the time that the consulting business came alive. Dean Butler, who had been my Ivory Liquid Brand Manager and sold LensCrafters to U.S. Shoe, suggested I reach out to its CEO. Their shoe and specialty retail business (Casual Corner,

Petite Sophisticate etc.) was troubled. I drove in my purple and gray minivan, trashed by the four kids and their friends, to Madisonville, where their headquarters is located, to meet with CEO Ban Hudson. I parked the minivan far from the front door to avoid the possibility of business executives sighting it.

A former P&G manager, Ban offered a consulting project – analyze and find a way to reverse the downward business decline of Hahn's retail shoe chain – about 20 stores in the Washington-Baltimore area. My ensuing proposal offered six months of work, nearly full time, for compensation of $25,000.

Six weeks later a letter from Ban arrived explaining that *"while your references are excellent, management has decided to hire an expert in the shoe industry."*

I wrote back: *"Good luck hiring an expert in a dying industry."*

That should have closed the door. But it did the reverse. Apparently, Ban took it as indicative of independent thinking. Besides, he knew I was right. Ban called me back into his office and offered the opportunity to work on the Capezio business. This time I proposed a three-month part time project for $75,000. He hired me.

I had to learn how to consult. Functionally, the job of consultant mirrored my P&G work, especially on those projects including various group vice-presidents, going from one business to the other. Yet, there was a world of difference. At Procter, all the tools existed down the hall or within easy elevator reach. Need an attorney? Call the legal department. Need information? The library and research assistants were at hand. Puzzled by an R&D question? The product development folks have answers.

Outside of the company, I had to figure out how to get things done – starting with typing.

Fortunately, my first P&G brand manager, Gordon Wade, had started a consulting firm called Cincinnati Consulting Group.

When we got together, Gordon announced that he was going to teach me "how to get excellent results by working out of a telephone booth." He did.

Gordon taught me how to use LexisNexis, an early computer-driven information service. It was the first source to actualize the vision in which end users would directly interact with computer databases rather than going through professional intermediaries like librarians. Information at my fingertips. We had started using it at Procter. Then he told me about Priority Mail Service with delivery guys on bicycles and introduced me to the FAX (facsimile) system which, pre-internet, transmitted documents via telephone. Best of all, he introduced me to his first-class secretarial office. I was in business.

Regarding what to wear and how to look, Gordon recommended a "uniform" – one or two suits of the same dark color with white shirts, substituting two scarfs for ties. Make it simple. This was before Steve Jobs made the black turtleneck famous.

When it rains, it pours. Doug Cowan, a former colleague, called the next day asking if I would consider doing some strategic planning work for the Drackett Company, a division of Bristol-Myers. The call launched a two-year, part-time consulting career. This would be the first of a series of ventures that would be squeezed into my life as wife and mother of four: consulting, flipping houses, selling real estate, managing a venture capital fund and developing real estate.

I worked for U.S. Shoe for several years. I also worked for The Drackett Company, a company founded in the 19th century which developed Drano and Windex and other specialty household cleaning products. It sold to Bristol-Myers in 1965 where it served as a cash cow misfit to that pharmaceutical enterprise.

Doug and CEO Bill Flatley engaged me; they were searching

for new businesses with profitable growth potential, just as John Smale had. Although we acquired a few companies, Drackett and Bristol didn't belong together – which was conveyed to Bristol-Myers Chairman Bruce Gelb – with Drackett later being acquired by S.C. Johnson.

Gordon hired me to work with him for CEO John Bryan, a Mississippian who had sold his family meat company to Chicago's Consolidated Foods. Gordon was behind helping John change the name to Sara Lee Corp. and the focus from meat packing to a consumer products conglomerate. We studied and then bought new consumer businesses for Sara Lee, including gourmet and more nutritious food products.

John Bryan was a gentleman and art collector – the force behind the company's $100 million art collection as well as Millennium Park. Being on the executive floor was like working in an art museum.

Now it almost felt like I had multiple jobs – real estate agent, entrepreneur, developer, consultant, coach and Seven Hills School volunteer – all because I just kept saying *"I can do that."*

WINNING THE TRIFECTA

"I am a great believer in luck, and I find the harder I work, the more I have of it."

– Thomas Jefferson

WE TOOK JACKIE to Princeton in September 1992. Three years before, I had driven Jackie and Missy on a tour of the East Coast, mostly Ivy League schools which, beyond obvious academic excellence, offered the most competitive squash. Cornell, Williams, Harvard, Trinity, Brown, Yale and Princeton.

After years of staying close to home, I was ready for a road trip and intended that the trip be done my way. There would be no fast-food stops. There would be visits with friends as well as college tours. Efficiency took second place behind time with the children and with friends.

In Amherst, we stayed with my college professor Bruce Carroll and his wife Gail. After a couple of scotches and dinner, we relaxed on the deck overlooking their private woods with its bubbling creek. For the college bound, Bruce expounded on the value of working hard and treasuring the upcoming four years. And then without any set-up or coaching, he told Jackie and

Missy (later Tim and Chris): *"Your Mom was the hardest working student I have taught in over 30 years of teaching."*

Bruce may have said that to the children of other returning students. Nevertheless, it made me smile.

He also shared memories of the summer of 1966 when I lured their family to the mountains of Grenoble, France without compensation – just to handle the rare unanticipated emergency caused by the 250 teenagers and their inexperienced traveling teacher chaperones.

"Gail and I never worked harder," he reminded me.

After Amherst and Williams, we drove to Harvard where a sophomore working in admissions scrutinized Jackie's application:

John Henry Wyant
Seven Hills School
Leadership Positions:
Junior Board of U.S. Squash
Seven Hills School: Class President
Captain: various Soccer & Softball Teams
Achievements:
Member US Junior Men's Team
Ohio State Squash champion
City Squash Champion
Winner number of junior squash tournaments
National Squash Ranking; #2
Source of News: Sports Illustrated
Essay Subject: The Squash Match

Looking up, he asked: *"Jack, do you, by chance, have any interest at all in anything academic?"* Pausing for one brief moment, Jackie responded: *"Not much."*

At Yale, the tour guide, wore sandals, spoke with a touch of intellectual arrogance and conveyed a non-committal attitude. When asked if he liked Yale, he said, *"Sometimes yes, sometimes no."* Not a match.

We stopped in Newport, Rhode Island for a couple days to visit the "cottages," see longtime friends the Pages and walk around the cliff. NYC brought a Broadway play and a visit with the Fishman family, squash friends from Brooklyn Heights since Jackie, at age nine, played Eddie Fishman in his first national tournament in Philadelphia. As may have been evident from my wreck with a police car when I started sales training at P&G. I am not an able driver. Going north on the Avenue of the Americas in rush hour, New York cabbies took note with loud honking and "Go back to Ohio lady!" shouts. Seventeen-year-old Jackie insisted on taking the wheel. I gladly relinquished it, even if it meant putting my child into Manhattan traffic. It was the last time he would ever again be a passenger in a car I was driving. Rites of passage start with baby steps.

Up to now, none of the colleges we visited lit Jackie's fire. Campuses were beautiful; coaches interested; academic opportunities unlimited. But Jackie has a way of cutting through to the heart of the matter without being distracted by any superficial or irrelevant things. Leaving one famous campus, he observed: *"Why would any college boast about the 12.8 million books in their library when all any undergraduate needs is a few hundred?"*

When we got out of the car at Princeton University, where Coach Bob Callahan met us, Jackie's eyes sparkled. For many summers, he had gone to Princeton squash camps. He admired and followed in the footsteps of Cincinnatian Tom Shepherd, who was the city's first junior national champion.

Tom graduated from Princeton. And Bob Callahan had sent several hand-written letters to him over the years. Princeton felt like home.

"This is where I'm going," he stated. And that was that. In the coming months, Jackie objected to applying anywhere else. With honors performance, yet not among the top scholars Princeton typically required, his college counselor, Susan Marrs, warned against such focus. Risky at best.

When Director of Admissions Dean Hartigan sent the "yes" letter welcoming Jackie to Princeton, I couldn't help remembering a couple of elementary school experiences. I served on the Board of the Seven Hills School and in the early eighties had a leadership role in a strategic planning project. In an executive meeting, Headmaster Peter Briggs asserted that "the school could identify by the fourth grade the kids headed for the premier schools." Finding the statement too rigid as well as somewhat offensive, as our children were not academic scholars in elementary school. I remember thinking: "No, Peter, that's not true. Not our kids."

That night I said to Jack, *"Let's take him out of Seven Hills"* and the next morning set up an appointment with the head of Summit Country Day, another good private school in town. Ahead of time we talked about what Jackie needed in a school to motivate better performance. Discipline primarily. But that wasn't what my husband had in mind. When we sat down with Summit's headmaster, Jack asked, *"How many students have you sent to Princeton?"*

I was thinking, I couldn't believe it. Have you lost your mind, Jack? Are you connecting the dots?

Actually, he was. Not connecting a report card with admission standards as one thinking conventionally would have done. Rather, Jack connected his natural optimism with his unshakable confidence in our eldest son and he saw Princeton in Jackie's future.

Over the years, Jackie's superb athletic accomplishments dwarfed his lesser interest in academics. I wrestled with taking him away from squash and its demanding schedule so he could focus on school. I never did. Then, in the eighth grade, he made honor roll and commented:

"It isn't even that hard. Just like squash. All you have to do is work."

Connecting the dots.

The trip to Princeton was difficult. We arrived and did the things parents do. We helped him unpack. We met his roommates — all seven, including Justin Sulger, a rower, who remains one of Jackie's good friends. We met their parents. We toured. We talked to Coach Bob Callahan. We went to the orientation lecture which ended with the Dean's admonition to parents: "It's time to leave."

We hugged goodbye. Dressed in khakis and a blue oxford, Jackie turned around and headed towards his dorm. He never looked back. Tears streaming down my cheeks, we watched for a few minutes, until he disappeared behind gothic stone.

Jack and I walked back to the car and began the 10-hour drive to Cincinnati. We didn't speak a single word to each other all the way home. The recognition of a new era — one which we did not welcome — was too sad for a couple so deeply committed to family to talk about.

Two years later, in the spring of 1994, Missy decided to join her brother at Princeton. Jackie welcomed her, introducing her to his friends who were and are an awesome group.

Missy has always been my best girlfriend. During middle school, we walked there together every morning and talked. We went to spas and exercised together. She gave dinner parties and brought her friends around. We shopped together and, even today, on occasion, wear each other's clothes.

When she was 12, I met Diane Firsten, then a personal shopper at Saks and later owner of her own shops in Cincinnati and Palm Beach. I asked Diane if she would help Missy build a great wardrobe. My Mom, being a one-time model, dressed with style, but I veered all over the place. We went to Saks and Diane picked a several-hundred dollar, Ralph Lauren navy blue blazer saying: *"Missy, you can wear this for years and look good with jeans, loafers and a white-T."* Diane has been dressing the two of us ever since.

The year after she graduated from Princeton, the University's admissions magazine had a full page spread on Missy. The photograph showed her hanging photographs for her art museum show. She was wearing the Ralph Lauren navy blue blazer, a white-T and loafers.

From the beginning, Missy was a kind, thoughtful, tons-of-fun girl. Confident that would last, I also hoped she would become a strong, independent leader. As the only girl growing up with three brothers and as a competitive athlete, the odds seemed good.

Graduating with a liberal arts degree, Missy struggled. She worked for a year in Washington D.C. for an internet start-up in telemarketing. No excitement there. Perplexed as to what to do she decided to take a plunge and off she went – alone – to Thailand to teach English as a second language at the University of Chiang Mai. This was part of Princeton University's Princeton in Asia Program. Describing the experience years later Missy said: *"I was scared out of my mind, I cried the whole flight over. I didn't know a soul there, didn't know about the Thai culture or how to teach English. I was more scared going into that year than anything I had ever done before. It was also the biggest growth experience of my life."*

Missy returned to the United States as burgeoning leader. Yvo and real estate would get her to the finish line.

In the spring of 1996, Harvard admitted Tim to the class of 2000. When applying, Tim asked me: *"Would you mind if I went to Harvard?"* I didn't answer. Rather, I just asked him to listen to the question. Tim played soccer as a walk-on for two-years and squash all four.

As a "cool" guy and a two-team athlete, Tim had the opportunity to join one of Harvard's selective and prestigious final clubs. Porcellian, for example, dates back to 1791 and boasted members such as the poet James Russell Lowell and Justice Oliver Wendall Holmes. Tim said no. I tried to convince him otherwise as clubs were an important part of the social life in Cambridge. But he stood his ground saying: *"Mom, surely you would not want me to join a group that excludes women. Would you?"*

There are 11 single gender clubs now on campus. Since the early nineties, the University no longer officially recognizes them.

Later Chris, would join Yale's class of 2005. He wanted to go his own way and Yale proved to be the perfect place as Harvard was for Tim.

Spring of sophomore year at Yale, Chris who was president of his fraternity, and a couple of his buddies left a party late and hungry. Perhaps influenced by a beer or two, the trio decided to break into one of the food halls. To get into the basement, the boys slit a screen, a felony, opened the window and jumped in. Running down the hall with a box of Cheerios, Chris was blinded by policemen shining flashlights in his face and demanding that he stop. New Haven police monitor college buildings rather than campus police who err on the softer side. Chris spent the night in jail, sharing a cell with a 40-year-old man who said: *"You little shit, you know what my kids would give to go to a place like Yale? And you're blowing it."*

His telephone privileges were used to call his brother Jack and, to me, only after being released the next morning. Crying, Chris asked: *"What should I do?"* I felt his pain but chose – though hurting inside myself – a tough love response. I loved him too much to take charge of his problem: *"Chris, you got yourself into this, you need to get yourself out of it. Call a lawyer."*

As it turned out, on the advice of a not-so-able attorney, he pled no contest to a felony and was sentenced to a year of good behavior – no speeding tickets, no false ID, no bars for 12 long months. Only with sustained law-abiding behavior plus community service would the court expunge (erase) his record. Perfect behavior is challenging for a 19-year-old college student.

After sentencing, I recognized the harshness of my approach. Could he possibly grasp the potentially dire consequences? He was so young. A criminal lawyer and friend of ours, Jack Rubenstein, agreed to spend an hour with Chris telling him what it meant to be a convicted felon. I went with him. Jack explained the implications in a slow, sober voice. If the sentence held, he would not be able to vote or run for office, work for a bank, be a real estate agent, lawyer, doctor or pursue any position which requires "trust." Chris was visibly shaken.

For the next 12 months, we all stayed close to Chris. Motivated by his own radar as well as the watchful eye of every member of the family, he behaved perfectly. At the end of the year the court exonerated Chris. The experience had an unexpected benefit. To fulfill his court ordered public service Chris volunteered for a young David Pepper in his City Council office. This ignited his interest in politics and public service.

Chris would go on to hold a position in the White House under

President Obama. Like his wife, Lauren Kidwell, he worked for the Obama administration for the eight years, notably as Executive Director for the Agency for Trade and Development. It required the highest level of security clearance. I called him and said: *"There was an exoneration but, just to be safe, perhaps you want to tell the Secret Service about the Cheerios incident. Who knows what they are able to uncover?"* He replied: *"I already have."*

If we had bailed him out, would Chris have ended up in the White House?

People sometimes ask: *"How did you raise four kids, all of whom earned top 10 national rankings in squash and went on to Ivy League schools?"* In fact, when the admissions letter came from Yale, Squash Coach Dave Talbot called, excitingly exclaiming, *"You guys won the trifecta. You guys won the trifecta – Princeton, Harvard, Yale!"*

Thanks to Jack's insistence on joining the Cincinnati Country Club and our family's good fortune to embrace the game of squash and to be embraced by Coach Mills, each child became a recruited varsity athlete. That means that the admissions officer at selective schools put their application in a separate and much smaller pile.

The day Chris received his acceptance letter, we listened to a message on our home phone answering machine (both devices now relics of the past) from Peter Briggs, Head of Seven Hills School: *"It just goes to show you what an outstanding secondary school, exceptional headmaster and mediocre parenting can accomplish."*

Starting a Venture Capital Firm

"I grew up with three sisters and no brothers and therefore recognized from an early age the energy, imagination and competence of women. So when I received Peg's invitation to invest in her new fund and join her Advisory Board, I was excited to do so."

– Edward Goodman, Investment Partner, Activate Venture Partners

B Y 1998, JACKIE and Missy were working in NYC and Washington D.C. for venture-backed start-up enterprises. The internet – which I first learned about in Missy's freshman year at Princeton when Netscape went public – was getting to be a hot topic.

Tim and Chris were halfway through Harvard and Seven Hills, respectively. For years, I had been straddling the workplace – resale shop, consulting and real estate – and home – homework, coaching, cooking and driving. I just squeezed it all together, whatever and whenever, as best I could. Thinking back to Tom Laco's comment about volunteer work, I thought: "Maybe instead of a patchwork quilt, it's my time to move forward with a career of my own."

Jack had started Blue Chip Venture Company in 1990. It was the first such firm in Cincinnati and one of the first in the Midwest.

Venture capital is placing a high risk bet in hopes of making an above-average return. Said another way, it is raising money from high-net-worth individuals and institutions like banks and pension funds to invest in relatively young, fast-growth businesses in order to get a higher return on investments than in stocks, bonds or real estate. The business has sex appeal in as much as VC backed companies like Apple, FedEx, Uber, Netflix and Intuitive Surgical have delivered incredible returns for the venture investors.

It is also risky, given that young companies trying to grow fast are susceptible to failure. When I was raising money for my own venture capital fund and explaining the risk, a potential investor commented: *"Oh I see, the investment might not make any return at all."* To which I responded: *"No, the risk is that you could lose 100% of your investment."* The partners contribute financial and intellectual capital to help these start-ups get to the next level. It takes years.

I travelled every once in a while to VC conferences with Jack. Surprisingly, the gender demographics in the '90s mirrored the corporate world of the '60s. It was almost all men in expensive pinstripes, focusing (now) throughout meetings on their cell phones as is prevalent among this group. Almost never was there a female CEO on the dais, presenting a fundraising opportunity. Similarly, there were no female venture capital partners listening to their pitches. It seemed the only women present were the wife of the speaker and me.

A little research showed that what I experienced represented industry norms. Only about 5% of VC money found its way to women-led companies and about 6% of the decision-makers were female while women founded a quarter of all new companies and their success rate exceeded male counterparts.

It looked like an opportunity: a field with little competition and lots of talent, an opportunity to make money for investors as well as the managers, an opportunity to build new entities and create value. There were some side benefits as well – most women know little about money. Unfortunately, death and divorce are the events which prompt learning. My new venture, Isabella Capital, would expose more women to a new asset class.

In a moment of supreme arrogance, I predicted: "I can change one more industry before I hang it up."

Jack tried to discourage me: *"Why don't you start a real estate fund?"* Echoing my Dad's sentiments in a World War II letter in which he wrote, *"I love to do hard things and hate routine,"* I said, *"That's too easy."*

So, I went on the road to raise money. The name Isabella Capital came from the Portuguese queen who financed Christopher Columbus' discovery of America; it stands as history's most successful investment. Interestingly, Queen Isabella funded her venture by borrowing money against her jewelry. It took two years for me to raise $10 million dollars, most from high-net-worth individuals (notably women played a big part) as well as three institutional inventors.

Several friends invested: community leader Anne Zaring, Trish Smitson, top attorney and Managing Partner for her firm, Smith graduates – Francie Pepper, Randy Fletcher, Leslie Carothers, a pioneering environmentalist from Hillsdale – Lynn Paul, my D.C. roommate and IBM's first female programmer and many others. Their trust meant the world to me. Always supportive, Jack raised some capital as well, mostly from venture capitalists.

The strategy – investing in an underserved market segment – was sound. The problem was that I had no experience at all in the industry. One of Jack's partners, John McIlwraith, agreed to help. It was also my good fortune that a local venture investor that I knew through my friend Liz Lanier suggested I reach out to a savvy New Yorker, experienced and highly regarded in the industry – Edward A. Goodman. He agreed to invest and become an advisor. He recently explained why:

> *"Having grown up in a family deeply rooted in the fashion industry and securing my first job out of college and after military service at Bergdorf Goodman, I worked for several women executives who were movers and shakers in the space and yet, at that time (1963), women were almost invisible in the venture community. In due course, after entering the VC business, I was eager to accept Peg's invitation to support her insurgent efforts with a VC fund focused on women entrepreneurs.*
>
> *We had an adventurous, 10 year run which helped many women establish their businesses while paving the way for comparable female-focused funds."*

It was, however, a frothy time on Wall Street and Sand Hill Road. Given some early successes in the high-tech field, money poured into venture funds as well as into NASDAQ. Valuation went through the roof. Companies with little income, let alone profit, commanded valuations of up to $75 million and people fought to get into such deals.

Venture capital dollars had swelled to an all-time high of $120 billion, double the year before and 24 times the $5 billion of 1994. It was the internet frenzy which, like the tulip mania of the 1600's, drew tons of speculators and dollars, dramatically in excess of good investment opportunities.

Being new in the field, and blissfully unaware of the extent to which venture capitalists were throwing money at overvalued start-ups, I decided to invest only in companies that experienced VC firms backed. This turned out to be a bad decision – like following lemmings off the cliff. During the early months, I also didn't access my advisors much – too cocky.

I invested $5 million or 50% of the capital in the first two years in technology startups with a big dream and an inexperienced CEO.

We had our first annual meeting in October 2001 at the Queen City Club where about 80 concerned investors showed up. I stood at the dais all alone. Serious old men stared down from the oil portraits hung on walls. I faced people who had put their faith in me. The portfolio companies were all operational. However, the times were tough, the road, long. Follow-on rounds would likely crush our investments.

First, I announced that half the fund had been invested in companies that would return nothing. 100% gone. Zero. Hopefully, we would do better going forward with the second 50%. Then, I asked investors to send the second $5 million.

Investors, for the most part, accepted the loss that had already occurred. However, many wanted us to call it a day and close the fund down. For reasons that defy logic, (there was absolutely no basis for believing our fund could recoup), I was determined to stay the course. Neither failure nor turning back was an option.

At this point in the meeting, I clicked onto the slide which announced "Now it's time for investor participation." That cued the waiters to bring in and place on each table buckets of tomatoes. Ensuing laughter broke the tension.

From the beginning, the industry proved unfriendly. Big firms showed little respect for small funds, less for women in the field. And, given troubled times, swimming with the sharks would prove particularly challenging.

A bridge round is an investment made before a young company gets a commitment for the full amount, which is needed to take it to the next level. The risk is great as the next investment round may never happen. In return for the higher risk, bridge investors get extra shares. Fund Isabella made a $250,000 bridge loan on a Boston-based company called Market Max, fully expecting a 25% equity advantage. We were a small piece of a $5 million bridge round. However, when the mega venture guys came around, they gave the bridge loan investors two choices – take your money out now with zero uptick or leave it in, but accept a 5x preference for the new money.

All the other bridge round investors accepted one of those two offers. I refused, saying that our investors took a risk and deserved a return. After putting pressure on me proved ineffective, a prestigious lawyer threatened legal action. Nevertheless, I told them that Fund Isabella would not accept their terms. We would sign nothing, would agree to nothing. Rather we would stay the course – as a dangling participle.

The bridge loan investors who stayed in all lost all their money. Not long after the standoff, Market Max needed a multi-million-dollar loan. Fund Isabella's $250,000 loan, with its priority position, stood in the way. I negotiated a buyout which doubled the money for our investors. However, standing up to the pressure that the sharks put on me took its toll mentally.

There were many other similar incidents. I was excluded from meetings, ignored, cut out of the conversation and – openly at times – forgotten. Procter & Gamble in the sixties was far fairer in dealing with women and open to new ideas than venture capitalists in the nineties.

From my perspective, old fashioned business building approaches and values didn't align with the industry. It's a dog-eat-dog business. Besides the orientation of many VCs is to make money as fast as possible for the firm – focusing on their own investment round rather than building long-term value in the entity. It is not the way I think. Most women don't.

We did make money with the second $5 million. Abandoning the get-rich-quick approach, Susan Schieman, who became CFO, and I returned to the principles learned at Procter & Gamble. We sought solid marketing companies, listened to knowledgeable advisors – Ed Goodman, Bill Butler and Frank Wood among them. We also developed a 10-point, evidenced-based analytical system for rating companies.

That's how we found OnTarget Media. Frank, a longtime friend and successful investor, introduced it. The CEO, Mike Collette, had P&G experience. For a decade, the company had placed Pharma brochures advertising Rx drugs in doctors' offices on a media board. Mike's new idea was to use the internet and TV screens to provide health information along with ads. Since prescriptions are monitored, the model offered a measurable return on investment. This was in the early stages of pharmaceutical marketing.

Fund Isabella invested $250,000. A private equity firm bought shares in OnTarget two years later, returning 10 times our original investment to the fund. When the analytical rating system we had been using indicated it was a stronger investment going forward than when we first invested, we asked Mike to sell us a piece of his equity (the private equity firm said no) and we invested again – an unusual move. Two years later, the $500,000 invested the second time returned another home run.

At the end of the day Fund Isabella did fine, performing in the top quartile of vintage '99 funds and delivering an IRR return of 4% for investors. Whereas the average '99 fund lost about 50 cents on the dollar. Every investor made money. But it would be 20 years before delivering the final check.

Sadly, Isabella Capital didn't change the landscape. The industry invests less in women-led businesses now than in '99 – 5% then, about 3% now. While the reason isn't clear, advisor Ed Goodman suggested and I agree it has a lot to do with comfort. Men are simply more comfortable with themselves than with women. Dollars are limited. Investment opportunities are not. Why not stick with the familiar?

I also speculate that the concentration of testosterone in the industry has to do with money and power. It is human nature for people who wield power to protect it. High finance – venture and private equity – is arguably where it's most concentrated. It's about the money, honey.

Another contributing factor is the way women think – long term and risk adverse.

At a Procter & Gamble conference, I gave a talk on entrepreneurship from a woman's perspective. I had one piece of advice. Women need to exaggerate – exaggerate their talents, exaggerate their revenue prospects, exaggerate projected profit. Exaggerate everything because most men do. And if women, with their tendency to be analytical and cautiously accurate, stick to unvarnished facts, their projected returns will fall way short of the men with whom they compete. To win, exaggerate everything. And then deliver.

PART VII

CLUBS AND NETWORKS

STARTING A CLUB
OF MY OWN

"An adult life . . . is a slowly emerging design, with shifting components, occasional dramatic disruptions, and fresh creative arrangements."

– Jill Ker Conway, Speaker Women's Capital Club Inaugural Dinner and first female President of Smith College

CLUBS HAVE BEEN around since antiquity. The "gentlemen's club," which grew out of 19th English society, is a group of people or the place where they meet, generally around a common idea. Many have a dining room, bar, library and sports facility such as billiards, golf or squash.

Often called private and social, they are actually a place where influential people gather to make contact, to make deals, to get ahead professionally and economically. Historically, the influential members all look alike.

Cincinnati's Queen City Club is one of the oldest and most prestigious private clubs in the Cincinnati. Founded in 1874 as a "gentleman's gathering place," it serves influential professionals as a place where "congenial people could gather in fellowship and common interest." It boasts thickly upholstered furniture, mahogany walls and fine art including portraits of President William Howard Taft and Speaker of the House Nicholas Longworth, who were early members. It is very quiet.

Procter & Gamble executives would sometimes take promising managers to the more exclusive, men-only second floor for lunch and personnel reviews. I was never invited. Sadly, men only membership rules remained that way throughout my tenure with the company.

About the same time, I called the University Club of Cincinnati, also an all-male club at the time where Jack was a member, to reserve a squash court, requesting a court at noon. The receptionist matter-of-factly stated, *"We prefer that the ladies play between 9:00 and 11:00 am."* I responded, *"I prefer to play between 11:00 am and 1:00 pm. Please put me down for noon."* I showed up and played, but there was no ladies locker room.

As women entered the workforce, some men became nervous. One defense was to tighten their hold on private clubs. It would take a lawsuit to break through. In the late 80s, Lorna Bade Goodman, wife of Ed Goodman, who would become a Fund Isabella investment advisor, represented the city of New York. In her capacity as Head of the Affirmative Litigation Division of the NYC Corporation Counsel's Office of the city of New York, she brought a lawsuit against the 122-year old University Club, one of the largest of the all-male clubs in New York City and one of the most prestigious. She won the case, thereby, effectively, ending the barring of women for club membership at the University Club and several others in NYC and beyond. On a personal note, had she not won, Jack and I probably would not, with the Goodmans, be members today.

The courts determined that "private clubs" which only accept personal payments for dues, as distinct from payments from employers, for example, could maintain membership policies which exclude women.

Several years later, in 1993, an offhand comment made at a Queen City Club lunch prompted me to conclude that "in my lifetime I will never be treated as an equal in this club." Some places of power and influence remain the preserve of men. I walked away from the club after lunch, down 4th Street for a couple of blocks feeling down. Then an idea struck. "I'll start a club of my own. No building. No history. No bylaws. No name. No money. No matter. I can do that."

A year or so later, Anne and Allen Zaring entertained a group of us at their Beaver Creek, Colorado, home for a weekend of skiing. At dinner one night, Stella Hassan suggested we start a women's investment club. As she said at our first meeting, *"I'm tired of other people losing my money."* Bingo. In the car on the way to the airport, Allen suggested the name Women's Capital Club. It had enough gravitas.

Trish wrote the by-laws. It would be a by-invitation-only club, with admission based on one criterion only: leadership. Leadership skills in one's chosen field of endeavor.

Many women with leadership skills at the time operated in silos – the lone female VP at P&G or Scripps, or the lone female partner at law or financial firms. Women weren't part of the old boy network. And some career women like me didn't have many "girlfriends."

Also, our club would – unlike many other membership institutions – have diversity and professional balance from day one. With WCC, we could create a strong, diverse, powerful network of our own.

We made a list of Cincinnati's top women leaders and invited each to send $5,000 to become charter members of what was then only an "idea." It struck a chord. Virtually everyone sent money: $150,000 in the bank in two weeks. Charlotte Otto, P&G's highest-ranking woman, Denise Kuprionis of Scripps, federal judge Susan Dlott, Ginger Kent, COO of Kenner Toys, Janet Reid, global consultant on diversity, among other leaders, joined. At the first Queen City Club dinner, which Anne orchestrated, new members were so excited about introducing themselves that we didn't adjourn for hours.

In 1994 none of Cincinnati's leading organizations had a female CEO. The internet was not yet a factor in our lives. Retail meant shopping centers. We ordered little by mail. Women didn't engage much in stocks or, for that matter, money.

Our investment decisions were solid, at times progressive. We bought Nokia, the first portable phone, in year one. We bought Amazon shortly after the IPO. We made opportunistic buys on Apple, Google and Netflix. We even bought shares of a security company that didn't exist. My recommendation.

We learned about stocks, and we made money. Beyond financial, there were other returns – delicious dinners, even an unprecedented Maisonette carryout, trips to Canyon Ranch and to NYC. We visited the stock exchange, saw Broadway plays and got an insiders' tour of Sotheby's and the High Line. Valentine dinners, learning lunches and more.

A few years later, I asked a few members why they joined. Charlotte's note summarizes WCC best:

"I joined because I was lucky enough to be included by you and the other founders. I could immediately see it was a unique opportunity to get to know outstanding women leaders in the community but didn't realize in the beginning how meaningful it would be. There was nothing like it. While it was ostensibly an investment club, to me investing was a side-dish. The true value was getting to know amazing

women in ways I never would have otherwise. WCC was/is uber-networking among the women leading the community in every aspect."

Also, I joined The Committee of 200, an invitation-only membership organization boasting many of the world's successful women entrepreneurs and corporate leaders. The Committee, with more than 450 members, represents 100 industries. The mission is to foster, celebrate and advance women's leadership in business by providing access to unique programming plus a professional and personal network of their peers. It's similar to YPO, of which Jack is a member. Networks make a difference.

PROCTER & GAMBLE ALUMNI NETWORK

"We created the network to connect and enrich the lives of members as well as to give back. The reason it works is shared values."

– Ed Tazzia, Founder, Procter & Gamble Alumni Network

ALTHOUGH I LAST worked at The Procter & Gamble Company in 1984, one never actually leaves. P&G is not just a company, it's a culture and way of life.

So, it wasn't surprising that, in 2001, Ed Tazzia, Mary Beth Price and two other former Procter & Gamble executives decided to form an alumni organization so we all could stay connected. I served for a short while on the founding board.

The group, particularly Ed, was driven. With increasingly frequent meetings and conference calls, the time commitment for the alumni board project demanded too much time from me as I was trying to dig myself out of Isabella Capital's early losses. As a solution, I offered to put together an Honorary Advisory Board – people whose names would give credibility to the fledgling network. The challenge we faced was legitimizing the organization and attracting members. Endorsement by our most successful graduates would be a way to say: "We're here. We're real. We believe in this start-up. Join us."

My first call was to John Smale who said he would talk with then current CEO John Pepper. Two days later he called back saying that he and Pepper would both like to serve. Scott Cook, CEO of Intuit, agreed. Then I called Meg Whitman, CEO of eBay at the time. We had been on a panel together, but she didn't know me. Even so, it required 23 calls for me to get her on the line. Apparently, she eventually realized that I would not give up without a discussion.

"Meg, you are the most successful female to have worked for P&G. We need you on the Alumni Board." She declined, saying that she and her neurosurgeon husband were just too busy with careers and teenage boys. She had agreed to join the Princeton Board, but that was it. I understood her resistance. However, we needed her name. We did not need her time. When I promised to be her gatekeeper – no contacting her except through me – she agreed.

The P&G Alumni Network is now a vibrant, global organization with local chapters on five continents and 30,000 members. At the bi-annual gatherings, the Network gives a few awards. It gave me the John Smale Management Award which honors one making a major contribution to the world of business. I got it for bringing diversity to the company. I was the third recipient after John Smale and Meg Whitman. The gala occurred during a snowstorm which blanked the entire eastern United States and grounded the airlines. Not deterred, our children rented a car and drove nearly 24 hours to get there in time for the presentation.

Chairman Ed Tazzia, in his 2019 letter, thanked the Advisory Board for lending "your names and credibility at the outset of this journey . . ." I haven't done much but am pleased to still serve on the Advisory Board.

And, speaking of The Procter & Gamble Company, it is doing exceedingly well on the business and diversity fronts. Performance slipped for nearly 10 years, reminiscent of the late '70s and early '80s. But, thanks to David Taylor and his people, the irrepressible company is alive again. The world's current focus on healthcare and cleanliness is P&G's sweet spot.

When Charlotte Otto said being a woman at Procter in the late '60s when I started was a disadvantage but an advantage a decade later (when Charlotte started), she accurately described the company, not corporations in general. I like to think P&G and I lucked into each other before other Fortune 500 companies, helping us both get an early start on empowering women.

Women now represent about 50% of management and Board talent. In advertising, the company's emphasis on female strength is manifested by showing women in powerful positions – astronauts for example – and by sponsoring women's soccer. Amazingly, the personnel people now seek out "brain dead" moms who spent a few years on the mommy track. They offer flex time and generous leaves; P&G routinely appears on best company lists for women, moms and dads.

The company is empowering men with advertising showing men washing dishes and cleaning house, even installing thousands of diaper changing tables in men's restrooms. How sweet it is.

The remaining challenge, of course, is that there is no woman CEO. But that will soon change. Meanwhile, the stock is soaring.

BOARDS

"Peg had the courage to ask difficult questions and the wisdom to demand intelligent answers."

– Paul Sittenfeld, Former Board Chair, The Seven Hills School

WHEN MERCY HEALTH, a leading hospital system, made a woman its CEO, I asked her to play golf. We had gone through Leadership Cincinnati together. Arriving at the Cincinnati Country Club on a crisp spring afternoon, we started playing. After driving from the third tee, Julie Hansen surprised me: *"Peg, would you consider joining the Mercy Board?"* Private clubs apparently spark invitations.

One of my biggest mistakes in life was starting to smoke and continuing – given my addictive Irish genetics – far too long, until 14-year old Jackie presented a couldn't refuse challenge: *"I'll make good grades if you give up smoking."* After stopping 30 years ago, I became a non-smoking zealot.

After joining the Mercy Health Board, I learned that our network allowed smoking on the premises. For four years, my efforts to convince hospital leadership that we needed to ban smoking entirely, failed. Trustees reasoned that such a ban would prompt nurses and technicians who smoked to seek employment elsewhere.

Exasperated, I asked for time at the end of a Board meeting. Handing a copy of the Hippocratic Oath to our Board Chair, I asked him to read it. *"Though shall do no harm."* Then I added some perspective: *"If we had a person at our front door with a gun to his head, I suspect we would do something about it. And yet every day we walk through those doors to see people smoking and we do nothing."*

Trustees around the table still shied away from taking a strong stand given the personnel risk. My response was: *"Perhaps there's a story for the press. If not us, then who?"*

This prompted the Board to offer me a path. If I could convince every hospital in the area to give up smoking, Mercy Health would do so as well. I made an appointment with all the CEOs. The first was a woman who headed a recently formed three hospital alliance. She agreed on the spot. *"If you get Mercy, I'll get the Alliance."*

Then I went to Children's whose CEO Jim Anderson hesitated at first: *"Peg, it may not be the right time to burden the parents as we have children here who are dying."* I answered with a statement that still surprises even me – *"What good does it do to save the life of a child while enabling the death of a parent."* He agreed. Jim was so respected in the industry that all the other healthcare institutions quickly came around. The smoking ban effected 30,000 employees right away. Within a couple years, the city began to expand the prohibition.

Before and since I have served on a number of profit and non-profit boards. Phyllis Sewell, my female mentor, who served on several Fortune 500 boards, gave a succinct explanation of a director's responsibilities: *"To ensure survival of the entity and to have a capable CEO at the helm."*

After leaving The Procter & Gamble Company my stature in the eyes of the CEO and other directors seemed to shrink. Being an entrepreneur simply doesn't carry the weight of being a corporate executive. That is strange, in a way. It takes financial and intellectual capital as well as courage and a special something to build an entity from the ground up. And there are no guardrails. It takes time to regain respect.

POLITICS

"Mom and Dad insisted that the family have dinner together and once more, politics was an even helping with meat and potatoes."

— Tim Hogan, brother

RIGHT AFTER GRADUATING from Manhattanville College and watching the Democratic Party nominate Senator John F. Kennedy for President, Nancy drove to Washington D.C. to work on the JFK campaign. She and Fred focused the balance of their lives primarily on government and politics. She became an addict. Eventually, they would become engaged in changing the structure of the Democratic Party through the McGovern commission, which took power away from male bosses in of smoke filled back rooms in favor of more diversity. Betty Friedan called Fred "the papa bear of women's lib."

When Nancy said, *"politics is habit forming,"* she could have been speaking for the entire family for three generations, now four. It started with the Attorney General and extended through the Judge, the Kennedy years, my brother Tim's county commissioner and Democratic Committee roles and son Chris's work with President Obama and Hillary Clinton's Presidential Campaign.

I have been involved, not ever full time, but involved,

throughout my life. We contribute to campaigns, give parties and, almost every year, I work the polls.

When the Watergate scandal escalated, it cost Richard Nixon much of his political support. Jack and I were among those early on to lose faith in Nixon. It was 1974 and there were three special elections for congressional seats. Results of these elections would become a public expression of opinion on Watergate. Our heavily Republican district seat was among those up for grabs and attracting national attention. Tom Luken, a popular Irishman, ran on the Democratic ticket. Jack and I volunteered to work for him, running Tom's advertising campaign. Keying off an oft-used Procter approach, we used consumer testimonials.

Tom won the elections in an extremely close race which moved the needle toward impeachment. That summer, the tapes which Nixon tried to suppress on the basis of executive privilege, ironically the subject of my thesis, were released. Faced with almost certain impeachment and removal from office, Nixon resigned on August 9, 1974, the only time a U.S. president has done so.

Dad's work in politics contributed to his appointment to the federal bench. In the courtrooms of federal judges, portraits hang of the judges who have presided there, older grey-haired men sitting impressively in their formidable black robes observing the proceedings. Dad was a humble man. For years, he refused to allow his portrait to be painted. Instead he hung a dolphin which he had caught in Florida. It shook up the formality of the court room and the lawyers who argued there.

When asked: *"Why a fish?"* His response was. *"The fish ends up on the hook for the same reason most people end up in this courtroom. There is plenty of food in the sea, but the fish who gets caught, gets caught out of greed."*

Ahead of his time, he criticized early on the country's growing materialism that the "me" decade of the 80's made apparent; America seemed to be moving further and further away from the "greatest generation" that sacrificed so much in WWII to a more self-centered one. When Dad died, several friends and associates asked for a memento or remembrance of him. There was nothing to share. Aside from a couple of rosaries, he had already given everything away including all of his books and all of his money.

Son Chris, who gave up a Wall Street job in 2007, said *"I don't enjoy making rich people richer."* He resigned to volunteer for Barack Obama, landing a job in South Carolina a few months later. As part of Jeremy Bird's team, Chris helped develop the ground game that would be critical to Obama's election.

Timmy and I went to Denver for the Democratic Convention which nominated Obama. It was 50 years after the March on Washington. I wondered how many of us from that March were there to see and experience the fulfillment of King's dream and Bobby Kennedy's prediction. A proud moment for us as parents and for the country.

We attended Bush's inaugural with our friends the Prices, and Obama's with Chris and his future wife Lauren Kidwell. Lauren was the first employee to work on Obama's senate campaign in Illinois. Because I am known as a liberal Democrat, people sometimes question my presence at the events honoring Republicans. It's important to reach across the aisle.

Chris followed Nancy and Fred's example and worked in the White House before heading the Agency for Trade and Development and managing the Ohio campaigns for Obama and Hillary Clinton. His boss at the Agency nicely told us that Chris, at the age of 26, was the best crisis manager she had ever encountered, to which we responded, *"Perhaps that makes sense as his older brothers used to hold him by his ankles over our second-floor balcony. A national economic crisis pales in comparison."*

Today, divisiveness and a leadership vacuum mark politics – suggesting we are engaged in a battle for survival itself – raging fires, global warming, pandemic, exploding unemployment, racial demonstrations, insidious meddling from the Russians and impending collapse of industries ranging from Broadway to cruise ships. It's reminiscent of the 60's.

But because I grew up at the Hogan dinner table believing that politics – public service – is the highest of all callings, I believe, we will see better times.

The Judge's explanation of politics is worth repeating: *"When the Democrats get elected, they get in the rowboat and paddle as fast and as far as they can toward open waters. When the Republicans get control, they turn the boat around and paddle as fast and as far as they can toward the shore, never quite making it all the way back. The difference is called progress."*

SPORTS

"Alone we can do so little; together we can do so much."

— Helen Keller, American Author

ALWAYS, I HAVE been immersed in sports from learning to ride horses to joining the kindergarten kick ball team. Interest intensified on the hockey fields, basketball courts and baseball diamonds at Hillsdale.

In high school, I played tennis competitively and vividly remember matches with boys during which my debate was whether or not to win, as males so hated to lose to a girl. Nor did the boys find athletic girls anywhere near as attractive as prom queens. Deciding always to win, if I could, influenced my ability later to hold my own in the business world. As an athlete and coach, I saw how sports strengthen young people. Sports imbues a competitive spirit (women need that more than men, who seem to be born with competition in their bones), fitness, discipline and the determination to win.

Of the legal protections that have been enacted, the one that seems particularly effective to me is Title IX of the 1972 Education Act, requiring that educational institutions seeking federal funding provide equal opportunities to participate in all programs including sports. Recognizing the obvious differences, this legislative act requires schools only to offer both sexes the opportunity to participate fully in sports – not to spend dollars equally on men and women or to offer the same sports. This law has made a difference.

Our children played multiple sports growing up and trained hard to excel in squash. The boys took to competition naturally. Missy, who early on looked outside herself to parents and coaches for encouragement, eventually learned to compete as fiercely as her brothers and – as a four-time, first team All-American – at a skill level above most men.

Missy is San Francisco's #1 female real estate agent. Her advertising claim from day one has been "work with a winner." It's a slogan that telegraphs success.

In sports, the scoreboard, and the scoreboard alone, determines who wins. Bias has no sway. And, while many women have been heard to say, "I play but don't like competition," we need to understand that it's not practice but the competition that makes us better.

Since Jack has a similar love of athletics, it's not surprising that our sports focused family began investing in the arena. After the Cincinnati Red's baseball team suffered through five straight losing seasons, the team's longest losing streak in 50 years, Carl Lindner, Jr. announced that he planned to sell the Red's franchise. The Reds are the oldest team in professional baseball. Founded in 1869, the Reds enjoy a storied history that includes World Championships and a number of "firsts" in its long history.

Cincinnati native Bob Castellini, who owned and ran a national fruit and vegetable wholesale business, came forward to get into the bidding fray. He partnered with the Williams family who owned the franchise during the Big Red Machine era which includes Pete Rose and Johnny Bench. Bob, like Carl, had an interest in keeping ownership local with a strategy of stewardship, owning, managing and building a public trust, not just a commercial enterprise. He sought partners of the same mind.

There would be about 15 units offered with a preference given to Reds fans with a Cincinnati connection. To determine who would be the co-investors, Bob held a series of one-hour meetings with interested parties. The Castellinis would be the largest stockholder, followed by the Williams family.

Jack expressed interest, although we didn't have that kind of money, but scarcity of assets wouldn't deter Jack. He's the guy who advocates, *"If you don't make enough money, make more."* To his credit, he invited me to join the interview – the only woman in that session. I knew something about baseball, having been a fan, a player and a coach for Missy's team. But I knew almost nothing about investing in the sport.

As a typical Procter & Gamble graduate, I researched the subject and then made a list of about 20 significant questions on my yellow pad – questions on financial history and projections, team record, the role of technology, plans to end the five-year slump, small market versus big market issues and others.

We entered a small conference room where Bob held court accompanied by Joe Williams and Bob's CFO Christopher Fister. Of Italian descent, Bob is an imposing figure with a strong voice, large personality and easy smile.

Conversation started. Nothing serious. After a while the talk moved to baseball, focused on Jack's long history of youth coaching. Bob shared some stories about growing up with the sport and Jack about his father's passion for the Reds. My husband didn't ask a question about the investment. No talk of financial risk or projected return. Nothing about baseball's future or a turnaround plan. In the time that passed, the only words spoken about dollars were a sentence or two from CFO Chris Fister about Bob's previous investments in sports teams – the Baltimore Orioles, the Texas Rangers and the St. Louis Cardinals.

After 15 minutes or so, I put away my yellow pad and pen.

It seemed to be about who you know, love of sports and if you like each other. In the circles where power is concentrated, I was observing how big boys play ball.

And success wouldn't be limited to performance on the field, revenues at the gate and profits on the bottom line, as an outsider like me anticipated. Proper stewardship of a community asset was a goal of the group.

There are only 30 Major League Baseball teams. There are very few investment slots that open up. But there are lots of people who long to be in an elite club – pro sports.

Bob and Jack are lifetime members of Young Presidents Organization and fierce squash opponents. They were co-investors in other projects, and we were neighbors.

As is typical in major league sports, the deal put all the power in the General Partner's hands, none with limited partners. Supply and demand. Fun. Connecting to our youth. And the expectation that the franchise value would be increased.

The deal closed in January 2006 for $270 million. We had made our largest investment, and in a benevolent dictatorship. It has been an excellent experience. Good fun. Good people. Good to reconnect to more youthful days.

About 10 years later Jack, Jr. suggested that we explore an investment in soccer. Given its popularity worldwide, its U.S. growth trajectory and our son's enthusiasm, Jack started to explore the idea.

Within a few weeks Jimmy Gould, a friend, invited Jack to his office to meet a Dutchman named Mike Mossel who owned the nearby Dayton Dragons. It drew about a thousand fans a game. Mike hoped to move the franchise to Cincinnati, a larger market. Jack and I connected with Jeff Berding, former city councilman and 20-year veteran of the Cincinnati Bengals. Jeff was exploring a soccer launch. No definite plan but there was purpose.

About the same time, we met with Steve Hightower and George Joseph and we each committed to be the first to invest in the franchise.

In 2015, to help Jeff and the initial entrepreneurs get off the ground, Jack gave them full use of his office to launch the enterprise. Originally, we anticipated investing $100,000 as part of $1,000,000 to get the team off the ground.

Later Jeff engaged Carl Lindner whose family formerly owned the Reds and who loves soccer, and the dream became bigger.

In March 2016, play started in the United Soccer League, two levels below Major League Soccer, and the team began to set records. Three years later FC Cincinnati became a Major League Soccer team, opening the season with a sellout crowd of 30,000 fans.

In 2019, FC started construction of a new $300 million stadium located in Over-the-Rhine. A nice twist is that Meg Whitman with $100 million became the team's second biggest investor. We hope that a women's team is not far behind.

Now, 15 years after that first meeting with the big boys, I get it. Whether sports stimulate family debates, following the news, attending games, or playing together, sports can rally families and communities.

*   *   *

In the beginning, the group of men at P&G who comprised the invitation only "lunch club" never included me. And I, like other women still sometimes experience a cold shoulder. But times have changed. Now, we are in many of the rooms where it happens, including some of the most influential and exclusive clubs.

PART VIII

BUILDING GRANDIN PROPERTIES

Magic Money

"Peg's belief in taking control was something she naturally passed on to others. There was no sermonizing about trail-blazing, she just led by example. Her willingness to take on new challenges and to assign over-the-top tasks to the staff led to our development and confidence that was not previously held. I cannot imagine any other person who would have given a high school educated employee the opportunities and responsibilities with which she trusted to me. I am forever grateful."

— Kathy Meier, Board, Grandin Properties

IN THE DARK year of 1988, we took the risk of purchasing 2337 Grandin Road before we sold 2386 Grandin. The new home was a worn out, raccoon and bee filled house a block away with a leaking roof and falling plaster. We become the second owners after the Hoadly family. It had enviable bones, lots of light and – like all attractive real estate – a very good location.

We were aware that this was a good time to sell high-end Hyde Park real estate in as much as recent Cincinnati corporate acquisition activity prompted the move of several executives from the New York area to come to Cincinnati. Cincinnati prices were low in comparison to, for example, Greenwich, Connecticut. The time to sell was favorable.

Over the preceding year we had become fearful that the educational trust my parents had set up might run out of money before our four children would graduate from college. So I – granddaughter of a landlady and daughter of a man who invested in a 400-acre farm after World War II – turned to real estate as a way to fill the gap.

2386 Grandin sat on one acre, along with an adjacent, wooded acre and one-half, next to the Cincinnati Country Club. We bought the property for only $35,000, included in the $355,000 purchase price, as it was considered landlocked. After talking with my brother Tim, an appraiser, we concluded there might be a way to set it free.

Our entrance was from a private street called Crabapple. The house at the end of Crabapple controlled the street and the utility rights for our land and home. Since the Crabapple homeowner was thrilled to be living in the privacy of the woods, he had no interest in offering us access to utilities so we could build two houses in his forest. Nevertheless, we would try to find a way to unlock the parcels. We hired a surveyor, an architect and a lawyer to investigate. No one could come up with a solution.

Undeterred and driven by the goal of making certain we had tuition money for all four children, we persisted, starting the process again. We hired the same developer and attorney but a new surveyor, this time an older country gentleman from Clermont County named James Smith. My brother Tim recommended him. There had to be a way.

After surveying the property, Mr. Smith asked me to walk to the end of Crabapple Lane and take a look at the house which controlled the utility rights.

To my amazement, he announced matter-of-factly: *"That guy isn't going to cause you any trouble."*

"Why?" I inquired.

"See that tree at the corner of his lawn? You own that tree."

And he went on: *"See that driveway? You own his driveway."*

It turns out there was a marker inaccurately placed in the 1920's on our property. Jim Smith discovered it whereas none of the others had.

There was some legal wrangling afterwards from the Crabapple homeowners which our attorney David Todd managed to win, including compensation for survey, architect and legal fees. As it turned out, we sold our home as well as the land to the same buyer. The house itself brought enough money to buy and renovate our new home. No mortgage. Plus, we had $400,000 left in "magic money."

We closed on the Hoadly House March 1, 1988, putting our house on the market shortly thereafter. As hoped, we got a strong offer in June from one of the New Yorkers who was coming to Cincinnati as a top executive of the Federated Department Stores, now Macy's. Both the buyer and his wife were attorneys. Also, they engaged a personal real estate lawyer as well as Federated lawyers.

Understandably, the buyer's team exerted pressure on us to move earlier than the October closing date that we set. However, our new house was not going to be finished till then and my father was very ill. Our four children were active and demanding, while Jack, who had sold NTC to a New York Company, was traveling weekly to the city. I stood firm on the closing date for all those reasons, but mainly because I wanted to spend as much time as possible with Dad.

The buyer was offering an attractive price. We had a lot to lose if the deal went down. Then, the buyer presented an inspection report asking us to correct 26 items.

"Not going to do anything" was the message I gave David to

convey. *"Tell the buyer that there are always 26 items to fix in a home of this size and stature. And if he can't handle it, he should not buy the house. "*

David thoughtfully responded: *"Peg, you and Jack can't afford to carry two houses."*

"I know, David, that we can't and you know we can't. But the buyer doesn't."

It worked. The property sold "as is." We stayed in the house till October.

And we sold the land for $400,000. Virtually all profit. As income taxes were high in the 80s, Tim and David both suggested we do a like kind exchange, saving taxes, by investing in another property.

"OK, that seems like a good idea. However, I don't know anything about real estate. I'll have to learn."

And that's what happened. I would just start . . . and figure it out.

Over the ensuing three months, the legal "window" allowed before naming the intended exchange property, I looked at all kinds of options including industrial warehouses, commercial buildings, apartments, office buildings, even land. We investigated places down the street as well as fairly far away. We looked at leveraging the money.

At the end of the day I settled on buying a six-unit investment in Hyde Park Square, the Peebles, which was located less than a mile from our house. We purchased the property from a friend and former P&G associate, JoLynn Gustin. We knew the Square. We understood the Square. We knew the type of people who lived there, and we patronized the first-floor businesses.

This was "magic money" – turning $35,000 into $400,000. We used it to start Grandin Properties.

After the move, life changed. We told the children why we

were moving. We could no longer afford the old house. We had always treated them like little people rather than little kids.

We remained committed to private schools and squash (which meant country club, lessons and travel expenses). With limited financial resources, we dramatically cut the amount of help around the house. Suddenly, the kids had to pitch in rather than be waited upon – with cleaning, cooking, laundry. Even Chris, age seven, started doing his own laundry and cleaning (if you call it that) his own room. The trajectory toward spoiled children morphed to helpful and self-sufficient young people. It was a very, very good thing.

Their becoming more hands-on helpers started right away. That summer, we renovated our new home. I worked with the construction crew, along with the children who ripped off drywall, scraped and painted, stripped carved wood, cut grass and hauled trash. It was definitely a "family" project.

They also made creative suggestions that only children could conceive. When Eve expressed concern about the absence of a backstairs, fearing that the boys living on the third floor could die in a fire, 15-year old Jackie suggested a fire pole. We installed one. It became a neighborhood attraction. Tim and Chris wanted secret rooms so under the eaves we dry walled and carpeted two hidden places for play and, as they got older, for who knows what.

The process of looking around and deciding to make investments in real estate close to home and within our sphere of knowledge led to the strategy: "Grandin will buy, renovate and manage historic properties in best of class walkable urban neighborhoods." At the time, the trend for residents as well as businesses was moving to the suburbs. Grandin would look beyond current trends – to the future.

Two years later, we bought a second very similar property –

ironically called The Grandin Building. Listed by John Frank, Cushman and Wakefield broker, who would become our primary real estate agent and longtime friend over the next 30 years, the building was selling for $495,000-down from $550,000. With an offer of $415,000, we put The Grandin Building under contract. It housed four apartments, a beauty salon, antique store, exercise studio and the BonBonerie, Cincinnati's best bakery. Bonnie, who had a superior eye (the building oozes character) came to see it with me. She said: *"Buy it."* And so I did.

It was the reverse of our first purchase when Grandin paid almost entirely in cash. For this one, we didn't have enough for the down payment. However, the children had recently inherited $50,000 from Mom's sister Ruth which, as trustee, I could access. By combining this with profits from selling some P&G stock, I pieced together a 30% down payment. The bank offered to finance 80% rather than 70%, but that seemed too risky for me. We had been managing real estate for just a year.

We closed in December 1989 and, for a few months, it was smooth sailing. Then the salon abruptly closed, leaving in the middle of the night; then, the two guys who leased apartment #1 got into a fight, walking out as well. I didn't panic. My Procter training provided marketing and sales skills. I thought that I could always find more tenants.

On August 8, the Iraqi government invaded and annexed Kuwait. Right away President Bush sent U.S. Air Force fighter planes to Saudi Arabia as part of a military buildup dubbed Operation Desert Shield. The world stood still. For weeks, we advertised our vacancies, but marketing generated no calls. And when there's nobody to talk to, there is no chance of making a sale.

Had we borrowed more money we would not have been able to keep up on payments to the bank and PNC could well have shut us down. The lesson – avoiding too much leverage – became a guiding principle and we stay close to a 50%/50% debt to equity split.

We now had two historic properties, located in walkable, urban neighborhoods, which we also knew well. Both represented an age-old approach to real estate: retail on the ground floor with living quarters above.

As a result of Ruth's inheritance, which I borrowed initially and later converted to equity, the children became owners of Grandin Properties. Though they were young – 7 to 16 – the company provided opportunities for them to learn and contribute. Taking out the garbage. Showing apartments. Helping with renovations. Weighing in on acquisitions.

Part of the thinking regarding the children's involvement was, first, that they were smart and closer to the age of our target audience. This meant each could contribute to shaping the business. Second, Grandin could help finance college tuition if the money in Mom and Dad's educational trust didn't stretch far enough. Third, if the trust lasted long enough to finance their education and if the company ended up being a valuable part of our estate, those that helped build it would be disinclined to squander the spoils. Gifts carry a greater risk. All four have served on the Grandin Properties Board for 20 years and contributed to its growth.

Over the next decade we would buy a similar property every couple of years. To manage the business, I was fortunate enough to re-hire Mac, who had worked with me during the P&G days. Her operational excellence, strong character and people training skills proved instrumental to the company's success. During my years running the venture capital fund, Mac ran the company on her own and ran it well.

Coincident with launching Isabella Capital, I bought, in 1999, the Weston and San Carlos in Hyde Park – adding another 40 units. Don Mills labeled that Wyant trait "stacking." Good thing Mac was on board.

Our business model was "always" to buy in Cincinnati's best neighborhoods, add value by renovating (starting with exterior and common area beautification), then raise rents on new residents. For financing, I had the good fortune to work with two women. Initial funding would be a signature note from PNC – Kay Geiger, President, and Pam Weber, Head of Commercial Banking. After renovating and stabilizing, another bank, usually CBank, would refinance with a permanent loan at a higher value. We would use the extra money to buy another building. That way we avoided having to put more equity dollars into the company while keeping debt/equity in the 50%/50% range.

As the time required to manage Isabella Capital lessened in 2003, I turned my attention back to real estate, putting my foot on the accelerator. The company was poised for growth. We added new neighborhoods – Covington, Kentucky, and Walnut Hills, moving closer to the center city. We believed young professionals and empty nesters as well as businesses would eventually move back to the urban core – attracted by the built and natural environment. The magnetic pull associated with historic architecture in the most convenient locations with the cultural advantage of diversity seemed irresistible.

Located just north of Downtown, Over-the-Rhine (OTR) is among Cincinnati's oldest neighborhoods. It was settled in the early 19th century largely by German (and Irish) immigrants who crossed over the newly opened Miami & Erie Canal, which they called the Rhine. Street after street of fine Italianate buildings – the largest collection in the United States – distinguish the neighborhoods. The homes are human scale. Livable. Imbued with the spirit of lives lived there. Those lives built breweries,

Cincinnati's iconic Music Hall, Memorial Hall, theaters, schools, churches, meeting halls, Washington Park and Findlay Market all in the OTR neighborhood.

OTR was once home to 43,000 working class people. However, with suburban flight and the influx of poor Appalachian and African Americans, the neighborhood suffered significant economic decline, dropping to 3,500 in 1993 with the median household income of about $5,000 a year. At the doorstep to three Fortune 500 Company headquarters, it had become a low-income and dangerous neighborhood.

That is when – in 1994 – Grandin Properties made its first OTR purchase. It was an attractive but decaying 10-unit brick building on 12th Street, anchored by a center circular staircase with four occupants. Tenants included a deadbeat artist skilled in the art of avoiding service for payment, a 90-year-old retired secretary who kept her gas stove on 24/7 to keep warm, a mentally disabled man on welfare and a mystery man who neither opened the door nor paid rent.

I signed a contract to purchase the building for $50,000. In search of financing, I took Dan Groneck from US Bank, and one of his associates, and Jack on a tour. It was in rough shape and a crazy mix of tenants were evident. As we exited, there were two men across the street shooting heroin right there in the open. That prompted Dan, whose discomfort was apparent, to say, *"Peg, just so you know, we're not going to give you any money for this property."* Jack added, *"Nor am I."*

There was a pause – silence for a moment. As I reflected on living in Georgetown and New York's Upper East Side as well as on what OTR would become – I responded. *"Gentleman, it's a damn good thing I don't need your money."* And I proceeded to buy it.

The venture proved to be a nightmare experience. While

praised by the Cincinnati Preservation Association, on whose Board I served, I was attacked in the newspapers by Buddy Gray, an in-your-face advocate for the poor. I failed to collect any rent and found, after getting bids, the redevelopment economics just didn't work. I sold that building ($5,000 profit) but was not deterred, buying two more in OTR over the next five years. Then in 2001 the Cincinnati race riots occurred and our four children, speaking as both Grandin Board members and concerned children of an adventurer, said in our first meeting, *"Mom we really don't want you to get shot. Why don't we sell the last OTR building?"* Though reluctant, I did. During my early forays into OTR, I never saw the falling plaster and leaky roofs. All I ever saw was what those red brick buildings, with their hidden stories and secrets, would one day become.

It was a race riot that shook the establishment into action. City government led by Council members John Cranley and David Pepper and the business community including The Procter & Gamble Company joined forces in 2003 to quick start development efforts. They created and funded The Cincinnati Center City Development Fund (3CDC), a non-profit economic development agency which could bring critical mass to restoring OTR. By 2010 it started making a difference. Along Vine Street, a few restaurants and bars opened. Adventurous young people bought the newly developed condos.

Grandin turned its eyes back toward the neighborhood. This time, however, we would start by working with 3CDC. The organization financed (with a $400,000 city grant) the $1.6 million renovation of a five-unit building next to Music Hall, overlooking the newly renovated Washington Park. Led by Mac, Grandin did the work. Personally, I know almost nothing about plumbing, roofing or the mechanics of construction. Design is another story. I have good taste. And I surround myself with experts who have better taste – architect Denis Back, graphic designer Heather Vecellio, interior designers Aubrie Welsh and Lara Roller and Peter Frey, who worked for Grandin.

For our first project with 3CDC we envisioned a much higher-end product than had been attempted in OTR. When 3CDC pushed back on spending the money for marble countertops, antique chandeliers and Pella windows, Mac and I asked for a meeting with Steve Leeper, 3CDC's Executive Director. It proved hard to get. Then, I emailed Leeper saying that we would like to get together and Jack would join. Leeper promptly complied.

After confidently suggesting that high-end finishes would get higher resale prices and the project would be profitable, we asked Steve how the profit would be handled. He said: *"We've never made a profit."* I said: *"This time we will – how about a 50-50 split."*

We completed the project that summer of 2013 with the high-end finishes.

The condos went on market August 2, 2013. Approaching the sale as if we were in the on-fire San Francisco market, we staged the units, priced them at over $300 per square foot which was $94.00 over the existing OTR high water mark. We held an open house and stated we would open offers the following Sunday just like our daughter Missy, by now a top five real estate agent in San Francisco, does.

Cincinnati is not a hot, coastal market. However, following her plan, we sold them within two weeks over the asking price in a competitive bidding situation. The project made a profit of $250,000. 3CDC had to figure out how to recognize a profit on their books.

THE STRIETMANN CENTER

"There are two types of developers that take on historic buildings, leaders and followers. Grandin Properties is a leader in so many ways. Its projects regularly push the boundaries of what people think is possible, both in terms of location and quality. When its adaptive reuse projects come online, others see what is possible and follow. Cincinnati has benefited from such visionary leadership in preservation."

– Paul Muller, AIA, Executive Director,
Cincinnati Preservation Association

"You're playing with the big boys now, Mom."

– Jack Wyant, Jr., son

M Y EXPERIENCE WITH commercial leasing at the squash center gave me the confidence to look for another office building. I spotted the Strietmann Biscuit Company factory and asked George Verkamp, a Sibcy-Cline agent, who had long focused on OTR, to find out about its availability. As soon as he learned it was quietly on the market, we toured the seven-story building. Essentially abandoned for decades, it had been used by the Wegman family to store discarded grey metal office furniture too old and clunky to see service again.

For me, it was love at first sight. High ceilings – as high as 30 feet where the ovens once stood – huge beams, wooden floors, big windows, skylights which once served an air conditioning function (when bakers opened those windows to let out the hot air) and fire doors throughout. The fire doors gracing every floor were large, angled hunks of metal, held at the highest point by a rope that, when burnt, made the mechanism slam close, protecting the space yet not catching fire themselves.

I didn't know the stories and secrets associated with the building then, but it was located in an exploding area near Music Hall, the planned Shakespeare Theatre and the newly renovated Washington Park. Always when I look at distraught buildings, my mind only sees the vision of what will be. This is so dominant a trait that "after" pictures prompt the query: "How could I possibly have taken that on?"

That afternoon, I saw potential – 15,000 square foot plates, huge wood beams, ceilings up to 18 feet and construction, spanning as it did five different decades, that provided a historical tour of architecture, design and building from 1899 through the '30s. I fell in love.

After walking through six floors of decrepit furniture, we took a 100-year-old, manual elevator to the top. When the door opened, we saw – no metal furniture – only a high-ceilinged empty room. As the door closed, the word "Penthaus."

And then there was the view. It was an unimaginable 360-degree view of so much that happened in this part of the world:

To the East: Procter & Gamble, Kroger and Macy's.

To the South: the Richardson Romanesque City Hall, Plum Street Temple (where reformed Judaism started) and the Greek Revival Catholic Cathedral of the Archdiocese of Cincinnati.

To the West: the Art Deco masterpiece called Union Terminal

(now the Museum Center) and nearby future site of FC Stadium for the MLS soccer team.

And to the North: Washington Park, Music Hall (Cincinnati's cultural epicenter which boasts the orchestra, The Pops, ballet, opera and several theaters), William Howard Taft's home and University Hospital (where the Sabin vaccine and Dr. John Tew's laser brain surgery were developed).

On a clear day – and on that day, it was – it seems that one could see most of the region's landmark buildings, the past and the future, and the people who would take us there.

"What's the asking price and square footage, George?"
"$1.5 million and 100,000 square feet."
"That's about $15 per square foot – less than I pay for a good dress."
"George, I'll offer asking price."

Later that day when he reported that the building was under contract, I asked: *"Has the seller signed?"* When the owner responded in the negative, we went to his office and presented the asking price offer. I got the deal.

Few things worthwhile come easily and this was no exception. We negotiated a one-year due diligence period starting January 2015. Our first goal was to secure parking. 3CDC's Executive Director Steve Leeper agreed. By St. Patrick's Day, he wrote a note committing to provide us 175 parking spaces in the neighboring Washington Park Garage. The garage is city owned but controlled by 3CDC. Parking is crucial to any office development project. 3CDC knew that OTR needed office space to get to the next level and giving us parking would be required to take the first major step. 3CDC didn't have the money to develop office buildings itself at the time.

The contract provided 175 spaces for 15 years. What Grandin had to do was start construction by July 15, 2016 and to substantially complete the project by January 15, 2018.

It would be Grandin Properties' most ambitious project. I was excited to sign the contract in September, and at the same time give Denis Back, our architect, the go-ahead to develop final plans, move forward with city approvals and start getting construction bids. Separately, we sold a property to help finance the project, and lifted contingencies toward a January 15, 2016 closing.

In November Denis presented the plans to the city's Historic Conservation Board, which was the first step. It was considered a routine meeting. But, because it looks good to have the owner there, he asked me to join. All we needed from the city was a parking variance and parking variances had been routinely issued for decades, especially in a neighborhood like Over-the-Rhine which desperately needed renovation. Also, we had a contract with 3CDC for more parking spaces than needed for 15 years. A similarly sized building down the street – Rhinegeist – received permits with virtually no parking.

Shockingly, the board voted us down. The stated reason was that "15 years is not enough." I countered at this and other follow up meetings with explanations relating to other granted variances and ". . . After 15 years we may not even be driving cars." Months later Mayor John Cranley and Luke Blocher in the city solicitor's office took an innovative approach and proposed to City Council a zoning change. It exempted 12th Street where The Strietmann Center is located from all parking requirements.

With that obstacle behind us, I pushed forward for a construction permit. Again, the city put one roadblock after another in front of us. For example they refused to permit outward swinging doors, though there were dozens nearby. Who was pulling the strings?

Clarity came when we received an email on July 8 from Daniel Lipson, 3CDC's top development officer: *"The parking contract is null and void since you have not started construction."* What were they thinking? Grandin started work in February and had spent over $450,000 as dumpsters on the street made clear. Then it dawned on me – that was demolition, not construction work. We could be stopped on a technicality. Who would have thought?

Nine months had passed since we first applied for a construction permit. It should have taken a month or less. We still didn't have it. Now we had only a week before the July 15, 2016 deadline. We turned our little world upside down and, with the help of our architect, lawyers (several) and The HGC Construction Company we got the appropriate permit and kept the contract in place. But now we knew who the opponent was.

The final "aha" moment and plausible answer came from a question Councilman Smitherman asked: *"This doesn't happen. Who wants your building?"* It wasn't the building somebody wanted; it was the parking.

A few weeks after agreeing to give Grandin parking, 3CDC was awarded nearly $43 million in new market tax credits. This was enough to build two office buildings. It seemed that the non-profit, which was now a development company and competitor, didn't need us anymore to bring offices to OTR. What 3CDC needed was our parking for their projects.

Spending even more than anticipated, because of the hurdles put before Grandin, we needed leases more than ever. We hired Cushman & Wakefield's Scott Abernethy to begin signing tenants. He generated interest, only to find that 3CDC signed our most promising prospects.

And when we "substantially finished" the building, we gave

three 3CDC's executives a tour so they could witness our compliance. On the tour, Leeper, in front of six other people, agreed that it was "substantially complete," only to renege in an email the next morning.

Then the deal changed again. He said despite the contract: *"We will give Grandin Properties parking for The Strietmann Center when you get tenants."*

I contacted 3CDC board members, city leaders and several on Council. There was no evidence, apparent to us, that a single one of these people took affirmative action to stop 3CDC. One said to me in a face-to-face conversation that: *"I don't care. 3CDC moves the city forward."* I responded: *"If that's the kind of city we are creating, it's not where people will want to live."* And I walked out. The breach was incredibly damaging to Grandin Properties.

No one wanted to stand up and do the right thing. Certainly, not openly. In a board meeting, as Jack, Jr. said: *"Welcome to the NFL."*

Throughout this ordeal our entire team was immersed. Mac and I counseled with first class legal minds: two friendly federal judges, a common pleas judge, several real estate attorneys and litigators – those paid and those in the friends and family circle. According to these judges and lawyers, the validity of the contract as well as the breach were beyond dispute. Damages would have been harder to prove if they were in the hundreds of thousands of dollars. One roadblock after another for months and months proved extremely costly. In the end, Grandin's survival was at stake.

Mac and I were on the verge of legal action when my friend Valerie Newell – a successful businesswoman and intelligent leader – talked me off the cliff, saying, *"Peg, you'll be suing the entire city!"* She suggested that I talk to Mark Jahnke, President of Katz Teller, a corporate attorney in town. He was known for his unique ability to resolve conflicts without going to trial. We initiated an offer to give back 25 spaces in Washington Park for the schoolteachers who were also being pushed out by 3CDC. Jahnke skillfully helped negotiate with the city, especially Greg Landsman, for 200 spaces in nearby Town Center Garage. 3CDC backed off.

Meanwhile Andy Keene, founding partner of GoDutch, on his own created a brand and logo to help us: The Strietmann Center – a place where creativity can breathe.

The Strietmann Center started signing tenants – the breakthrough was a global creative powerhouse, Saachi & Saachi X. At the opening party, I stood watching creative leaders from all over the United States talking to clients from Procter & Gamble, Kroger and Wendy's. The Saachi X speakers praised the building's beauty and ability to help attract top talent – the very purpose for which it was renovated. I listened quietly and, for the first time in three years, felt confident that our speculative investment would work out. Grandin wasn't alone anymore.

OTR is getting its due these days as one of the nation's premier historic districts – urban revival at its best, booming as it is with some 150 new restaurants, the School for Creative and Performing Arts, the Art Academy, craft breweries, gastropubs, shops and businesses that have opened in the last few years while also boasting hundreds of condominiums and market- rate apartments.

The long vacant Strietmann Center now bubbles over with praise. The fire doors are conversation pieces; the stories of what happened there, inspirations. It was originally financed by a woman in the 19th century for her sons. The Strietmann boys invented the soda cracker (Zesta), chocolate chip cookies and the Ferris wheel conveyer belt. They used electric cars for delivery. Now the building boasts environmental accolades including Gold LEED certification. It also has solar panels – the first to power a commercial building in Cincinnati. It is the place where Girl Scout Cookies, originally baked in a mother's oven, were first manufactured. The Penthaus is an event center.

When putting $15.00 per square foot on the proverbial napkin, I had no idea that the project would cost nearly $20 million. I had no idea that banks don't loan money for empty buildings. Nor did I understand the challenge of bringing marquis tenants to an office desert or how tough playing with the big boys would be. As S.L. Green, a leading NYC developer, said at an urban squash event, *"in real estate, you launch the ship, or you have paper in file cabinets."* I launched the ship.

At Grandin, I keep launching ships. The four children and Mac still serve on our Board. Every once in a while, someone tries to break my propensity to buy another building, but in the words of Jack, Jr., *"We Wyants don't break, we accelerate."*

As the saying goes, when God closes one door, She opens another. And that's exactly what happened when financial pressure forced us to sell our first Grandin Road home. We were able to find a place that proved better for our family plus buy a small apartment building on Hyde Park Square. That started Grandin Properties. The company proved to be a homerun financially. More importantly, it opened up an opportunity for me to be an entrepreneur and to lead the family in building an enterprise together. The enterprise makes folks who live and work there happy (most of the time) while also contributing to the environment, historic preservation, and a more beautiful city.

I remember well the months, even years, I agonized over whether or not to leave P&G, too structured but loved all the same for its talented people, endless opportunities and 'do the right thing' principles. It was heady being a high ranking somebody. It was comfortable being enveloped by the prestige of working at an acclaimed company. It will always be my favorite book. Besides I was good at it.

Even now there is a tinge of "I could have been . . . I would have been . . ." regret. But just a tinge. Beyond building a company my way, I got to live through all the chaos at home. If you miss too much of the chaos who knows what will happen to the children.

PART IX

LOOKING FORWARD

TEA LEAVES

Betty Douglas served as my administrative assistant for 13 years at Grandin Properties. Her going away present to me was a jar filled with tea bags, each with a saying. She described the gift as *"Steeped in Wisdom."*

LESSONS LEARNED FROM PEG WYANT

1. Don't take no for an answer.
2. You can be strong and feminine.
3. Predictable is boring. Erratic is more interesting.
4. The secret to making a good cup of tea is clean and extremely hot water.
5. There is no such thing as a closed door. You just need to learn how to knock loud enough.
6. Don't wear shoes when dancing on a table.
7. Crash parties.
8. Never have a bad day.
9. Everything is negotiable.
10. Never give up on what you want, even if it seems the odds are against you.

11. How to write and speak fluent P&G.

12. P&G is not just a company. It's a culture and way of life.

13. Under contract does not mean sold.

14. You're never too old to be hip.

15. To stay relevant and sharp, surround yourself with younger people.

16. With each passing year, choose to improve, not age.

17. If you have fabulous legs, flaunt them.

18. Taking a good photograph is all about lighting and minute details.

19. Dream bigger. Aim higher. Be larger than life.

20. Be persuasive.

21. Whether or not you have shoes on your feet is a minor detail.

22. Wear your shirt inside out. Or backwards. Or both.

23. Anything boys can do; girls can do more efficiently.

24. Girls have more fun.

25. Behind every great man is an extraordinary woman.

26. Sadly and gladly, there is only one Peg Wyant.

27. Marketing, marketing, marketing.

28. You can convince almost anybody of anything with the right spreadsheet.

29. Don't be ashamed to admit you've lost your keys, phone, purse, car, or mind.

30. Whatever you pursue, do so wholeheartedly.

31. If you leave a car running on the street, it will still be there when you return.

32. It's good to be the Queen.

33. Bring a robe when skinny dipping in a neighbor's pool.

34. If you don't get a response, call every hour on the hour.

35. Refuse to take typing tests.

36. Do what you love, and the money will follow.

37. Only hire smart people.

38. Invest in relationships.

39. Cut out the busy work and focus only on what matters.

40. Educate yourself. If you want to accomplish a goal, find out all about it.

41. Discover who you are and be happy with what you find.

42. If people disagree with you, you are standing your ground and walking your own path.

43. Sometimes when you're doing things considered crazy by others, you're doing the right thing.

44. Don't fear the judgments of others.

45. You know in your heart who you are and what's true to you.

46. Make the world a better place.

47. Follow your heart but take your brain with you.

48. When you are truly comfortable in your own skin, not everyone will like you, but you won't care about it one bit.

49. You must let go of the old to make way for the new.

50. Eat healthy and work out.

51. There are no failures, just results.

52. Don't settle for less than you deserve.

53. The secret to winning is sheer persistence.

54. You always think you have more time than you do.

55. Get your priorities straight.

56. If you want good things to happen, you have to make them happen yourself.

57. Grace.

58. Be clear about what you want. Clarity gives you focus and the power to think and act intelligently.

59. Be careful not to confuse the things that are urgent with the things that are important.

60. Look for time wasters and eliminate them.

61. Do your homework.

62. Start before you are ready.

63. Stay one step ahead. Be proactive. Take the initiative.

64. Self-love. Become your own priority.

65. Finish what you started. Avoid the urge to stray.

66. Great achievements involve great risk.

67. Learn the rules so you know how to break them properly.

68. Share your knowledge. It is a way to achieve immortality.

69. Individuals can make a difference and change the course of the future.

70. Don't be afraid of change.

71. Step outside of your comfort zone.

72. Don't ever feel like you have to conform to society.

73. You determine the course of your own destiny. Don't let anyone hold you back.

74. Set goals. Make lists.

75. It's okay to let people go, the important ones never go far.

76. You can't always be agreeable.

77. Pour yourself into your children.

78. Have confidence in yourself.

PAST IS PROLOGUE

"Ever since women began entering the business world in the second half of the twentieth century, they have been fighting an uphill battle. One of these women was my mother, Peg Wyant ... Hopefully, one day, men and women will be treated equally. Hopefully more women like my mom enter business."

— Chris Wyant,
excerpts from middle school essay 1994

"While I may be the first woman in this office, I will not be the last."

— Kamala Harris,
Vice President, United States

ETCHED IN STONE at the entrance to The National Archives is Shakespeare's line from the Tempest: "What is past is prologue." All that's happened to me and others up to now simply prepares us for a future that is ours to write. The Judge told me that at the beginning of my career, when I realized that there weren't any female managers: *"Don't worry about the past. Focus on your own career going forward."*

If Emily Del Greco is right, my story offers lessons that might be applicable to today's challenges.

ON WOMEN

Over two centuries have passed since 1776 when Abigail Adams wrote her husband John, as he and other founding fathers prepared to declare independence from British rule:

"Remember the ladies and be more generous and favorable to them than your ancestors. Do not put such unlimited power into the hands of the husbands. Remember, all men would be tyrants if they could. If particular care and attention is not paid to the ladies, we are determined to foment a rebellion, and will not hold ourselves bound by any laws in which we have no voice or representation."

John didn't empower the ladies. Nor did the generations and generations of men who came after. The ladies made it happen. It took the suffragettes, their marches, protests and hunger strikes to convince men in 1920 to pass the 19th Amendment giving women the right to vote. It took ladies after World War II going to work in ever growing numbers to get Congress in 1964 to pass the Civil Rights Act which made discrimination illegal in employment, pay, accommodations and in the voting booth "on the basis of sex."

Women have made progress in the last few decades. However, after all the marches, laws, court decisions and pioneering breakthroughs, the power balance favors men. Women hold less than 20% of positions of influence – such as CEO's, senior partners, governors, producers, directors and boards of directors. Pay for women is about 70 cents on every dollar paid to men versus 60 cents when I started working. Women account for more than 50% of law and medical school graduates. However, if you look at positions of power in these fields – high paying litigators and surgeons, for example – these remain the overwhelming province of men.

Laws help. Laws establish rules, but they don't change attitudes. At the 1970 Xavier University graduation, upon receiving an honorary degree, my father the Judge explained:

"Never in our history have we been so devoted to the proposition that human conduct can be controlled by human edict – law if you please. Our reaction to anything undesirable is a new law. But the prevention of evil is not now and never has been the resultant of constitutional or statutory command. Human conduct responds only to the extent that such law is expressive of the prevalent morality of the times."

Whatever barriers I broke open, change happened because I raised the issue. *"All I can do is think. Don't you have a test for that?" "I want to try the fast lane." "I don't intend to stop working just because I am pregnant."* **At the end of the day, it was up to me to kick start the process. Then thoughtful leaders helped.**

Going forward, it is up to us, ladies, to change the prevalent morality of the times. Yet, just as I needed leaders, like Pepper and Smale, to help by taking chances, we need power brokers on our side. P&G's CEO David Taylor is doing just that. With ground-breaking, controversial commercials and approaches, he is challenging us all to look again at people who are different, to see good, to do better. This is the kind of risk-taking that has the power to move us closer to equality - to bring the prevalent morality of our time to a better place.

ON MAD MEN, ME TOO AND NOT ME

Jack, Jr. has a perceptive way of defining the difference between the sexes: *"men are stupid, and women are crazy."* **There's a lot of truth in that definition.** School boys will speak without knowing the answer; girls won't because getting it wrong might cause a breakdown.

Mad Men will always be with us. So will Peggy Olson.

The Me Too movement needed to happen; and, like Black Lives Matter, it will bring the world closer to achieving equality. Sexual harassment is obviously a way of holding women down and as such needs to be eradicated both in the workplace and home.

Beginning with my internship on the U.S. Congressional Committee through gun threats and the switch blade incident, I experienced unwanted advances. However, I never allowed myself to be a victim. Having privileges and a powerful mother helped give me the courage to say no. I recognize just how fortunate that was. Hopefully, more women will stand up for themselves and avoid saying "me too." The better answer is "not me."

ON CONFIDENCE

The key ingredient seems to me for women to have more confidence. And, when we look at extremely successful women, we find they have confidence in abundance.

For example, when looking to move to a new house, Missy and Yvo found a lovely home on Lombard Street in the Pacific Heights neighborhood with its breathtaking views of San Francisco Bay and Coit Tower. Lombard Street is known as the "crooked street" given a series of sharp hairpin turns built in the twenties to offset its incredibly steep grade.

Touring with them was Missy's mother-in-law, Neelie Kroes, a Dutch political and business leader who was Vice Chair of the European Commission and serves now on several Boards. When Neelie enthusiastically suggested buying it, Missy objected saying, *"Neelie, this won't work. The street attracts millions of* visitors a year. It's a nightmare given traffic jams and constant noise."

Neelie responded, *"We'll just arrange to have the street closed."*

To which Yvo added, *"Mom, that's not possible. It's San Francisco's second most popular tourist attraction."* Not deterred, Nellie added: *"No problem, we'll figure out how to close the street."*

Yvo and Missy passed on the purchase, but there's little doubt that Neelie, who has a history of deftly and successfully solving problems, would have tried. Her singular ability to act with confidence is an irreplaceable asset.

ON UTOPIA

As a country of immigrants, American's unique strength is its diversity. The constant influx of driven people coming here to give their families opportunities brings new energy, new thinking. It shakes us up. Barriers breed prejudice and hate while inclusion makes us stronger and wiser. To quote Richard Brodhead, former Duke University President:

"In this country, those who have stopped thinking are typically those who have stopped interacting with people who might make them think; namely, people who do not already think more or less the same as they do."

In the words of my friend Janet Reid, renowned consultant and author on the subject, wrote, *"There is so much that our divided world needs to do to get to a better place; focusing on diversity, equity and inclusion can help."*

The prevalent morality of our time is moving in the direction of diversity. However, to tackle the remaining issues – flexibility and bias – it is, once again, up to us. Flexibility is the issue which forced me to leave line management at P&G. Since then, companies have opened up, especially as almost all managers are working from home during the pandemic. Covid-19, though inherently tragic, holds the potential to solve the flexibility problem or – with childcare and school options limited and responsibility tossed back to parents – set us back significantly. Time will tell.

Jack, Jr.'s wife Amelia, CEO of Eastern States, commented that *"the key to having it all is a flexible partner."* The other way to have it all is to do it sequentially rather than all at once.

And as for bias – conscious and unconscious – it will lessen when we walk in each other's shoes, when the sexes share each other's roles – women as wage earners and men as caretakers and vice versa. To reach our full potential, we need for the dads to take an equal role in caring for the playroom and moms to become boardroom leaders.

That's happening in our family – among our children's households, all four men take on more responsibility for the children and home than the previous generation. When I asked Chris what was the home life/work life split between Lauren and him, he said, *"About 50%/50%. And I like it that way. I want to know my sons."*

At the risk of stereotyping, what the world needs now is more of the skills women seem to have in greater abundance. As Lauren said, *"Women thrive on facts more than bravado, long-term goals rather than quarterly targets and bringing-everyone-to-the-finish line over a winner-take-all approach."*

Countries headed by women, including Germany, New Zealand, Iceland, Taiwan and several Scandinavian nations than countries led by men such as the United States and Great Britain whose blustering, non-scientific, self-adulterating leaders have proven less effective.

And when will we see utopia? When men consistently put the

dishes in the dishwasher rather than the sink and when women stop counting.

ON MARRIAGE

Jack and I – the State Department and the War Department – remain happily married, active in sports, business, politics and the community. When a six-year-old Julian grandchild proudly exclaimed: *"Bet I am the youngest to wakeboard on all of the Chesapeake Bay,"* I agreed, adding: *"We have something in common. I bet I am the oldest to water ski."*

We are still focused on our family, especially now on the grandchildren. Until the pandemic, we travelled frequently – within the last 12 months to Russia and Scandinavia, to Kathryn Herskovits inspirational 40th in Cinque Terra, Italy, to Gigglemoor, Sea Island, Charleston, and several times to Wilmington, San Francisco, Tahoe, Chicago and Brooklyn to visit the children. We will again.

There have been ups and downs as there are in all relationships. But the ups outweigh the downs. Pal said, *"seldom have a bad day."* Seldom, not never. The adventure Jack promised me goes on. I used to look at older couples having dinner at restaurants and be saddened when couples have nothing to say to each other. For us, conversation is never lacking.

Always, we seem to be doing something new. Jack recently founded and teaches in the Center for Law and Entrepreneurship of the Salmon P. Chase College of Law. I am writing a book for the first time. And yes, we are still in love.

ON ENTREPRENEURSHIP

Men are the architects of legacy systems. If, for example, women invented the game of golf, it would be a 14-hole game.

That is a key reason why they still hold power. If moms were to establish the workday, more likely it would be 4:00 a.m.-7:00 a.m. and 9:00 a.m.-2:00 p.m. – before anyone else in the family wakes up and before the children get out of school. If women work in an organization that doesn't accommodate their needs, perhaps the best choice is leaving. It's a tough decision. Or start something of your own. Skills are transferrable.

Women do well starting enterprises. Creating your own entity can be the best way to take control of your time and your life.

REFLECTIONS ON MANAGING THE PLAYROOM AND THE BOARDROOM

Decades after first giving the "Playroom and Boardroom" talk, I still believe in all the basics espoused. However, I want to close out *One Red Shoe* by adding current perspective:

Look ahead: When I missed a deadline at work or forgot to decorate for a holiday, it seemed like the sky was falling down. It reaffirms the importance of taking the long view.

Normally, I do. It led me to opening world travel to high school students, getting to work for John Smale on planning for the next millennium and building Grandin Properties around walkable neighborhood before walkable was chic.

Start: Start before you're ready. Following the Boy Scout "be prepared" mantra leads to good but never great work. Just do it. Launch the ship. Take the risk. If I had not started AEI – when I knew nothing about business or Europe or language competency – P&G would never have opened its doors for me.

Figure it out: The problem with some young people is that they don't know how to do even the simplest things by themselves. Examples would include getting to the airport and getting a job. It's what happens when helicopter parents do the thinking work for their children.

At the University of Pennsylvania's new squash facility, coaches Jack Wyant, Jr. and Gilly Lane posted these letters on the women's locker room wall: "FIO" which means figure it out. Another sign says, "don't defer." Good council.

Fail: Failure is hardly the worst thing that can happen. As Coach Mills said, *"players learn when they lose, not when they win."* Without the bankruptcy, disastrous marriage and divorce, being unemployed and unemployable and a series of bad venture capital investments, I would probably be an unhappy suburban housewife.

Expect the best of people: In Sea Island this April, 3-year-old Sachin and I were making brownies when I gave him an egg to crack. His mother Meeta Agrawal intercepted saying, *"I think you overestimate the abilities of our child."* At that moment I realized I have been doing that all my life.

Overestimating the abilities of children and people we work with is the trait that most contributes to whatever success I enjoy.

Expect the best of yourself as well. On an International Women's Day symposium, I was privileged to share the podium with John Pepper. The first question to me was: *"Did you expect to be a legend in your own time?"* My answer: *"No, I expected to be president."*

On the secret to success: *"I can do that."*

ACKNOWLEDGEMENTS

WHILE THIS BOOK title starts with the word "One," there are others to thank. And because I list too many, the blame falls on my Dad who sent thank you notes to people who sent him thank you notes. Alternatively, we could point to headmaster Peter Briggs whose every speech for the 20 years our children attended Seven Hills started with *"thank your parents, thank your teachers, thank . . . ."*

I am grateful to my editor Polk Laffoon, former P&Ger, who showed patience and skill when I had nothing written, then both improved the manuscript and kept me on schedule for months. Thanks to others who read, re-read and made it better – Patty Hogan, Kathy Meier, Jack Wyant, Tim Wyant, Meeta Agrawal and 12-year-old granddaughter Finn Smit.

Thanks to Empower MediaMarketing and the Prices, another former P&Ger, who designed the original Red Shoe poster as a birthday present, to graphic designer Heather Vecellio who turned the shoe around and managed the visuals, to my current and former executive assistants, Tricia Collins and Betty Douglas, who did the real work and to Shannon Hogan Kulik who helped determine who might want to read the story and how to market.

All the above did their very best to lower the volume of my screaming from the hilltops *"Hip, hip, hooray world. Look at how great I am!"* But the influence seeps through George Corrigan who long ago started calling me 'the legend', Coley Laffoon who bows low to Queen Isabella, and the always enthusiastic Pete Blackshaw.

The audacity to suggest that I belonged in unwelcoming places came naturally from my lineage: the great-great grandparents who immigrated from Ireland and Wales, Ohio's Crusading Attorney General, the Judge who championed outsiders, Mom who raised the bar, speaking her own mind well before it was fashionable and siblings who pulled me along.

Having the courage to knock on the door is one thing, getting into the room is quite another. The Seven Hills School and Smith College provided the education, and The Procter & Gamble Company gave me the tools.

There is only one P&G. It trained me, my husband and our oldest child. There were, of course, a few Mad Men at the company but most were exceptionally talented and played fair. Back then, it was risky for people in charge to give power to a woman – untested and unknown – but they took the chance. A special thanks to: John Pepper, Tom Laco, John Smale, Gordon Wade, Sandy Weiner and Bob Wehling.

It wasn't risky but it was challenging for the men who worked for me, as they didn't grow up expecting to report to a girl. They figured it out – among them, Jack Wyant, Larry Plotnick, Jack Balousek, Tom Herskovits, Dean Butler, Mitch Wienick, Doug Falk, Jerry Gramaglia, A.G Lafley and Dirk Yeager.

There are not enough words for the team who helped plan for the next millennium. Nor for Ed Rigaud who, as the pioneering African American, walked down the same road I travelled. Or Ed Tazzia who started and leads the P&G Alumni Network.

And then there are the women who began coming to P&G, bringing fresh thinking and vibrancy – among them JoLynn Gustin, Lynn O'Shea, Mary Beth Price, Claudia Kotchka, Charlene

Trimmer, Lynn Boles, Marje Kiley, Janet Reid, Charlotte Otto, Kay Napier, Meg Whitman, Susan Arnold, Mel Healey, Erika Brown and Shannon Hogan Kulik.

The P&G Heritage & Archives Center, through Greg McCoy, provided many of the photographs related to P&G.

Thanks to those who helped build the real estate business: Mac, my business partner of 40 years, Tim Hogan, David Todd, John Frank, George Verkamp, the Grandin Team and 3CDC. I am grateful to the 80 people who risked their dollars by investing in Fund Isabella and those who helped make it profitable, Ed Goodman, Frank Wood, Mike Collette, Cynthia Fisher, Jenny Floren Sozzi, John McIlwraith, Gary Antonius and Susan Schieman.

All the Wyants appreciate Don and Judy Mills who taught us to love squash as well as U.S Squash, the Squash and Education Alliance and the Cincinnati Squash Academy for making the sport better. I am grateful to the 30 women – diverse women – who paid thousands to join the Women's Capital Club before it even existed. Especially Stella Hassan who came up with the investment hook and our good friends the Smitsons and Zarings.

Thanks also to those men who – as men of their times – resisted change and made me and other women work harder and be stronger, as well as to the people who helped navigate crisis, Judy Wizmur, Magistrate Timothy Hogan and Valerie Salkin.

Last, and most importantly, a warm shout out to Jack, who made everything possible, including our children and grandchildren. Life continues to be the grand adventure he promised.

The gang of four grew up with a Mom whose working lifestyle fell outside the norm. I worried a lot about that. Was I spending too little time with them? Was my working being selfish? Would they grow up valuing family? There were so few of us travelling down that road, it was hard to know.

All survived and, I like to think, thrived, partially because of our dual working household. They, too, learned to jump in and figure it out. All are independent thinkers and able leaders who "run" something and run it well. The quality of partners who married them provides real proof – Amelia Wyant, Yvo Smit, Meeta Agrawal and Lauren Kidwell. They are raising bright, active, well behaved children.

We have nine grandchildren: Finny, Johnny, Palmer, Charlie, Sam, Sachin, Owen, Reva and Henry. Being a grandparent is a joyous experience, simply because of the fun and energy it brings to life. In the gang of nine, the continuity of life is evidenced.

Experiences echo the past – I've seen that squash stroke before. Isn't that laugh familiar? As Finny perceptively noted, *"my sister Palmer pushes the envelope just like Eve."* There are glimpses of the future as well. There's an artist, zookeeper, writer, chef, squash player, politician, naturalist, thinker, lawyer, homemaker, comedian, teacher, coach, singer, entrepreneur, model and CEO.

The family continues to be close and strong. We just celebrated Jack, Jr.'s opening a new squash center at Penn, followed a month later by the 25th Anniversary of the Squash and Education Alliance at a dinner in New York City. The siblings all came to support and celebrate as did several cousins, aunts and uncles. Tom Herskovits warned Amelia, the Wyants show up and celebrate everything – no matter where or when.

Often, I feel like the luckiest person.

The grandchildren promise to make the world a better place. If they find something in this book that will help us get there, it will have been a worthwhile effort.

CPSIA information can be obtained
at www.ICGtesting.com
Printed in the USA
BVHW041927240121
598636BV00017B/685